AUSTRALIAN UNIVERSITIES

A HISTORY OF COMMON CAUSE

GWILYM CROUCHER is a Senior Lecturer in the Melbourne Centre for the Study of Higher Education, and Program Director at the LH Martin Institute. He is a co-author of two histories with Stuart Macintyre and André Brett: *Life After Dawkins: The University of Melbourne in the Unified National System of Higher Education*; and *No End of a Lesson: The Creation and Consequences of Australia's Unified National System of Higher Education*.

JAMES WAGHORNE is a Senior Research Fellow, who leads the University History Program in the Melbourne Centre for the Study of Higher Education, University of Melbourne. He is the co-author of *Liberty: A History of Civil Liberties in Australia*, with Stuart Macintyre, and co-editor of *The First World War, the Universities and the Professions in Australia, 1914–1936*, with Kate Darian-Smith.

AUSTRALIAN UNIVERSITIES

A HISTORY OF COMMON CAUSE

GWILYM CROUCHER & JAMES WAGHORNE

UNSW PRESS

A UNSW Press book

Published by
NewSouth Publishing
University of New South Wales Press Ltd
University of New South Wales
Sydney NSW 2052
AUSTRALIA
newsouthpublishing.com

© Universities Australia 2020
First published 2020

10 9 8 7 6 5 4 3 2 1

This book is copyright. Apart from any fair dealing for the purpose of private study, research, criticism or review, as permitted under the Copyright Act, no part of this book may be reproduced by any process without written permission. Inquiries should be addressed to the publisher.

 A catalogue record for this book is available from the National Library of Australia

ISBN   9781742236735 (paperback)
          9781742244860 (ebook)
          9781742249377 (ePDF)

Internal design Josephine Pajor-Markus
Cover design Luke Causby, Blue Cork
Cover images Front: Students at the University of Western Australia, 1967 (National Archives of Australia: Australian News and Information Bureau, Canberra; A1200, L65198); *Back:* Quadrangle, University of Sydney, Camperdown, Sydney, c. 1935 (EW Searle, National Library of Australia, nla.obj-141966769)

All reasonable efforts were taken to obtain permission to use copyright material reproduced in this book, but in some cases copyright could not be traced. The authors welcome information in this regard.

CONTENTS

ACKNOWLEDGMENTS vi
ABBREVIATIONS vii
INTRODUCTION 1

1 A PRACTICAL FEDERATION 5
2 AUSTRALIAN UNIVERSITIES 25
3 CONTROL AND INFLUENCE 51
4 COMMONWEALTH AND STATES 78
5 SYSTEMATISATION 108
6 FREE AND ACCOUNTABLE 132
7 A UNIFIED SYSTEM 154
8 INTERNATIONAL UNIVERSITIES 179

NOTES 204
BIBLIOGRAPHY 242
INDEX 285

ACKNOWLEDGMENTS

In writing a history as complicated and multifaceted as this, we have benefited from the support of numerous individuals. Most significant of these have been the advisory group of historians associated with the project, Stuart Macintyre, Vin Massaro and Julia Horne. This group read numerous drafts of the manuscript and offered detailed advice, pointed out areas to which we had devoted insufficient attention and helped us immeasurably to improve the text.

This project was commissioned by Universities Australia to mark the centenary of formal relationships between Australia's universities. We are grateful to Universities Australia for its support in the preparation of this book.

We thank our colleagues in the Melbourne Centre for the Study of Higher Education who offered a wide range of perspectives about Australian universities. Several colleagues reviewed the text, which assisted us in constructing the narrative, most notably William Locke, Andrew Norton and Peter Noonan. We thank Hamza Bin Jehangir and Zoe Vlahogiannis, who provided invaluable research assistance. We also thank the great team at UNSW Press for all their support.

While we have drawn on the expertise of many people, all errors remain those of the authors.

ABBREVIATIONS

AIF	Australian Imperial Force
AUBC	Association of the Universities of the British Commonwealth
AAUCS	Australian-Asian Universities' Cooperation Scheme
AARNet	Australian Academic Research Network
AAEC	Australian Atomic Energy Commission
ABC	Australian Broadcasting Commission
ACDP	Australian Committee of Directors and Principals
ACER	Australian Council for Educational Research
ACTU	Australian Council of Trade Unions
AINSE	Australian Institute of Nuclear Science and Engineering
ANU	Australian National University
ARC	Australian Research Council
ARGC	Australian Research Grants Committee
ASIO	Australian Security Intelligence Organisation
ASTEC	Australian Science, Technology and Engineering Council
AUC	Australian Universities Commission
AUQA	Australian Universities Quality Agency
AVCC	Australian Vice-Chancellors' Committee
CAE	College of Advanced Education
CFAS	Commonwealth Financial Assistance Scheme
CRTS	Commonwealth Reconstruction Training Scheme

CTEC	Commonwealth Tertiary Education Commission
CSIR	Council for Scientific and Industrial Research
CSIRO	Commonwealth Scientific and Industrial Research Organisation
FAUSA	Federal Association of University Staff Associations
FCUSAA	Federal Council of University Staff Associations of Australia
Go8	Group of Eight
HECS	Higher Education Contribution Scheme
HELP	Higher Education Loan Program
HESF	Higher Education Standards Framework
ISI	Institute of Science and Industry
MOOCs	Massive Open Online Courses
NASA	National Aeronautics and Space Administration
NBEET	National Board of Employment, Education and Training
NHMRC	National Health and Medical Research Council
NTEU	National Tertiary Education Union
NUAUS	National Union of Australian University Students
OUA	Open Universities Australia
PhD	Doctor of Philosophy
QIT	Queensland Institute of Technology
RMIT	Royal Melbourne Institute of Technology
SAIT	South Australian Institute of Technology
TAFE	Technical and Further Education
TEAS	Tertiary Education Assistance Scheme
TEQSA	Tertiary Education Quality and Standards Agency
UA	Universities Australia
UNS	Unified National System
UGC	University Grants Committee
UWA	University of Western Australia
UNSW	University of New South Wales
UTS	University of Technology, Sydney
WAIT	Western Australian Institute of Technology

INTRODUCTION

Universities have played a profound role in Australia's development. Over the past century, they have worked together to widen access to many more students, construct a national research system, and promote shared engagement with industry, government and international partners. Their joint endeavours have shaped Australia, yet it has been little explored. This is the story of how Australia's universities, each fiercely independent, gradually came together to work in common cause.

The connections between Australia's universities are complex and multilayered. All produce graduates, conduct research, provide service to the community and foster intellectual inquiry. They share many attributes and conventions, including the names of their degrees, and significant common core curriculum in degrees for professional qualifications. Each of them fosters the health of our democracy and civil society, helps to grow and diversify Australia's economy, through their skilled graduates and research breakthroughs advances knowledge for its own sake, as well as for immediate application. Yet, independence is crucial to each of these institutions and their ability to serve their public role. Created to meet the needs of local communities, universities were established under state government legislation as separate statutory entities. This story is one of safeguarding independence, while pursuing common cause.

The idea that Australian universities have shared interests first arose in the early decades of the twentieth century. Before then, interaction had been infrequent, and universities had developed largely in isolation from one another. They had closer ties to universities in Britain than with each other and felt strong kinship with their counterparts across the world. Capturing the national sentiment of Federation and the First World War, they came to look increasingly to each other. The catalyst for action came in 1917, when a group of students from the Riverina region of New South Wales enrolled at the University of Melbourne, rather than studying at a university in their own state. Up to this point, interstate movement of students was uncommon. This group of cross-border enrolments prompted the first meeting of universities later that year. A national conference in 1920 formalised relations.

These ties anticipated and, as this book shows, encouraged the growing interest and involvement of the Commonwealth Government in the state-run institutions. The increasing importance of science, and particularly the belief in applied science to support Australian primary industries, captured the public imagination. The establishment of statutory Commonwealth organisations to manage funding, first for industrial research and later with the creation of commissions that funded the breadth of university activities, both strengthened and gave purpose to a national university system. It also brought new challenges as the new funding bodies imposed their own will.

The ties between universities deepened further with the appointment of full-time chief executive officers, who adopted the title of Vice-Chancellor. These leadership roles had responsibility for the needs of the whole institution, both in internal and external decision making; they acted simultaneously as servant and champion of their institution. Their appointment created continuity and each university now had individual leaders who communicated

INTRODUCTION

directly with each other, as well as with Government, the media and the Australian public.

In 1920 Australia's universities created a standing committee to facilitate that interaction and define issues of common interest. In 1935 this became a committee of vice-chancellors. Originally, there were just six universities. By 2020, there were 39. At times, the Australian Vice-Chancellors' Committee (AVCC) formulated a common policy stance for Australian universities. At others, it provided a forum to resolve differences. Yet neither it, nor its successor body Universities Australia (UA), as it became in 2007, had powers to make binding decisions on its member universities.

In 2020 each Australian university remains a self-governing institution. But over the past century, they have seen value and wisdom in working together on major issues. By providing a forum and support for universities to discuss a common position, the peak body provided a collective alternative to separate negotiations between individual universities and governments. Cohesion has relied on regular interaction, convention rather than rules, and consensus over edict. It has been forged through deliberation, conciliation and advocacy. National organisations were also formed to represent students from 1938, and staff from 1952. They added to the voices speaking for universities, their constituent parts, and the communities they serve.

This book joins a rich international literature on university systems.[1] Australian historians have mostly concentrated on individual institutions, and analysis of the university system by economists and political scientists usually has a limited historical dimension, with some exceptions, including the work of Simon Marginson.[2] Most university histories focus on the internal workings of the institutions, tracing in detail the decisions of governing bodies, the changes in structure and operations, and the contributions of their significant professors. A minority emphasise universities' public role and their connection with the communities they serve, arguing universities should be read through these connections 'from the inside out'.[3] An alternative approach sees universities as generators and protectors of knowledge, driven by networks of individuals attached to institutions, but also moving between them.[4] Other research identifies the significance of universities' relationship with government, tracing changes in public policy.[5]

Insofar as system-wide analysis has been undertaken, it comes from policy reviews commissioned by state and Commonwealth governments. The university system has often been shaped by politicians, such as Robert Menzies or John Dawkins, or authors of formative reports, such as Keith Murray, Leslie Martin or Denise Bradley. This history contextualises the contributions of these figures, and highlights many others, as well as analysing the role played by universities themselves to determine their collective fortunes.

Universities cannot be understood in isolation. Their interaction has been key to their collective development. It was in the national forum provided by AVCC, and then UA, that they adopted common standards, won a scheme for awarding research grants, and interacted with overseas institutions and international benefactors. It was together that universities welcomed international students from the 1940s, and in the 1990s established the infrastructure that was the forerunner of the internet in Australia. Together they ushered in an era of much wider participation in higher education.

1
A PRACTICAL FEDERATION

The delegates who gathered around the old Senate table of the University of Sydney at the 1920 Conference of the Australian Universities had travelled by train and steamer from the other state capitals. The Sydney Chancellor, Sir William Cullen, offered his colleagues, senior professors from the six Australian universities, a 'hearty welcome'. A noted champion of Australian Federation decades earlier, Cullen now looked forward to the prospect of universities working together.[1] Yet he also recognised that there was no precedent for such an association, and indeed there were obvious limits. The six Australian universities were self-governing, funded by their state governments, drawing their students largely from within their states and serving state needs. As Cullen told the representatives of the other universities, 'We take pride and pleasure in hearing of your successes. We sympathise with your difficulties'. The universities were similar and recognised each other's academic standing, but had no direct connections. There was anxiety about what ends a university conference could achieve, or where agreement might lead. Cullen urged the gathered delegates to view their separate contributions as working 'for the honour of Australia'. Any friction, he declared, should be seen merely as sibling rivalry.[2]

The meeting brought together university leaders and senior professors from across the country, seeking to strengthen collaboration in a common cause. It was the first such gathering, although the apparently simple achievement of bringing together the universities had required an extended process of building trust. While Cullen offered a warm welcome, he also cautioned those present to act in the interests of the universities and not bend to external pressures. He warned against adopting too enthusiastically the current preoccupation with ideas of 'national efficiency' or following the false idols of modern 'materialism'. He urged universities to recognise how far their 'obligations' to the state and benefactors had already 'been met'.[3]

The national gathering showed how much universities were changing. Before this meeting, when the universities looked beyond their local communities, they saw themselves as part of a wider international network of British universities.[4] Their professors, most of whom were still recruited from Britain, enjoyed close ties back 'home'. In the most literal sense, universities had no national character at all. Rather they existed simultaneously as local and international organisations.

This was changing with the national sentiment nurtured by Federation in 1901 and the First World War, which raised questions about the state-based universities' national responsibilities, and thus their relationship with the Commonwealth Government. The existence of universities in each of the state capitals, combined with improved communication and transport links, including the recently completed transcontinental rail network, created the conditions for greater interaction. Common issues were emerging, yet unavoidable tensions were also developing. There was the question of whether all the universities should seek to be comprehensive in their curricula and disciplinary coverage, as many within them assumed. In addition, the greater emphasis on research, and the cost of new laboratories raised the prospect of coordination to avoid duplication.

These changes cast the universities and their histories in a new light. In coming together, the universities began to redefine themselves in relation to one another, and they forged a new identity as 'Australian'. The 1920 conference was a new beginning and the first step in the emergence of a national university system.

LOCAL AND INTERNATIONAL UNIVERSITIES

By the end of the First World War, Australia had a university in each capital city. The oldest universities – the University of Sydney, established in 1850, the University of Melbourne in 1853 and the University of Adelaide in 1874 – were founded as city universities in colonial capitals.[5] In practice, however, they served their entire colonies, and this was formally acknowledged by the naming of the universities that followed, the University of Tasmania in 1890, Queensland in 1909, and Western Australia (UWA) in 1911.[6] The University of Tasmania had campuses in Hobart and Launceston, broadening its reach.

All had been established in a pattern that borrowed from English, Scottish and Irish institutions. They were secular and non-residential, with tuition by lecture and little in the way of small-group teaching. They were funded by a mixture of lecture and examination fees, gifts from donors and annual state government grants. They adopted the curriculum of modern universities, combining humanities with the new sciences, such as Chemistry and Biology. Vocational courses in the learned professions, such as Medicine and Law, were introduced from an early stage, both to demonstrate their utility to government and attract students.[7]

Universities had internal governance structures that ensured they fulfilled both their civic and academic missions. The Act of Incorporation of the University of Sydney provided the template from which later universities diverged in small, although often important ways. Universities had a governing board, named variously the senate or council, consisting of government appointees and others elected by graduates. Some universities required policies to be approved by a general assembly of graduates, known as the convocation. Beneath the central governing board stood an additional body comprised of all professors. This provided advice on matters of academic policy, and in practice it was most often determinative. All universities were non-residential institutions, with only a minority of students living on campus in affiliated residential colleges. Most of these colleges were established by religious denominations and were separate from the university, although sometimes they had representation on university governing bodies.[8]

A complex network of rules and conventions was developed at school and faculty level, as well as by the council and academic board, and gave professors and students significant influence over academic policy. Specific courses of study were led by professors, who dominated activities in their disciplines, and whose interests shaped the curriculum at each university.

In 1920 these universities were still modest in size, but they were growing quickly. The University of Sydney had 3397 students and Melbourne 2360. Adelaide was the next largest with 1300 students. The fledgling foundations of the University of Tasmania (179), Queensland (291) and Western Australia (332) had far fewer students. In total, across the six universities there were 100 professors, and 337 lecturers and demonstrators.[9] Each was small enough that its community, including students, graduates and their teachers, were well known to one another.

Table 1.1
UNIVERSITY STATISTICS, 1920

	Sydney	Melbourne	Adelaide	Tasmania	Queensland	Western Australia
STUDENTS	3397	2366	1300	179	291	332
PROFESSORS	32	23	14	7	8	10
OTHER TEACHING STAFF	133	76	73	16	20	19
GOVERNMENT GRANT	£83478	£37542	£24577	£11215	£16400	£14248
FEE INCOME	£33324	£67375	£18137	£2640	£6650	£2294[10]
ENDOWMENT	£501218	£234205	£179535			

SOURCE *Commonwealth Yearbook* 1922, pp. 746–47.

Universities were embedded in each state's system of public education and they depended on state government support to supplement income drawn from student fees and endowments. The proportion provided by these three sources varied. Sydney had the largest state allocation, and this was supplemented by the largest endowment, which at £501218 was more than twice as large as that of Melbourne, and almost three times larger than that of Adelaide.[11] The University of Western Australia did not charge tuition fees, a first in the British Empire, owing to a bequest of more than £425000 from the proprietor and editor of the *West Australian* newspaper, Sir John Winthrop Hackett. For universities other than Western Australia, students who could not pay the full fees had to secure a free place or scholarship provided by the state, a benefactor or a community organisation, such as a church, as well as find paid employment; many undergraduates studied part-time in evening classes.

The differences between the states stood as a barrier to cooperation between universities. Even minor changes could have unforeseen consequences. For instance, matriculation examinations, used to determine admission, differed. They were developed by universities in consultation with the state government and school representatives, but their influence on the curriculum in secondary schools had been a matter of debate since the first matriculation examination was held in Sydney in 1852 and Melbourne in 1856.[12] The test also came to be seen as an indication of success in secondary schooling and a prerequisite for some forms of employment. It was also meant to be open to all regardless of whether they attended a private or state school. However, in practice very few schools, whether independent or government, prepared students for the exam.[13] But by 1920, the universities drew in students from a wide range of schools, including country high schools and the new selective state schools established by state governments around the turn of the century.

Universities made various arrangements with governments to make higher education more accessible, using a network of scholarships and fee concessions, as well as government-supported 'free places' for students in courses that served a public need, such as Education. Universities also maintained 'extension' programs, using government subsidies to teach accessible subjects to members of the public. There were other examples of such outreach, such as the policy of the University of Melbourne to relieve country students in Arts and Law from attending otherwise compulsory lectures.[14]

Australian universities were proud institutions. They identified with the long traditions of British universities, in particular Oxford and Cambridge. Like those universities, they established their own grand buildings, heraldic crests and Latin mottos.[15] They defined their role as the transmission and extension of knowledge, as well as the training of professional graduates. Professors were prominent members of the community in their capital city, participating in public debates, setting up local institutions such as museums, observatories and learned societies, and enjoying high public standing.[16]

UNIVERSITIES OF THE BRITISH EMPIRE

Although each university was shaped by its internal policies and embedded in its own state, academic staff knew their counterparts across the country, at least by correspondence. With notable exceptions, the majority of professors were recruited from British or Irish universities, so they also retained connections with former colleagues back 'home'. Academic networks extended from Australia and New Zealand back to Britain.[17]

Professors were more likely to travel to universities of the empire than other Australian ones. Travel between the state capitals was by ship or railway, and those living in the other states would pass through Adelaide, Sydney and Melbourne as the network's hubs. Respite from heavy teaching loads was infrequent. For Australian professors who obtained sabbatical leave, the opportunity to work in more established overseas institutions, observe developments there and reacquaint themselves with academic networks eclipsed any interest in moving between states.

In the sciences in particular, Australian universities identified themselves as part of an imperial network, sharing in the achievements of British laboratories that had brought international renown to many of their postgraduates.[18] Select students were given the opportunity for further study in Britain, with travel supported by free passage provided by shipping companies; from 1891 there were the prestigious scholarships of the 1851 Exhibition Trust; and Rhodes scholarships from 1904.[19] Hackett, the benefactor of the

University of Western Australia, captured the sentiment by telling an audience at Oxford University that 'colonials were unable to recognise Oxford University as the property of Oxford. They regarded it rather as a possession of the whole Empire'.[20]

The importance of imperial connections was revealed during the jubilee celebrations of the University of Sydney held in 1902, and Melbourne in 1906. These events drew representatives of universities from across the world, but professors from other Australian universities made up the majority of the participants, attending as representatives of the British universities from which they had graduated.[21] Such representation more often brought members of Australian universities together to affirm their wider links, rather than to promote closer domestic relations. In many ways they were as isolated from each other as from their British peers.

Rather than pursuing a national network, universities looked to efforts to improve communication between universities across the imperial network. Sustained efforts led to a 1903 conference of Colonial and Allied Universities, held in London. Australian universities did not send delegates directly because of the lack of prior notice, but Sydney and Adelaide arranged for representatives who were already in London, including former professors.[22]

The conference agreed to improve cooperation between universities to harness the empire's global reach and to support the exchange of students, but few firm commitments came from the meeting.[23] A council was formed to coordinate further meetings in 1907 and 1912, leading to the formation of the Universities' Bureau of the British Empire. The Universities' Bureau had limited powers, serving chiefly as an information 'clearing house', and as a vehicle for informal collaboration between British universities and those of the colonies and dominions, including Australia.[24] Friction among the universities in the United Kingdom impeded repeated attempts to create a stronger organisation, let alone allow the

Universities' Bureau to do more than aspire to support the dominion universities. For the Australians, its most important offering was the *Yearbook* of British universities, which provided consistent information on the universities and listed their professors.

The Universities' Bureau held congresses in 1917 and 1918, inviting Australian and other dominion representation to discuss exchange of students across the empire and the development of research. Central to proceedings were plans by many British universities to adopt the new postgraduate qualification of Doctor of Philosophy (PhD) to ensure there was no repeat of 'the traffic of scholars and scientists' who otherwise went to German universities before the First World War.[25] Sydney University's lecturer in English, Ernest Holme, was an early voice for Australia in the organisation. As a former chairman of the Universities Educational Committee of the Australian Imperial Force (AIF), which educated First World War troops awaiting repatriation, he was well acquainted with many of the professors involved in establishing the Bureau. Holme saw the Bureau's shaky start in 1912 first-hand, and in 1918 he cautioned his fellow Australians that the organisation was badly in need of strengthening if it was to fulfil any of its promises for the dominion universities. This did not happen. The only significant achievement of the 1918 conference was to establish a standing committee exclusively for British universities, the forerunner of their Committee of Vice-Chancellors and Principals.[26] Despite its promise, the Universities' Bureau remained peripheral to Australian universities during the interwar period, but its very existence served as a reminder of the difficulty Australian universities faced in turning the idea of a community of empire universities into reality.

Pressing national issues were emerging that went beyond the relationships of universities with their state governments. The First World War had mobilised industrial and human resources.

Large numbers of students enlisted in the armed services and the medical corps, while many staff and students undertook war work in munitions factories or in the provision of professional services. These undertakings involved working with the Commonwealth Government, rather than the states, and the universities took steps to coordinate some of their activities. Hence Sydney, Melbourne and Adelaide adopted equivalent measures to reduce the length of their medical degrees in order to meet the shortfall in the numbers of doctors and surgeons in military hospitals.

The First World War also produced heated debates about Australia's place in the British Empire. Many senior academics were prominent members of the Round Table, an exclusive association with local branches that promoted closer imperial ties.[27] The loyalty of university lecturers of German origin was challenged at Melbourne, Queensland and Tasmania.[28] The divisive conscription plebiscites of 1916 and 1917 also drew in the universities, pitting critiques of British militarism against arguments that universities should do more to compel their students to enlist.[29]

THE CHANGING POLITICS OF UNIVERSITIES

Universities' contributions during the war renewed long-standing debates about academic independence and the merits of offering professional degrees and programs in applied science. During the first decade of the twentieth century, a series of government reviews had recast technical education's purpose to focus on its benefit to national development, and universities were not immune from this new orientation.[30] Central to the concern of many inside and outside universities was a view that vocational degrees departed too far from universities' scholarly mission. Some argued that the technical and professional disciplines were overly 'materialistic' in their quest for solutions to current problems, and failed to inculcate a deeper understanding. Universities risked becoming the mere servants of 'technical improvement', rather than nourishing a community of scholars.[31] It was assumed university study would benefit the student materially, but critics argued that education tailored for a particular purpose was too narrow and the knowledge it imparted was too shallow. Others disagreed. At the 1902 Jubilee, the Dean of Arts at the University of Sydney, Mungo MacCallum, countered that critical thought could be fostered in any professional discipline.[32]

Australian debates over the degree to which government could direct the activities of universities and determine areas of national priority echoed those overseas. In the United States, the desire to solve problems in agriculture, science and engineering prompted the Morrell Acts of 1862 and 1890 and the establishment of the Land Grant Universities in addition to existing universities supported by private foundations.[33] The original American colleges had been small, whereas the American universities emerging in the early twentieth century were large and more oriented towards practical education and research. Liberal arts colleges, lacking access to these federal funds, continued the older model.[34] Australian universities walked a middle path, accepting the benefits of professional and applied programs, but injecting them with additional content. This meant that degrees such as Law, Medicine and Engineering required the completion of Arts subjects, to provide the next generation of public leaders with broader knowledge as well as professional skills and expertise.

In Britain, too, governments increasingly tied funding to specific purposes, most particularly the production of graduates trained in the professions and applied science. This was framed as 'national efficiency' – the application of scientific knowledge to the purposes of the state.[35] The Prince of Wales, later King George V, had returned from a tour of the European continent in 1901 with the exhortation 'Wake up Britain!', pointing to the extent to which British universities lagged behind those of France and Germany.[36] The French *écoles normales* and the reformed research institutes in Germany produced large numbers of research graduates who underpinned significant advances in the physical and medical sciences. These developments implied a degree of central control achieved in France under Napoleon and in Germany, 60 years later under Bismarck, that had not occurred in the British Empire. It was not clear that British universities would accept the same direction, let alone their Australian counterparts.

These questions were most acute in proposals to develop university research. This involved substantial expense in the construction and maintenance of laboratories, support for researchers and, most costly of all, time for university staff to conduct their own research. Universities could cite examples of the value of research, such as the geological surveys of Edgeworth David in Sydney and JW Gregory in Melbourne, which revealed major mineral deposits ripe for exploitation.[37] However, they also sought to ensure that university research was not restricted to 'applied' projects, for they thought it was also important to pursue research that would make new discoveries.

The public role of universities and their contribution to their states were key questions in royal commissions into the universities of Melbourne (1904) and Adelaide (1911), established to deal with the financial trouble in which both institutions found themselves. This was a central theme of the 1909 study of the comparatively recently developed Land Grant Universities in North America undertaken by the New South Wales Director of Education, Peter Board. He argued that universities must be public in their accessibility to all residents of the state but also in the production of graduates who were 'capable contributor[s] to the prosperity of the state'.[38] A similar impetus drove the establishment of the University of Western Australia and the University of Queensland, both seen as 'people's universities' and serving state development, including agriculture.[39]

This sentiment led to the introduction of new disciplines.[40] The 1904 royal commission into the University of Melbourne led to the establishment of courses in Agricultural and Veterinary Science for the express purpose of improving Victorian agricultural productivity. Agriculture courses were also introduced at the University of Sydney; Roseworthy Agricultural College in South Australia was affiliated with the University of Adelaide in 1905, and Hackett endowed a chair in agriculture at the University of Western Australia as part of its foundation.[41] These developments followed William Farrer's cultivation of the 'Federation' strain of wheat, which had dramatically boosted yields in the unforgiving Australian conditions. With greater scientific attention, a whole range of pests and diseases could be controlled, with the potential for further improvement of agricultural productivity.

The Commonwealth Government was also drawn into supporting research in the interests of national development. The introduction of disability pensions in 1910 gave it an understandable interest in promoting public health. The government backed the establishment of an Institute of Tropical Medicine in Townsville, with the assistance of the Medical schools at Melbourne, Sydney and Adelaide.[42] National development also motivated the decision of Prime Minister William (Billy) Hughes to establish a federal Advisory Council of Science and Industry in 1916, in consultation with the universities, to 'cure the diseases of the body economic and be its striking and producing power'.[43] This body was reconstituted as the Institute of Science and Industry (ISI) from 1920, and charged with making scientific advances to assist the development of Australian industries.[44] The ISI directed most of its support to agricultural and pastoral projects, usually through universities and their laboratories or in collaboration with them. There were major national success stories; for example, professors and staff from the University of Queensland helped lead the eradication of prickly pear, an invasive cactus that had consumed 10.5 million hectares in the grazing and farming areas of southeastern Queensland and northern New South Wales by 1919, and eventually controlled through the successful introduction of the cactoblastis beetle from South America.[45]

The push for scientific development was accompanied by some government investment in the new social sciences. The Victorian Government had made provision for the discipline of Political Economy when it funded the creation of a dedicated chair in history in 1912. Tasmania, New South Wales and South Australia all assisted the development of the study of Economics. Victorian Government research grants introduced in 1908 were subject to a review in 1916 that criticised the 'non-scientific' nature of the projects. A young Robert Menzies, editor of *Melbourne University Magazine*, wrote in defence of his friend Richard Mills' project on the prerogative of dissolution of parliament. He argued the need for this study as it built expertise, even if it did not produce immediate material benefits. 'There is an unfortunate tendency to esteem the utility which expresses itself in terms of iron and steel, or improved scientific knowledge, at the expense of the utility which is appreciated only by the expert or the man [sic] behind the scenes', Menzies wrote.[46]

NATIONALLY COORDINATED EDUCATION

As new 'practical' departments were created in universities, the question arose whether all universities should teach these vocational and applied disciplines, or whether students could travel to where they were offered. Interstate study had been necessary for students from Queensland and Western Australians until the eve of the First World War, and afterwards this was still necessary in fields such as medicine and architecture. The royal commission into the University of Melbourne examined whether a Professor of Mining Engineering should be appointed when the University of Sydney had already established a Mining School.[47] The Melbourne commissioners accepted the presumption of the time that universities mostly served the needs of their own states and local communities. The Professor of Chemistry, Orme Masson, argued that 'leaving it' to Sydney ran 'contrary to the spirit of the time, which is for an increase of local facilities rather than the opposite'. The Sydney Mining School was 'of no advantage to [those] in Melbourne and the neighbourhood, who wish to have a mining education of the highest kind'. Only the wealthy would travel to complete degrees. They would do as well to travel overseas.[48]

The debate about which universities should deliver which courses, and whether they could all ultimately aspire to offer a comprehensive suite of teaching for their local communities, forced discussion of their interaction. The need for a forum to resolve issues was compelling.

The case for practical arrangements between universities was starkly demonstrated in 1917, when it emerged that students from the rural Riverina region of New South Wales were enrolling in substantial numbers at the University of Melbourne rather than at Sydney in their home state. By doing so, they took advantage of the Melbourne regulations that exempted rural students from attending lectures. Conscious that this broke the customary jurisdictions between universities and shifted the costs between state boundaries, Melbourne wrote to Sydney in July 1917. The registrars of Melbourne and Sydney agreed that there was nothing to prevent students from doing this, and Sydney's Faculty of Arts wrote a terse response to Melbourne that it did not 'disapprove or approve' and would not intervene in the applications.

Sydney then called a hasty national meeting in August to clarify rules of entry. The conference, held in Melbourne as it was the most equidistant from the other Australian universities, agreed that more consistent entry requirements were desirable to give secondary students more choice about which university courses they might undertake and 'simplify … the transference of students from one university to another'.[49] However, as the agreements at the meeting were not binding, it was left to individual universities to follow up.

The significance of this first national meeting of Australian universities was apparent to participants. The University of Western Australia's Vice-Chancellor, AD Ross, saw it 'as a first step towards closer coordination of the work between the various Australian Universities'.[50] This was a confronting claim for the staunchly independent universities, and was dismissed by agreement because the delegates lacked the seniority to commit their institutions to any course of action. The universities had no chief executive officers and the position of vice-chancellor was simply to deputise for the chancellor.

Inter-university cooperation had been discussed before, but was usually met with vocal opposition. At the 1902 University of Sydney Jubilee celebrations, the classicist Thomas Tucker had argued that Australian universities must retain their distinctive qualities and rejected the idea that they could have 'precisely the same methods, standards curricula, and … teaching'. While this might appeal to 'those who love a pretty system', he declared, it would deny the inherent advantages of diversity. Rather than a fixed system Tucker proposed a 'practical federation' that was characterised by deliberation between them.[51] An 'informal conference' of Australian universities was held in 1906 at the Melbourne Town Hall, but the gathering was also joined by foreign delegates and achieved little of its broad agenda on common vacations and degree status.[52]

By 1917, this was set to change. At the same time as preparations were underway for the national Matriculation Conference, the Victorian Minister for Public Instruction, Harry Lawson, wrote to the Chancellor of the University of Melbourne, John MacFarland, with his firm 'suggestion' that the University should give 'early consideration' to the question of 'co-ordinating the development of university education in the Australian states', and that Melbourne call a conference at 'an early date'. Lawson reasoned that coordination was essential to ensure the 'strictest national economy' in developing the universities, as well as to ensure there was not an oversupply of graduates and that they had employment opportunities. It was 'better', he stated, to have 'two strong and efficient Faculties than to have several weak Faculties attempting the same work'.[53]

Lawson's request for regular university conferences met with mixed responses. Sydney was cautious about derailing the meeting's purpose, whereas others, such as Tasmania, saw this as an opportunity to discuss greater cooperation between programs. Tasmania had particular interest in becoming a centre of work in electrical engineering 'owing to the probability of great developments of Electrical Engineering in this State' through hydroelectric projects that were in development.[54] Universities agreed that regular meetings should take place 'at intervals of no more than three years'. This was a soft commitment, but it did reflect the growing acknowledgment of the benefits of regular meetings as universities continued to develop in scope and scale.

It was not until 1920 that the next congress was held, following a request by the Universities' Bureau's Alex Hill that Australian universities conduct preliminary discussions on issues they wished to be canvassed at the forthcoming conference of empire universities in London. In the preparations for this conference, the Australians decided local issues were more important. The first draft of the agenda raised the issue of improving the standing of Australian universities in the British world, encouraging teacher interchange and more Australians to undertake postgraduate degrees in Britain. The items on the agenda quickly evolved into strictly domestic questions such as the possibility of inter-university research projects within Australia, the desirability of allowing professors time for research as well as teaching, and the relationship between universities and government.[55]

By the time the universities met in May 1920, they had already agreed the need to establish a Standing Advisory Committee of Australian Universities to manage inter-university discussions, and to take responsibility for convening future local meetings and conferences. The emphasis was now on Australia asserting its own connections rather than operating through the Universities' Bureau. Australian universities came close to leaving the Universities' Bureau altogether, but decided on balance to persist, although enthusiasm for the organisation waned from that moment. In distancing themselves from the Universities' Bureau, Australia's universities also sought to form their own direct relationships with other countries. They decided to make contact with the United States' National Institute of International Education, and to seek exchange of speakers with the University of Toronto.

This national focus enabled common issues to be discussed. Regular discussion improved the prospect that common agreements would be implemented. Basic issues of entry standards and administrative arrangements began to be settled, including whether universities should employ a full-time and paid 'chief executive officer', to be called a vice-chancellor.

A PRACTICAL FEDERATION

AN EMERGING SYSTEM OF AUSTRALIAN UNIVERSITIES

Agreeing to cooperate was one thing; making it happen was another. The need for regular meetings was evident, yet there was no agreement on how they would operate as a system, what issues the new organisation could act on, and with what authority. Even basic questions about where and how often it was to convene were left open. The key difference between the new Standing Advisory Committee and previous attempts at inter-university organisation was its permanence. It had created a central office to which issues could be referred and resolved. The office was established in Melbourne on the grounds that it was then 'the political centre of the Commonwealth and ... also geographically central', and the honorary secretary was the Registrar of the University of Melbourne, Joseph Bainbridge.[56] For the first year Sydney and Melbourne would each carry just over a quarter of the costs, with the other four universities making contributions proportionate to their size. The less well-resourced universities were also the furthest from the population centres on the eastern seaboard, and the most affected by the limited transport links. An interstate journey required changes of train and many days.[57]

After 1920 universities met every year and there were biennial conferences of Australian universities with a wide contingent of university representatives to decide on major matters. The meetings held some interest for the public, and each was reported in syndicated news across Australia, with journalists covering the conference proceedings. Alongside the conferences, the smaller Standing Advisory Committee met in alternate years, usually hosted by Melbourne.[58] Many academics would attend regularly over the first decades, cementing personal relationships. The conferences and meetings were also joined by prominent scientists such as Sir Douglas Mawson and Sir Edgeworth David, as they were timed to coincide with the meeting of the Australasian Association for the Advancement of Science.

Although each institution was beholden to its state government, and governed by its council or senate, the ambition for collective action grew quickly. At a time of limited transcontinental communication, the new meetings provided the only regular opportunity to work through thorny issues arising from the universities' organisation and practices. From the outset universities deliberated over many areas of their operations. As well as the question of entry that had first brought universities together, in the early years they discussed examination standards, common curricula, degree structures, academic titles and staff salary levels. Through the committee, universities came to speak with a unified voice on many matters, despite the inevitable differences of opinion on some topics.

Although the advantages of appealing collectively to the Commonwealth Government would take some time to emerge, from 1920, universities sought to present a united front on national matters. They had begun to think of themselves as a collective of 'Australian' universities, as well as peers of other universities across the British Empire. Although brought together by necessity, the benefits of staying together quickly became clear. Indeed, in the lead-up to the 1920 universities conference in Sydney, a member of the University of Melbourne Council, Alexander Leeper, proposed a 'Joint Board of Australian Universities'. This would replicate the coordinating body of Scottish universities established in 1871, which ensured consistency and equivalent qualifications. Leeper was perhaps unaware that the Scottish universities had moved away from this form of centralised coordination.[59] Ultimately, it was the dramatic national changes and crises of the 1930s and 1940s that kept Australian universities together.

2
AUSTRALIAN UNIVERSITIES

After the achievement of the national conferences and the formation of the Standing Advisory Committee, attention turned to what cooperation would mean. This was no small task. The *Sydney Morning Herald* had editorialised against more extensive coordination, given the 'widely different' circumstances between the larger and well-resourced universities and those more heavily dependent on state subsidies. 'It is obvious', it argued, 'that complete uniformity is impossible, nor should it be sought after'.[1] Many people within universities, however, saw immediate advantages in cooperation. They argued that national political and economic developments demanded a response and that a consistent position was required to deal with the world beyond their gates. Universities' connections with the professions, many of which were forming national associations in the 1920s, added a national inflection to academic policy. Similarly, the organisation of universities in other countries gave impetus to the Australians to ensure they had standing to represent Australian interests. National agreements could serve as a vehicle for changes to all parts of university activity, including standards, curriculum, governance and structures.

COOPERATION

The first meetings of Australian universities combined enthusiasm with caution. Plans for greater collaboration were written into the terms of reference for the new Standing Advisory Committee. It was a body to 'make recommendations tending towards coordination of educational requirements'.[2] Yet from the small committee's initial meeting, held in November 1920, six months after the conference, attempts to bring universities together met with resistance. The idea of compiling a national year book, for instance, was first deferred and then abandoned as an unnecessary diversion of resources. Plans for the committee to serve as the 'medium of communication' between universities were quickly shelved as impractical.[3] Collaboration was a shared ambition, but progress was slow, and the committee's 'advisory' status confirmed that individual universities would continue to implement national agreements as they saw fit. Regional concerns and institutional interests were on show at each of the larger biennial conferences of Australian universities. Agreement often took years to be reached, and a settlement could be re-litigated soon after it was made.

Yet from these meetings an overarching identity gradually emerged above the interests of single institutions. Starting with universities committing to a common vacation week in their academic calendars to allow meetings to be scheduled, more sweeping problems were tackled, and practical solutions proposed. They agreed on national standards to ensure efficiency of operations and the quality of academic programs. New degrees would be defined in accordance with those already in existence elsewhere, so they would be robust and leave students well prepared for future careers. The duplication of effort and cost to establish more courses, such as Veterinary Science, would be avoided where it was possible to identify one or two universities to serve the whole nation.

Universities were careful to treat any major changes as recommendations to each university's internal decision-making structures to avoid them being seen as imposed from outside. Unlike in Britain, for instance, where a central University Grants Committee formed in 1920 shaped the development of British universities through the allocation of funding, Australia had no such Commonwealth funding arrangement.[4] Indeed, the Australian Constitution was held to prevent the Commonwealth from intervening in state education systems. Limited federal initiatives, including funding in 1908 to establish an Institute for Tropical Health with the universities of Sydney, Adelaide and Melbourne, and the establishment of the Commonwealth Serum Laboratories in 1916, were enterprises that extended across state boundaries and were not educational.[5] Instead, universities retained their distinctive characters, with changes reflecting their concerns to maintain academic standards and preserve scholarly freedom, as well as to promote efficiency and consistency.

The formalisation of communication between Australian universities after 1920 allowed them to respond to national and international organisations. It facilitated interchange with international associations, particularly the Universities' Bureau of the British Empire, as well as increasingly extensive connections to the wider world, most notably the United States, India, China and Japan. It gave them the capacity to respond to the demands of the national professional associations and professional institutions that emerged alongside the universities and pressed for changes in the universities' professional degrees. It was also able to present common cause to the Commonwealth and harness its growing significance for many areas that were once the province of the states.

In seeking greater cooperation, universities first sought to determine precisely what courses they offered. At the first meeting of the Standing Advisory Committee, the Warden and Registrar of the University of Sydney, Henry Barff, tabled a list of the courses offered and the fees charged by the six universities, compiled from their various *Calendars*, the annual handbooks published by the universities. This revealed the different titles of courses that often overlapped as well as different fee systems: universities used combinations of lecture and examination fees, and bespoke fees for special subjects.[6] Reconciling these differences across universities would not be straightforward. Yet universities agreed to the principle that new programs should be discussed centrally so that these, at least, could be consistent. This commitment was quickly downgraded the following year to 'desirable', and ultimately would be honoured only where there was some reason for a national conversation.[7]

One such area of national priority was Engineering, which bridged university and technical education, and was emblematic of the drive for national efficiency. It was organised differently in the various universities. While Sydney, Melbourne, Queensland and Western Australia had bachelor's degrees, at Adelaide Engineering was a postgraduate diploma awarded by the local School of Mines and Industries. A Faculty of Engineering was established at Tasmania in 1921. Moving towards consistent titles and approaches helped to consolidate the discipline, and brought it more emphatically into the university sphere to offer a more rounded professional training than in technical colleges.[8]

There was less agreement on the question of postgraduate study. Among the first issues raised by Melbourne was the introduction of the Doctorate of Philosophy (PhD), awarded for a research project undertaken under supervision at the university, and thus different from other doctorates that were awarded for a body of work undertaken externally and without supervision. English universities had introduced the degree in 1917, and it had long been offered in a number of other countries.[9] In 1920 Australian universities unanimously agreed that the PhD would not proceed and, although Melbourne presented detailed proposals in 1924 for a three-year degree for researchers working in Science or Arts under close academic supervision, the other universities resisted.[10] The resources it would require and the higher priority of other issues quashed the idea. While it made sense for Melbourne, it was premature for many other universities, which were still developing their higher degrees. In 1924 Adelaide first offered the Master of Law and Doctorate of Letters degrees; Sydney reported that it was considering the Doctorates of Letters and Economics in 1927; Queensland was still considering introducing Doctorates of Letters and Engineering in 1934.[11] In the interests of cooperation, Melbourne decided not to proceed with the degree.[12]

There was interest in other radical reforms during the early inter-university meetings. In 1923, the Vice-Chancellor of the University of Western Australia, Edward Shann, proposed a common first-year curriculum for all university degrees. Students would need to take one laboratory-based subject, such as biology or chemistry; one language, either classical or modern; and one subject from the humanities or social sciences, such as history, economics, logic or mathematics.[13] Such a scheme perhaps made more sense for the newer, smaller universities such as Western Australia than it did for the larger established ones with many more courses. Shann's proposal also ran against the tenor of the interwar period, which was marked by a proliferation of degrees, particularly in the social sciences, that became increasingly specialised.

Professional associations had also been calling for university training that would serve their advancement. Although this pressure was felt by all universities, and professional associations now operated on a national level, the legislation governing the professions was enacted by state governments, hampering a collective response.[14] An example of the pressure came after the Royal Australasian College of Surgeons was established in 1927, since it not only represented the interests of surgeons beyond the advocacy provided by the overarching British Medical Association (which represented all medical professionals), but also provided specialist postgraduate training, which provided high standing within the profession. A Royal College of Physicians followed in 1938 with a similar purpose. The provision of credentials outside universities challenged the standing of university degree.

The College of Surgeons, led by the redoubtable and veteran campaigner George Syme, urged universities to impose 'uniformity in the surgical degrees', a request referred to the respective medical schools.[15] The college's own postgraduate qualifications remained a thorny issue. In 1932 Adelaide and Sydney warned that 'control of higher degrees in Surgery' might 'pass to any outside body' unless Melbourne agreed to their request to establish specialist degrees of Master of Surgery, focusing on diseases of the eye, ear, nose and throat, and obstetrics and gynaecology, which had emerged as the principal specialisations.[16] Melbourne argued that the general Master of Surgery would still be pre-eminent, and that the proposal would only serve to create lesser tiers of master's programs. It introduced these degrees as postgraduate diplomas.[17] Changes were necessary to modernise the medical curriculum, but the exchange demonstrated the power of an organised profession to challenge universities. At least in the case of higher degrees, the college recognised the credentials of their own organisation alongside those of universities.

During the 1920s most of the academic questions that concerned individual universities were handled outside the national frame. The establishment of the Commerce faculty at Melbourne in 1925, for instance, took place without consultation, as did the elevation of the Sydney veterinary school as the only Veterinary Science school on the east coast.[18] Even the protracted negotiations over the establishment of the Australian chair of

Anthropology at Sydney in 1925, supported by a grant from the Rockefeller Foundation, Commonwealth funding and contributions from the Universities of Melbourne, Queensland and Adelaide, took place outside the national conferences.[19]

Since the national meetings had no power to enforce changes, they served as much as a forum to advocate proposals for university development as for common action. In 1928 Sydney proposed that universities include greater emphasis on statistics within the mathematics course; in 1930 the Sydney Professor of English, Ernest Holme, called for the creation of geography programs outside the existing work within Commerce, Science and Arts disciplines, while the Chancellor of the University of Melbourne, James Barrett, called for the establishment of university nursing degrees to support the work of public health nurses, a long-standing objective of the Australian Nursing Federation, formed in 1924.[20] Some of these programs were introduced, but not at a coordinated, national level.

Universities achieved more coordination on issues that concerned their operations and administration. They agreed on consistent academic titles – professors, associate professors and readers, and lecturers – modelled on the conventions of the newer Scottish and English institutions. Standards for academic promotion were circulated, which included the length of tenure and research achievements, including unpublished research, as well as the associated pay scales. While there was not strict adherence to these conventions, a common nomenclature and structure of Australian academia quickly emerged, with universities setting out the core responsibilities of their staff.

The question of what special provisions universities should make for students in rural areas was also pressing, and a special concern of state governments. Some universities allowed technical college students to transfer to universities in later years of study.[21] Some also accommodated country students by making lectures non-compulsory where attendance was not essential, and by holding examinations in country centres. It emerged from discussions that Queensland offered country examinations as a matter of course, whereas Western Australia had done so but had encountered 'problems'. Universities agreed in principle that such provisions were undesirable, reasoning that it was better for students to come to campus so they could use libraries and benefit from a 'community experience', yet the provisions persisted.[22] Sydney brought a proposal for a Federal Examining University to the 1924 conference in a bid to cauterise the problem, but this was roundly rejected by the conference as undermining the pre-eminence of state-based university education with a device that would 'make permanent an imperfect system'. The conference also rejected the suggestion that the University of London offer its examinations in Australia.[23] There appeared no appetite for a federal university either modelled on the University of New Zealand or the University of California, where the different universities – each with its own campus – specialised to some extent, having their own identity but relying on a degree of central control over budgets and planning.

Pensions were an issue that required discussion as universities expanded and many staff moved between universities around the country. In Britain, universities contributed to a common pension fund, which accommodated staff movement, while in Australia the different institutions had their own arrangements. Plans differed in the age of retirement or the years of service required to qualify. To explore how a common scheme could be administered, a subcommittee of economists was formed, including Richard Mills (Sydney), Douglas Copland (Melbourne), James Brigden (Tasmania) and Henry Alcock (Queensland). Related to this question was the tenure of chairs, and again universities adopted different standards. At Adelaide, professors were appointed for five years, while at

Western Australia and Queensland, appointments were made for seven. Universities agreed that new appointments should automatically receive tenure until retirement, except the few research professors, such as the Melbourne research chair in Economics.[24] As the discussions evolved during the 1920s on this and other matters, universities were mostly unwilling to agree to terms that might undermine their own identities, even though the national organisation proved useful. The increasing importance of Commonwealth support helped strengthen the resolve to work together.

TURNING TO THE COMMONWEALTH

While universities maintained a principal relationship with their own state government, the interest of the Commonwealth Government was mounting. The Commonwealth expanded its range of activity in the 1920s and began making specific-purpose grants for projects such as roads. It established control of state borrowing through the Loans Council, which further strengthened its command of national expenditure. The growth of the Commonwealth, and its relocation of some government departments to Canberra in 1927, raised concerns and new opportunities. Universities assumed that because education was a state responsibility, the Commonwealth could not become a source of direct funding. However, the expanding reach of the federal government and the growth of universities meant their activities began to overlap.

The universities' national conferences allowed them to agree a joint approach for relief of federal customs duties and sales tax on books and scientific equipment, as well as technical changes such as the preservation of wireless bandwidth for use in university laboratories.[25] They also lobbied for the creation of a broadcasting board, akin to the British Broadcasting Corporation, to ensure 'planned and balanced material', and urged government to recognise the 'constantly increasing educational and cultural possibilities of broadcasting', even if it decided not to establish a university radio station.[26]

The Commonwealth was also a potential source of research support, and this gained impetus from the establishment of the Council for Scientific and Industrial Research (CSIR) in 1926. The new organisation, replacing the Advisory Council of Science and Industry, was chaired by the engineer George Julius and included university professors, such as the chemist David Rivett, and aimed to foster research to solve industrial problems.[27] The formation of the CSIR, under a central council and with a much enlarged capacity to fund research projects compared to its predecessor organisation, provided an avenue to approach the Commonwealth Government. University science professors all urged the new organisation to make use of and extend the existing university laboratories, rather than duplicate them externally.[28] Thomas Laby, Professor of Physics at the University of Melbourne, urged universities to seek a 'federal subsidy' for university research work, under the aegis of the CSIR.[29] Medical schools were also successful in lobbying the Minister for Health, Neville Howse, to allocate funds for cancer research.[30]

From the 1920s universities jointly engaged the Commonwealth public service, which remained small and initially eschewed university graduates.[31] In the early years the service had a small number of technicians or experts compared to the overall workforce. It was an organisation built on the same principles as the pre–Australian Federation civil services, to which the new Commonwealth bureaucracy owed its lineage. There was no graduate intake. Some public servants undertook degrees, but without assurance of promotion. Partly for this reason, entry into the Commonwealth bureaucracy was not viewed by university graduates as an attractive career path. Only after the creation of the Commonwealth Public Service Board in 1922 did possession of a university degree become more desirable in the eyes of those in the service, although promotion by seniority remained the norm. After the First World War preference was also given to ex-servicemen; and this continued through the 1920s and left few openings to others at the senior 'officer level'.[32]

The civil-service's reluctance to hire graduates changed during the interwar period. After the First World War the service had grown to nearly 36 000, of whom 21 000 were permanent officers.[33] Sir Brudenell White, as chairman of the Public Service Board, sought to elevate public sector qualifications and expertise. Universities were willing to oblige. From 1923, after many returned soldiers from the First World War graduated, the Commonwealth Government and universities agreed there should be a system for graduates to enter the Commonwealth public service. This system was championed by the Vice-Chancellor of the University of Melbourne, Sir John Monash, who as well as being a decorated general was an engineer by trade and head of the State Electricity Commission of Victoria. Monash and civil service officials jointly developed a plan for recruiting university graduates directly into the administrative ranks of the service. A system of entry examinations was established that could be used to admit graduates to Chief Clerk and other Division II positions, which were senior positions in the service.[34]

The numbers of graduates were modest at first but grew as Monash and others petitioned the Public Service Board to increase the number accepted each year. In 1932 a joint committee of Commonwealth and university representatives began annually to select a very limited number of honours graduates for appointment.[35] By 1934, the federal government had amended the Public Service Act to fill 10 per cent of vacancies from a pool of university graduates, although the intake of degree holders remained small until the Second World War.[36]

Interactions with the Public Service Board complemented universities' efforts to build relations with the Commonwealth Government across its different functions. Direct lobbying of senior ministers became more widespread. Universities sometimes sought assistance, such as in 1920 when they asked for funding for the Commonwealth Pan-Pacific Science Congress, which was held in Melbourne and Sydney in 1923.[37] At other times, they attempted to dissuade the Commonwealth from a particular change in policy, for example in 1925 when the Commonwealth proposed to levy taxation on gifts made to universities.[38] This troubled the larger institutions of Sydney, Melbourne and Adelaide, for whom such gifts were a crucial source of additional revenue. Although mostly tied up in scholarships and prizes, these funds still provided an average of 37 per cent of their annual income.[39] Universities urged the Prime Minister, Stanley Bruce, to withdraw a planned change to the taxation regime, and the government obliged.[40]

The desire to develop Canberra and serve the public servants who had relocated there, as well as the growing demand for graduates, led to moves to establish university education in Canberra. An initial step, which demonstrated the capacity for higher education to be delivered in the Australian Capital Territory, was the Australian Forestry School. This replaced the school in Adelaide and became the pre-eminent university forestry school in 1927. Universities awarded a Bachelor of Science in Forestry, which required two final years of work in Canberra.[41]

The larger plan was to create a new, federally funded university in Canberra. This plan was developed by a committee, including representatives of the universities of Sydney, Melbourne and Tasmania. A university was preferred over a system of scholarships to send students to the existing state universities. The committee recommended programs in Economics and Arts, but argued against the establishment of other departments, such as Law, which should wait for the development of legal activities in Canberra.[42] The other universities also raised concerns about the creation of a Science faculty, arguing that resources should be directed first to the existing facilities in the state universities.[43] Although universities chafed at the lack of consultation across the sector, Canberra University College was duly established in 1928. It was affiliated with the University of Melbourne and offered courses under its supervision on 'similar' terms as those it recognised at Victorian technical colleges.[44] A similar desire to offer local higher education would lead in 1938 to the establishment of the New England University College at Armidale, affiliated with the University of Sydney.[45]

THE GREAT DEPRESSION AND ITS EFFECTS

Australian universities were growing significantly by the late 1920s. They had doubled their staff and student numbers, as well as their incomes, over the previous decade, and had established new fields of teaching and research.[46] Yet they would not be spared the hardships brought by the worldwide economic depression that followed the 1929 crash of the United States' stock market. The Commonwealth Government's response of increasing tariff charges and restricting further migration had little effect. By August 1930, a director of the Bank of England, Sir Otto Niemeyer, was brought to Australia to advise federal and state governments on how to deal with what was fast becoming a national emergency. He advised a sharp reduction of public spending. Despite opposition from the New South Wales Premier, Jack Lang, the state and federal governments agreed on the Premiers' Plan in 1931, which specified a more equitable reduction of income. The plan imposed a 20 per cent cut in federal and state spending, along with increased taxes. State governments had to find a broad range of budget cuts, and grants supporting universities were not excluded.

Universities had substantial insight into the unfolding crisis. Lyndhurst Giblin, a research Professor of Economics at Melbourne and a former Tasmanian politician, was a frequent adviser to the federal Treasurer, Joseph Lyons.[47] Edward Shann, former Vice-Chancellor of Western Australia from 1921 to 1923 and a vocal contributor to the national conferences, advised the government on the crisis as part of a committee of economists. A particularly important contribution came from Douglas Copland, Professor of Commerce at Melbourne. He advocated expert advice to government from universities, and ultimately chaired the government's committee to devise a response to the Depression. He was instrumental in developing the Premiers' Plan, which was originally known as the 'Copland Plan'. As well as the involvement of university economists, in August 1930 Robert Cameron, Professor of Education at the University of Western Australia, urged universities to consider a public response to the broader effects of the national crisis, such as ameliorating the consequences of widespread poverty.[48]

By August 1931, all of the state governments had slashed university grants. Government funding fell between 1931 and 1934 and universities struggled to pay their staff and balance their budgets. Sydney suffered the worst, losing 31 per cent of its annual state funding by 1934, and only half of that loss was offset by other income. Western Australia and Tasmania suffered similar cuts. Western Australia was unable to attend the universities conference in 1932 directly because of budget constraints. Melbourne and Queensland were slightly better off, but Queensland still had to reduce salary costs by 13–15 per cent to accommodate a 'financial emergency' that lasted until the end of the decade.[49] Adelaide imposed a 10 per cent salary cut in 1930 after its funding was reduced. By 1934, its overall government funding remained almost the same as pre-Depression levels because funding for the University's Waite Agricultural Research Institute increased by an equivalent amount.[50] Overall, universities did vastly better than most Australians. The country suffered a reduction of real GDP in 2010 dollars from $91 182 million in 1929 to a low point of $74 257 million in 1931, and hundreds of thousands of people were unemployed, while farmers' incomes fell disastrously with the collapse of prices for their produce. Those in tenured posts at universities at least remained in work.[51]

Table 2.1
REDUCTION IN GOVERNMENT GRANTS DURING THE GREAT DEPRESSION

	1929 state total	1934 state total	Difference between 1929 and 1934
SYDNEY	£81 170	£56 333	-31%
MELBOURNE	£66 716	£51 450	-23%
QUEENSLAND	£25 857	£19 560	-24%
ADELAIDE	£55 676	£54 100	-3%
WESTERN AUSTRALIA	£35 558	£24 800	-30%
TASMANIA	£14 826	£10 380	-30%
TOTAL	£279 803	£216 623	-23%

SOURCE *Commonwealth Year Book*, various years.

In response to the unfolding crisis, universities adopted a defensive position, determined to preserve what they could while awaiting improvements. The priority was to ensure that the 'present troubles' were not allowed permanently to alter universities and their international standing. A common response was a temporary blanket reduction of staff salaries. Professors approaching retirement were urged to stay on in their positions as the costs of their pensions, combined with the cost of recruitment, was prohibitive.[52] The retention of senior staff also preserved universities' public standing, ensuring senior positions were not filled by inexperienced academics brought in on lower salaries, while universities waited for conditions to be restored.

The Depression boosted university enrolments, which grew by 20 per cent between 1929 and 1934 as students sought refuge from unemployment and looked to university training as a pathway to a secure career. To accommodate the additional students, universities increased the number of demonstrators, tutors and junior lecturers by 20 per cent between 1929 and 1934, from 516 to 635. In the absence of new professorial appointments, all universities built their junior ranks.

The funding cuts tested the stability of national agreements reached between universities over the previous decade. The chair of Anthropology, for instance, was threatened after Victoria, Western Australia and Tasmania 'ceased to pay their grants'. The position only continued at Sydney with Commonwealth funding.[53]

CHIEF EXECUTIVE OFFICERS

The Depression meant universities had to grapple with reduced circumstances, giving impetus to rearrange their administration. At the 1920 universities conference, there was extensive discussion by representatives from each university about whether their institutions required 'chief executive officers'. Existing honorary and part-time roles could not adequately oversee the growing size and complexity of university operations. University leadership was also divided between executive officers who were prominent members of the community, and senior professors who provided academic leadership. As the shifting cast of delegates to the national conferences revealed, universities lacked consistent representation.

The need for a leader responsible for the whole institution had been discussed for decades but, by 1920, little consensus had emerged. The royal commission into the University of Melbourne had declined that university's request to recommend such an appointment in 1904, even while identifying the advantage this would offer in improving the university's approach to administration.[54] The universities of Queensland and Western Australia had not included this appointment when they were formed, following the older universities. The University of Sydney had elevated Henry Barff to a position of Warden in 1914, combining his former role as Registrar with other responsibilities, but this fell short of a full chief executive.[55]

In 1916 the University of Melbourne floated the idea of a full-time administrator owing to the 'growth in educational service' – reflected in the array of disciplines offered and the number of students. It also saw a need for a 'leader and seer' with an overview of the entire institution, who was not beholden to any one department, but responsible for 'advancing Australian higher education'.[56] The 'principal', following the Scottish designation, would have participated in all governing and faculty boards. The office required an individual able to provide both professional and academic leadership, and stood above that of the principal administrator at that time, the registrar. The officer would engage across the university, but there were protections against the principal becoming the 'autocratic type of the President of an American university'.[57] Following the British convention, the principal would not chair the governing board, but would be responsible for university management while governance would remain the responsibility of the council or senate. Melbourne's council recommended the appointment of such a 'principal', but the position was never funded.[58]

Universities recognised the need for dedicated leadership through an 'officer of high status' to represent both the educational and administrative functions, and to enhance the governance of universities. Sir John MacFarland, Chancellor of Melbourne, made a detailed proposal in 1916 for the role and duties of these new full-time senior administrators. He proposed that they should be supported by a salary so they could concentrate on all university business, and that they must have responsibly beyond ensuring efficiency alone. This officer would have an outward-facing role, to represent universities before 'other universities and the public generally', with greater purpose and urgency than was possible for a part-time, honorary position.[59]

Even after universities agreed on the need for a chief executive officer in 1920 and to use the title 'vice-chancellor' rather than 'principal' as Melbourne had advocated, one was not appointed until 1927 when the University of Sydney selected Professor Mungo MacCallum for the new position. At first this full-time administrator was to be deputy chancellor, but Sydney adopted the new convention in 1930, and the designation was changed to vice-chancellor. To clear up the confusion over titles, the duties of the honorary 'vice-chancellor', a position that deputised for the chancellor on the governing body, were assigned to a new role of 'pro-chancellor'.

Sydney and Western Australia (Hubert E Whitfeld) were the first to employ such officers, and at each the new roles took a significant overview of university-wide business. Melbourne finally secured funding for the appointment in 1934, after failed attempts in 1913 and 1927. Raymond Priestley, the geologist and university administrator most famous for his earlier part in the Scott Antarctic expedition, became the first full-time vice-chancellor.[60] Queensland's first full-time vice-chancellor, career public servant John Story, was appointed in 1938; Adelaide's physicist, Albert

Rowe, took up the position in 1948; and Tasmania appointed the economist Torleiv Hytten, in 1949. The need for central oversight of institutions that were clearly changing was broadly supported, even if this implied some loss of power by their governing council.

These appointments gave impetus to concerns over the effectiveness of the national meetings of universities. The difficulty of ensuring that agreements were carried through by the respective universities created frustration. In 1924, the Dean of Engineering at the University of Sydney, Henry Barraclough, called on universities to report on whether agreements on specific matters had been implemented, and for a process to follow up on decisions.[61] This suggestion was not adopted, and Barraclough repeated his request in 1930.[62] There were also other challenges to the fledgling system of national university advocacy. The University of Western Australia stopped attending the meetings in 1932, citing the cost of travel.[63] To resolve the issue, the Standing Advisory Committee was reconstituted in 1934 with a more stable membership, comprising the chief executive officers, the vice-chancellors or an 'officer of equivalent status'.[64] The committee became the Australian Vice-Chancellors' Committee (AVCC), which first met in April 1935. The new committee ensured greater follow-through and accountability. Sydney, Melbourne and Adelaide formed an 'executive committee' with authority to act on behalf of all universities on urgent matters, signalling the acceptance of greater cooperation, even if the executive committee proved unnecessary. The establishment of the AVCC also signalled another important change to Australian universities during the interwar years. By explicitly naming their new committee as a meeting of vice-chancellors, it recognised the growing need for universities to appoint chief executives to provide more concentrated administrative leadership.

OPENING TO THE WIDER WORLD

The formal creation of the AVCC empowered Australian universities to look beyond their own state jurisdictions and advocate their interests more directly, both nationally and internationally. At the first meeting of the AVCC in 1935, Douglas Copland, who was an adviser to the Rockefeller Foundation in Australia, and Frederick P Keppel, president of the Carnegie Corporation of New York, were in attendance to discuss their philanthropy. From 1927 the Carnegie Corporation of New York had provided significant funding to Australian universities for fellowships, research and adult education.[65] The Universities' Bureau of the British Empire acted for a time as a clearing house for some Carnegie Corporation grants, but Keppel now transferred responsibility for the awarding of travelling grants to the Australian universities.

The AVCC also sought influence over the awarding of other grants, but was turned down, in part because it did not include New Zealand universities. However, the picture of coordination presented by the AVCC was enough to secure the funding, and individual universities were permitted to bid for this money separately. Keppel stated that Carnegie could not promise 'large sums', but the first round in 1936 brought considerable amounts in the Australian context: £25 000 to Sydney for general research, £12 000 to Melbourne, and £8000 to Western Australia.[66] The varying amounts demonstrated the lack of coordination, and a bid from Tasmania was rejected for overlapping with the Melbourne project.[67] In 1935 Copland was asked to approach Rockefeller to discuss other philanthropic projects.[68]

Universities also turned their attention more fully to the Commonwealth, citing greater use of university facilities by government-sponsored research and the growing demand for research-trained graduates. The Commonwealth also drew on university staff to contribute 'expert services' to royal commissions and government committees, 'and generally in an advisory capacity at the request of the Government', as university economists had done during the Depression and elsewhere for the government.[69] In 1935 universities prepared an advocacy document outlining the case for Commonwealth support for university research. The argument was made that the CSIR and other federal research centres, such as the Mount Stromlo Observatory in Canberra, required trained research scientists, and universities should be assisted by Commonwealth funding to provide these.

The arguments were practical and stressed the advantages of efficiency. Western Australia argued that the case should 'appeal to the Statesmanship of the Commonwealth' and emphasise 'national well-being rather than national efficiency', but was outvoted. Such sentiments were misplaced in a pitch that was concerned with overcoming technical questions. The proposal sought to explain how grants for research, but not for teaching, could be constitutional, even if universities privately thought that the Commonwealth's power to make them was 'dubious'. Citing the corporations power, they argued that Commonwealth support to state universities was possible if concerns around the potential for political interference could be assuaged and state governments could be persuaded to agree.[70]

The pitch was also made personally to senior ministers with experience of university study, including the Attorney-General, Robert Menzies, and the Treasurer, Richard Casey; their support proved crucial.[71] From 1936 the Commonwealth appropriated an annual sum of £30 000 for scientific research, with the money channelled through the CSIR. Grants were allocated for projects and could be used for equipment, travel and salary costs of researchers. They were 'not meant for the relief of finances at any university'. On the recommendation of the AVCC, the CSIR apportioned the money according to staff and student numbers, so that Sydney and Melbourne received £7500, Adelaide £5400, Queensland £4200, Western Australia £3000 and Tasmania £2400.[72]

The division of scientific research funding was a point of continuing contention over the allocation of resources between the different-sized universities. Sydney and Melbourne agreed that universities should review the initial division to privilege the strongest projects, an arrangement that anticipated the competitive system of research funding in Australia based on projects rather than proportional distribution.

Both universities and the CSIR interpreted this funding as coming directly to universities. As David Rivett, CEO of the CSIR, related to the 1937 Australian and New Zealand Universities Conference, the research work of the CSIR and universities was indistinguishable and the result of a 'combination of effort on a basis of mutual trust'.[73] But in 1938 Casey informed the CSIR that the funding was technically made to the CSIR 'for such work within the Universities as it considered advisable from the standpoint of its own activities'.[74] Universities protested that the money was already committed and Rivett agreed to allow work that was underway to continue, but it specified a list of 'subjects in which the Council was directly interested' as guidelines. The CSIR would also award projects on the recommendation of universities.[75] There was some interplay here in the definition of the CSIR priorities, and universities advanced suggestions for areas of future work. For instance, universities urged the CSIR to establish a 'permanent scientific station' in the Antarctic following the recent purchase of a ship with the capacity to reach the Antarctic mainland, on the recommendation of former explorer and Professor of Geology at the University of Adelaide, Sir Douglas Mawson.[76]

Universities were careful not to recommend research projects in the humanities, as they had done under existing state government research programs, for fear this might jeopardise Commonwealth support and undermine the constitutional justification for funding. Direct Commonwealth support for social sciences finally came only in 1943, as part of Commonwealth plans for postwar reconstruction. The government sought 'research into reconstruction problems', and funded projects such as establishing the study of demography and social sciences and conducting political surveys of rural areas, as well as projects such as developing library resources and supporting fellowships to train early career researchers.[77]

Efforts had also been made by the AVCC in 1935 to promote the establishment of the National Health and Medical Research Council (NHMRC), an organisation announced in 1926 after the Royal Commission on Health, but not funded until 1937, when it was given an annual budget of £30 000.[78]

Throughout the 1930s Australia's universities expanded their connections with universities in Japan, China and India. Queensland promoted the concept of teacher exchange and urged universities to agree to maintain visiting scholars. The champion of the scheme, the Queensland historian Alexander Melbourne, had visited Japan and China in 1931–32 and chaired the Queensland and Commonwealth Advisory Committees on Eastern Trade. After a further trip in 1936, he published a report on the universities of Japan and China. He urged universities to extend connections with East Asia. He argued to the AVCC that 'Australian interest in relations with the Eastern Countries should not be restricted to trade, but should extend to education and culture'.[79] In the same vein, Australia's universities were asked by the universities of Madras and Calcutta to recognise their graduates and support them in postgraduate work in Australia. This suggestion was accepted by their Australian counterparts, although more work was necessary to attain 'mutual recognition'.[80]

THE GATHERING STORM

The relations between Australian universities that emerged in the 1920s were defined by a commitment to academic standing and to building up the existing teaching universities located in each state. These priorities tended to privilege existing structures, and although coordination between universities was assisted by making vice-chancellors the conduit for discussion, the affiliation remained loose. Universities had it both ways, deciding when collective action benefited them, and when it was better to act alone.

The fragility of national commitments was revealed after the death of the Vice-Chancellor of the University of Western Australia, Whitfeld, in 1939. Facing a looming financial crisis, Western Australia invited the Vice-Chancellor of the University of Sydney, Robert Wallace, to conduct a wide-ranging inquiry. Sydney released Wallace out of commitment to a national colleague, but his review undermined the agreements of the previous years. Wallace stressed the need for economy in a 'system of administration' he criticised as 'too elaborate, cumbersome and costly' for the university's size. Wallace argued the university should model itself, not on the agreements of the preceding two decades, but rather on the administrative systems of 'Sydney, Melbourne and Adelaide' of the late nineteenth century, when they were of equivalent size. The office of vice-chancellor might not be replaced, he argued, but if it was, this should be by a part-time appointment from within the existing professoriate, or from the Perth community on an honorary basis.[81]

There was some public sympathy with this view. An article in the Adelaide *Advertiser* in the lead-up to the 1937 Australia and New Zealand Universities Conference attacked the costly hiring of overseas vice-chancellors as wasteful.[82] Western Australia's response was to appoint George Currie as the part-time, salaried vice-chancellor and, two years later, appoint another inquiry chaired by a member of the local judiciary. This response by the University of Western Australia showed that a central academic leader who could engage with the other Australian universities as well as relate to state and Commonwealth governments and national organisations had become a necessity.[83]

The Western Australian crisis revealed the problem of resources and how these should be most efficiently managed. Universities' position was placed in sharp relief in 1939 when they were presented with a report from the United Kingdom's University Grants Committee, which showed the extent of the difference in government funding for universities. Between 1919–20, the first year of that committee's existence and 1939, the annual recurrent grants to British universities had increased from £692 150 to £2 007 900, including during the Depression.[84] When Australian universities came together in the 1920s they were already behind their British cousins in levels of funding, and they had continued to fall further back over the subsequent twenty years. If they wished to consider themselves of equivalent standing to their British peers, they would need to find new sources of revenue and, perhaps, advocate for the creation of an equivalent Australian committee to supervise the funding of universities.

The sector was also changing, and the parameters that defined it were increasingly influenced by external parties. The most important of these was the Commonwealth Government, which brought advanced proposals to establish a University of Canberra to the universities in 1937. Sir Robert Garran, a career public servant and the chair of the Council of Canberra University College, put forward a proposal for a

> university of a special type ... performing mostly postgraduate research in matters particularly affecting the

Commonwealth, such as International Relations (including Pacific Relations and Oriental Studies), Public Administration and economics, but eventually undertaking undergraduate teaching under predominantly residential conditions.

Garran argued that the potential loss of students from state universities would be 'outweighed' by the presence of a university in Canberra, which would 'help to make the people and the government of the Commonwealth more university minded'.[85] Universities welcomed Garran's support for postgraduate research but were wary of the implications. Despite their reservations, the proposal showed universities that their role might soon change. Their recurrent work in defining common titles and structures, and consulting on academic programs, and in some instances aligning them, had led them to become recognisable as a system in a way that would have been unimaginable two decades earlier. In their common deliberations, they had found a new mode of action. With the beginning of the Second World War, universities would be left with little option but to harness this and coordinate their response.[86]

3
CONTROL AND INFLUENCE

The Second World War reshaped the Australian university system that had emerged over preceding decades. War powers and a greater emphasis on economic planning reawakened old discussions about the role and public responsibilities of universities. They also prompted new conversations – such as their place in a wider system of higher education. Fault lines opened up over who should be admitted into university, the barriers to access and the meaning of academic merit. These debates led ultimately to a showdown over university autonomy. Who controlled universities and on what terms?

Against this backdrop, the growth of universities continued. In the years after the war a surge of returned soldiers brought a dramatic five-year expansion before a debilitating contraction. The establishment of the Australian National University in 1946 and the New South Wales University of Technology in 1949, the first new universities in over 40 years, embodied different ideas of what a university could be. Universities were scrutinised by government and they were assessed against new criteria, which considered the extent to which the full intellectual potential of the Australian population was harnessed.

THE WAR EFFORT AND UNIVERSITIES

The declaration of war in September 1939 had immediate consequences for Australian universities. The previous war had shown that their expertise would be called on to support the war effort, in addition to the service of their students and staff in combat, and universities were ready to respond to the call. However, they were now much more complex entities. At the most basic level, they were much larger. At the beginning of the previous war, the largest university, Sydney, had 152 staff, but by the second war it had 384. Melbourne had grown from 89 to 318, and Queensland, by this time the third largest university, had grown from 25 to 223.[1] Teaching was now more layered, drawing together a wider range of experts, research and public engagement.

As the Commonwealth assumed administrative control under its defence powers, the AVCC emerged as a central player. War measures affected all universities and the AVCC realised its potential to speak collectively on their behalf to government. The AVCC held quarterly meetings during the war as the chief connection to the Commonwealth, so universities could collectively meet the government's frequent requests and the changing regulatory framework enabled by the *National Security Act*.[2] The National Union of Australian University Students (NUAUS), which formed in 1937 to represent the interests of students at a federal level, was invited to attend some meetings to encourage this new organisation, and to inform the AVCC's advocacy on behalf of the whole university sector. The University of Melbourne Vice-Chancellor and Registrar, respectively John Medley and John Foster, continued as chair and secretary, with Foster's honorarium increased from £25 to £50 in 1941.

In the early years of the war, universities were concerned largely with administrative challenges. The vice-chancellors suspended programs such as inter-university sport to save funds. The British and Carnegie travelling scholarships were also suspended as shipping was commandeered for the war effort. In 1941, Frank Beasley, Vice-Chancellor of the University of Western Australia, proposed that Australia should investigate sending students to universities in the United States, but this proved too ambitious when the United States entered the war. Such schemes involved considerable preparation, such as matching qualifications, which was only achieved after the war. There were similar challenges in requests for Australian universities to take on the education of American medical students studying at British universities.[3]

Mobilisation at first was limited, although all unmarried men aged 21 were required to submit to three months' military training. After the fall of France in mid-1940 the call-up became more insistent, and after 1942 all men under 35 were required to serve in the militia for domestic defence. Nonetheless, universities sought concessions from military authorities where decisions had material or operational consequences. For instance, the vice-chancellors were assured that staff would be able to accept military commissions only with their university's consent. This gave universities the right of refusal while replacements were found, a task made more difficult by the complication that universities had to supplement military pay if it fell short of the previous academic salaries of staff who went into uniformed service. Throughout the war, a number of university staff would be seconded to undertake work in the civil and military bureaucracy, notably economists Richard Mills, Douglas Copland, Kenneth Walker and Sydney Butlin, and the lawyer Kenneth Bailey.

Some students volunteered immediately for overseas service with the AIF. There were also negotiations about students called up for training in the militia. They were required to attend training camps, and universities received assurances that student training would be conducted over the long vacation, with students back no later than 1 April.[4]

In these negotiations, universities and military authorities collaborated in shared recognition of the importance of university graduates for the war effort. To ensure the nation had a sufficient number of graduates in key professions, each university was granted a quota of students in Medicine, Dental Science, Engineering, Agriculture, Science and Veterinary Science who were reserved from compulsory national service.[5] The government also asked universities to reduce the length of time to complete degrees in Medicine, Engineering and the sciences. The most controversial of these, the medical course, was the longest and also complicated by the later years of clinical training. Medical faculties were reluctant to shorten their courses, knowing the pressure this would place on students, with consequences for pass rates and the quality of graduates. At first, Adelaide agreed to shorten its course, but it then fell into line with Melbourne, Sydney and Queensland, which had decided to await a formal directive before investigating the options. However, a meeting of the medical deans in Melbourne in April 1940 pre-empted the official request made the following year and reduced the courses from six to five years, preserving the full curriculum by shortening holidays and condensing teaching.[6] Engineering courses were also shortened, with some final-year students embedded in military workshops rather than on campus.[7]

The government also asked universities to establish new courses in areas of special military need. Universities responded, although government support stopped short of what universities might have liked. Queensland established a course in naval architecture, and Adelaide included subjects on radio location training in its science course.[8] Yet the government refused universities' request that it subsidise the relocation of students from across Australia to undertake these courses, threatening their viability.[9]

Universities accommodated these early war measures but otherwise attempted to continue as normal. This was not always possible. One issue was Commonwealth research funding, since the five-year term of the grant administered by the CSIR was due for renewal in 1941. Negotiations took place at an AVCC meeting between universities and government representatives in June 1941, at which universities tabled a 150-page report outlining the research work that had been done and how the grant money had been expended.[10] Universities argued that research was essential, not only for war needs but also for 'post-war planning' to assist the new reconstruction division in the Commonwealth Department of Labour and National Service.[11] Accordingly, universities requested research money for projects in the social sciences, as well as the physical sciences.[12] The government supported the idea, suggesting work on agricultural markets in Australia and overseas, as well as on labour supply and the employment of women, housing and transport. It urged universities to train researchers in economics and the social sciences to support the public service.[13]

The negotiations over Commonwealth support for university research were then taken up by the new Curtin Labor government, sworn into office in October 1941. It lifted funding for research to £33 300, of which £2300 was to be allocated for social science research into reconstruction. The government allocated an additional £6700 for other reconstruction research.[14] This enabled Sydney and Melbourne to continue as before, with the additional funds allocated to the smaller universities. Universities formed an engineering subcommittee to coordinate university contributions to the war effort, such as the manufacture of munitions, measures to improve ventilation systems in tanks, and the development of a 'Blood-Type Dryer' and other industrial machines. The Curtin government established a Scientific Liaison Bureau under Eric Ashby, a Professor of Botany from Sydney University, who had championed better means of connecting scientific problems with 'suitable scientific men', including in universities. The bureau supported botanical and agricultural work, as well as the domestic manufacture of optical glass for munitions, although these initiatives took place outside the meetings of the AVCC.[15]

THE UNIVERSITIES COMMISSION

The Japanese attack on Pearl Harbor that launched the Pacific War in December 1941 radically changed the complexion of these negotiations. The government's 'manpower' controls became more stringent, with immediate implications for universities. John Dedman, the Minister for War Organisation of Industry, emerged as a central figure. His ministry had sweeping controls over war production. Universities were a small but tricky part of this impossible portfolio, and Dedman agreed to universities' requests for a conference. The meeting was held in Melbourne on 19 January 1942, with government manpower controls the central issue on the agenda.[16]

Dedman's address to open the conference committed the government to work closely with those present, but he signalled that he would not be intimidated by them. Dedman had an unusual university career. He had broken off his science degree at Edinburgh to enlist in the First World War, and had then deferred his part-time commerce studies degree at Melbourne when he was elected to the federal seat of Corio in 1940. Although not a graduate, he had educated himself through wide reading. What he lacked in oratorical grace he made up for with hard work, and he expected the same from others.[17] He conveyed to the gathered vice-chancellors and professors the gravity of the war emergency and the scale of the reorganisation of industry that was underway, but he urged a measured response. He did not want universities to close down non-essential programs, but his government required them to deliver two 'specific services': first, they would undertake 'investigations and research into particular problems relating to the war effort', and second, they would provide 'the training of personnel with the special qualifications for armed services, war production and other essential needs'.[18] Students, like workers, would be subject to manpower controls.

This interpretation of universities as fulfilling a service role was new, and Dedman anticipated a reaction. 'I am sure the universities recognise', he told the meeting, 'that it is their new task and new responsibilities, rather than their old privileges, that count'. He wished to make clear that the immunity from national service enjoyed by students in reserved degrees had 'nothing to do with rights and privileges' and was 'not meant to protect the persons concerned'; rather, it was motivated wholly to overcome the shortage of skilled graduates. Similarly, the university authorities should not consider themselves immune. He exhorted the vice-chancellors that 'universities must become rather more flexible institutions than they have been in the past; and they must be willing to do untraditional things'. Their research efforts must be redirected to war requirements, and 'provide training not previously regarded as university work'.[19] The AVCC chair, John Medley, thanked Dedman, who then left the conference to attend the War Cabinet, leaving his stunned audience to work with military and government officials.

Medley set out a considered response to Dedman. He agreed that universities should not become places of 'refuge' for those seeking to avoid service and he supported the 'ruthless elimination of the undeserving at all stages' by directing students who failed examinations into military service. He also accepted that university research efforts should be devoted as much as possible towards the immediate needs of war. Medley believed, without foundation as it turned out, that 'the inevitable reduction in student numbers' as they enlisted for war service 'will make time and staff increasingly available' for research. But he was more apprehensive about the prospect of new degrees and the push to train more graduates. Universities could not, he stated, introduce courses that undermined their academic standing. Nor could they, with good conscience, 'persevere with the training of those who cannot take advantage of it' if they were compelled to take unprepared students to meet quotas in the reserved courses. Universities were complex organisations, he explained, and he warned that blanket directives could create unintended problems, but he undertook to work with government to ensure the best outcomes.[20]

Under the new controls, a hard line was drawn between reserved and non-reserved courses. In the reserved ones, military authorities directed universities to enrol a specified quota of students. These courses included degrees in Medicine, Dentistry, Engineering, Science, Agriculture and Veterinary Science. Students in non-reserved courses, including those in Arts, Law, Commerce and Economics, which made up the majority of the university population, were liable to be called up for national service. In order to preserve these faculties, universities secured a 'limited number' of protected places for outstanding candidates, chosen in consultation with military authorities. These faculties continued under the Damoclean sword of total conscription.

The changes placed university enrolments under the control of military authorities, and universities sought concessions that would give them greater certainty. The Vice-Chancellor of the University of Adelaide, Sir William Mitchell, asked that the age of conscription for students be lifted to nineteen to allow them time to complete three-year courses. Kenneth Bailey, the University of Melbourne's Dean of Law, asked that the number of protected places in non-reserved courses be fixed. However, the Adjutant-General, Lieutenant-General Victor Stantke, refused to compromise. The age of conscription would be no different for students than for others and remained eighteen, and the 'limited number' of students in unreserved categories would be determined by manpower prerogatives. Then Richard Mills, the University of Sydney's Professor of Economics, who also had Commonwealth responsibilities, pointed out that not all universities had legislative authority to exclude qualified applicants, so it was not clear how they would limit numbers to the necessary quotas. Undeterred, the government and military authorities indicated they would obtain legal advice to overcome this technicality.[21]

The regulations that followed empowered the Minister for Labour and National Service to nominate the number of students in these courses. Where demand was higher than this number, places would be awarded to students on a competitive basis, on their order of merit. The government required that any students who 'failed' in their studies would not be eligible to re-enrol the following year.[22] Yet there remained ambiguity in implementing this directive. Universities interpreted 'failure' in different ways, variously taking this to mean in single subjects or in the majority of classes within a year. Some universities obtained permission from local authorities to enrol fewer students than stipulated by the quota if they attracted insufficient 'students of proper calibre', whereas others followed the directive with 'literal obedience'. The 'limited' number of protected places in non-reserved courses was also different at different universities, but university authorities were careful not to push too far. In 1942, Sydney nominated only 24 students, Melbourne 23, while Queensland and Adelaide did not find it necessary to nominate any.[23]

Universities' total enrolments fell during the war. The student population of 14 236 in 1939 fell to 11 675 by 1943. It might have fallen further without efforts to urge students to enrol at the university at a younger age, so they might complete at least the rudimentary parts of their courses before they were called up. Women were also urged to enrol, which they did, but not in sufficient numbers to offset the number of male students who would otherwise have been admitted. Women made up a quarter of the total student numbers, comprising almost half of Arts students but a much smaller proportion in courses such as Law. Their number grew from 3942 in 1939 to 4474 in 1943, increasing their proportion of the total university students from 27 to 38 per cent.[24] Other measures included encouraging students who failed exams in unreserved courses to take up reserved ones. For instance, students who failed Mathematics could be advised to transfer to a Science or Engineering degree, so as not to lose their place.[25]

Under the logic of the manpower controls, a student doing a reserved course was considered to be undertaking national service. But while conscription into other military or civilian service entitled individuals to full pay, students were not paid, while remaining liable for university fees. In one case publicised in a letter to the Melbourne *Age* newspaper, a father explained the hardship this had placed on his family. He had himself been called up for military service and could no longer afford to pay his son's university fees. However, because his son was in a reserved course, he could not withdraw. The catch-22 reached Prime Minister Curtin himself, who promised to investigate providing financial assistance to students under these circumstances.[26]

The question of financial assistance fed into existing concerns about the shortfalls in the numbers of doctors, dentists and engineers required to meet the needs of the war. A government study found family financial incapacity was a determining factor in capable students not enrolling at university. Financial assistance achieved two related objectives: meeting the demand for university graduates and broadening the base of students attending university (or, as it was expressed at the time, reducing the 'wastage' of talent deterred from attending university). Several alternatives were considered. These included the idea of introducing a student loans system, rejected as further disadvantaging those already 'most heavily burdened', the 'direct enlistment of students' as well as where university study was a form of military service. This latter idea was rejected as introducing complexities over how to accommodate the medically unfit. A means-tested bursary system was recommended to remove a major financial barrier to attending university, although there remained questions about the obligations on recipients during their studies and in their choice of subsequent work.[27]

The introduction of student financial assistance was a major undertaking. Dedman appreciated the need for a special commission to administer the scheme and compile the necessary information.[28] Universities petitioned Curtin for a 'central bureau with permanent secretariat to deal with the numerous inquiries' from 'Government and other authorities', and offered to set up and administer it.[29] Curtin saw advantages from the government's perspective, but decided that government should retain control over its administration through a Universities Commission.

The Universities Commission first convened on 2 December 1942 in Sydney. It was chaired by Richard Mills, who had extensive experience leading major public inquiries, including chairing the 1942 Commonwealth Committee on Uniform Taxation and then the Commonwealth Grants Committee, which allocated Commonwealth funds to the states. The other members comprised Dr Lloyd Ross, a former lecturer in economic history and Workers' Educational Association tutor, and until recently the communist secretary of the New South Wales branch of the Australian Railways Union,[30] FP Barker, MHR, and James Darling, headmaster of Geelong Grammar School. Two days later, the commission met with the AVCC. Sydney Butlin, an economist with the Department of War Organisation of Industry, was invited to attend.[31]

The commission had an imposing program of tasks: to introduce and administer Commonwealth financial assistance to students, and review 'existing University facilities for providing training for various forms of National Service and the need for new buildings and teaching equipment'. It had significant powers, including the authority to compel answers to questions, and a wide remit for the 'preparation of post-war plans'.[32] The commission also proved to be an effective liaison body, providing advice to government and also consulting with universities over the numbers of reserved places.[33] Much of its work would be in gathering data on universities, a task supported by the AVCC and universities.

A function of the commission was to support the Commonwealth Financial Assistance Scheme (CFAS), which provided funds to pay for course and examination fees and paid a means-tested living allowance. It provided travel costs for students travelling interstate to enrol in reserved courses unavailable at their local university. Available to families earning less than £250 a year, with the assistance reducing for those of greater means, it was awarded on merit and open to students from all Australian universities enrolled in Medicine, Dentistry, Engineering, Science, Veterinary Science and Agriculture, as well as a limited number of students enrolled in Arts, Law, Economics or Commerce, and Architecture. The CFAS was supported by an information campaign in secondary schools about entering universities, which contributed to its success. By October 1943, the scheme had assisted 1595 students.[34]

The financial support had immediate effect, and the quotas in reserved courses were quickly filled, which introduced a new element of competition into university selection. Universities and the military authorities interpreted this in slightly different ways.

For the military authorities, this meant choosing physically and mentally robust students able to complete their courses and join the war effort, whereas universities wanted the best and brightest, and those prepared for university life. Mills expressed the government's desire to open up the matriculation examination to anyone who wanted to sit it. However, universities noted the examination itself was only the final hurdle in the longer matriculation process, including advanced secondary schooling. The University of Melbourne Registrar, John Foster, objected that the government's proposal would undermine the position of 'A' class schools, which prepared students to matriculate in Victoria. Others argued that it would lower the quality of university graduates. Thomas Parnell, Queensland's Professor of Physics, said matriculation standards were already too low. The Sydney Vice-Chancellor, Robert Wallace, worried that pressure on universities to fill quotas in unpopular courses was making the student cohort 'weak'.[35]

These issues became critical for those whose examination results placed them at the cut-off for entry into a degree course. Mills asked whether universities would consider psychological or medical testing of applicants on the understanding that this should not become a means of 'exclusion' but would nevertheless provide useful 'information' in deciding close cases.[36] The University of Adelaide announced its belief that selection for the final places should not be based on examination alone, but that references should be sought from headmasters and interviews conducted to assess 'character, aptitude, physical fitness, and health record, among other factors'. The University of Western Australia adopted a similar resolution, seeking reports from headmasters 'on the leadership qualities and sporting ability ... besides their personality and interest in general school activities'. At the University of Melbourne, all first-year students had been psychologically tested in collaboration with the Australian Council for Educational Research (ACER), as a test case. The University of Tasmania moved to interview all candidates.[37] These policies were mocked in places such as the populist tabloid newspaper *Smith's Weekly* for considering aptitude over an individual's interest in or ability for hard work, suggesting that interviews merely confirmed professional predispositions and class biases.[38] None of the schemes continued once quotas were lifted.

The idea of university quotas was also foreign to prospective students, who could previously have expected to enrol in the course of their choosing. However, in 1943, Sydney received 1111 applicants for only 550 reserved places, leaving large numbers disappointed.[39] In April, sixteen-year-old Robert King, who had missed out on a place in Science at Sydney, petitioned the full bench of the New South Wales Supreme Court for a writ of mandamus requiring the university to admit him. The application was referred to the High Court as it went to the constitutional validity of Commonwealth control over enrolments.[40] King withdrew his claim after he ultimately secured a place under the quota, but another prospective student, John Drummond, aged eighteen, from Artarmon in New South Wales, brought a separate action after he was denied admission to a medical degree. The government obtained leave to act as defendant in the hearing, it having previously agreed to indemnify universities against liability for applying the regulations.[41]

In a split decision handed down in June 1943, the High Court upheld Drummond's claim and directed Sydney to allow Drummond to matriculate on the basis that the federal government had no constitutional power to intervene in state education systems. However, it could not require that Drummond be allowed to enrol, as this was a matter of interpretation of the university's statute.[42] The government responded by gazetting new national security regulations that made universities responsible for determining the order of merit on which the manpower directorate would allocate reserved places. It also acceded to the AVCC's request that it give publicity to its action to stave off a probable influx of new claims and a public education campaign to counter media coverage that framed university study as a means of shirking national service.[43]

Although total enrolments at Australian universities declined during the war years, the threatened exodus of students never eventuated. As the war turned and the Japanese began their protracted retreat, the pressure on universities subsided. From October 1943, universities began planning to reinstate the normal duration of Engineering and Medicine courses as pressure for graduates reduced.[44] After January 1943, when HC 'Nugget' Coombs was appointed Director-General of the Department of Post-War Reconstruction, attention turned to planning for the transition to peace.

POSTWAR RECONSTRUCTION

When hostilities ceased and the servicemen and women returned home, much had changed for universities. The full mobilisation of the economy had demonstrated the urgent need for experts, and the government had shown a willingness to support their training in the national interest. Universities benefited from this policy, but they were no longer in full control of their activities, with government requests being thrust upon them. Student financial assistance had not been their initiative, although their administrators provided the statistics to support it. The wartime quotas were set by military authorities, even if universities secured small numbers of discretionary places. The Department of Post-War Reconstruction, of which Dedman became minister in place of Ben Chifley towards the end of the war, continued to set the agenda, bringing fresh opportunity but also some erosion of autonomy.

The largest contribution of postwar reconstruction was the transition from the CFAS to the Commonwealth Reconstruction Training Scheme (CRTS), which covered the tuition and exam fees of returned servicemen and women, and paid them a living allowance. In 1943 Dedman had appointed economist Ronald Walker to chair a committee examining the question of Commonwealth support for education, not only to universities but also to schools, to aid postwar reconstruction.[45] The CRTS was established under the war powers, however, the Walker committee recommended that the Commonwealth clarify the constitutional standing of its contribution to education. This led to the inclusion of the 'benefits to students' clause in the Constitution, a change adopted in the 1946 referendum. This allowed the Commonwealth Government to provide scholarships and living allowances after the war powers ceased.[46]

Prior to the 'benefits to students' power being added to the Constitution, the continuation of the financial assistance was secured by consultation with universities during the final years of the war. While the CRTS had overwhelming support, it did create concerns. The NUAUS and Coombs for instance, sought the liberalisation of the scheme. A 24-point plan agreed at the 1944 NUAUS conference urged larger quotas for the non-technical degrees, monitoring of the scheme, and careful planning for repatriation assistance. In practice, students were allowed to enrol in the course of their choice. The overarching concern was that financial assistance should be provided to students regardless of their contribution to government priorities, which was nominally the purpose of the scheme. While student groups sought to shape this agenda in the postwar period, the NUAUS campaign to lift the living allowance for CRTS students was unsuccessful.[47] Universities opposed a proposed means test on the grounds that education should be open to all, and urged concessions to enable supported students to undertake vacation work. They were unable to secure immediate concessions on each of these issues, although in practice no means test was applied.[48] The scheme enabled access but stopped short of providing more than basic support, with student income support payments set below the minimum wage.[49]

The CRTS presented universities with both opportunity and threat. Demobilisation promised a surge of new enrolments that would dramatically expand universities. As the scheme came into operation in 1944, state Education Departments reported surprising increases in the numbers of applications for public examination, including for matriculation. University enrolments almost tripled between 1943 and 1948, when they peaked at 32 453. Between 1945 and 1952, almost 60 000 students would attend university under the CRTS.[50]

These students needed to be supported, and given that student fees covered only around a third of the actual cost of a university place, the upsurge would also strain university finances. Universities convinced the Commonwealth to provide block grants for the construction of new facilities, and even for the appointment of special tutors. Labour and material shortages, however, left universities reliant on temporary accommodation. Universities also won additional grants to subsidise the full cost of the Commonwealth-supported places.[51]

To ensure that financial aid was efficiently applied, the Universities Commission undertook extensive and detailed surveys of student progress, working in collaboration with the AVCC. The commission's research reports admitted it was 'overloaded with numerical data', which it analysed using mechanical computer punch cards. It aimed to 'give facts and inferences based on facts after the application of statistical methods'.[52] This was a new form of reporting, and universities struggled to meet the requests of the commission. In 1943, for instance, the commission requested reports from universities on lecture attendance, which universities did not monitor.⁵³ In 1944 universities secured Commonwealth funding to cover the cost of such administrative work.⁵⁴ In exchange for Commonwealth financial aid, universities faced unprecedented levels of financial scrutiny, and the established rhetorical devices gave way to tables and charts, outputs and inputs.

The CRTS largely resolved the 'wastage of talent' problem by opening universities to a broader spectrum of students. But two other issues also loomed. First, the need to produce sufficient numbers of graduates with technical and professional skills, which in turn raised the question of whether universities undertook technical training. Second, the continued question of university research, and how the training of researchers could be supported and expanded.

These issues could have radical or modest solutions. Some argued that technical training could be provided, with fewer resources, directly by technical colleges rather than through universities. The CRTS comprised both university and technical college training, and the overwhelming majority chose the latter. The New South Wales Government established an Institute of Technology out of the existing Sydney Technical College in 1946 to fill this gap, and Victoria investigated similar options in 1948.⁵⁵ The issue of 'wastage' arose again in this context: if the cost of university study excluded talented candidates, could cheaper ways of providing such education be found?

Meanwhile, the Commonwealth prepared to establish a national research university, including a medical research school, in Canberra. This was an old idea, dating back at least to the 1920s, with different proposals as to its proper role. Champions such as Thomas Laby, the University of Melbourne Professor of Physics, who had also led the push for the introduction of the PhD, had urged the creation of a research university allied to the CSIR.⁵⁶ Universities had also discussed the idea in the 1930s. The notion of a new university in Canberra was then taken up by public servants in the Curtin government, notably the economist and Director-General of Post-War Reconstruction, 'Nugget' Coombs, the University of Melbourne Professor of Physiology, RD 'Pansy' Wright, and Mills. It was given impetus by the visit of the Australian Nobel laureate, physiologist and pharmacologist, Sir Howard Florey, who had helped to develop penicillin in 1940. During a speaking tour, Florey criticised Australian research facilities, spurring proposals for a John Curtin School of Medical Research in Canberra, which was established as one of four schools of the national university in 1948.[57] The Australian National University (ANU) Act of Incorporation passed in 1946.

John Medley expressed universities' anxieties in the 1945 Macrossan Lectures, which The University of Queensland had invited him to deliver. Medley was chosen for his capacity to speak generally about the needs of all universities, drawn from his experience chairing the AVCC, and his lectures were later published.[58] They combined a general defence of universities with bold claims for the necessity of massive expansion. He was acutely aware of the pressures facing universities in the transition back to peace, pointing out the contradictory demands made on them:

> We are, for example, nothing but technical schools, but on the other hand our graduates are theoretical and impractical individuals who cannot take a place in the real world. We are hotbeds of Communism and at the same time playgrounds of the idle rich. We stand aloof from the community but are accused of neglecting University duties to indulge in outside work.[59]

Medley countered these misconceptions by taking 'universities as they were'. He reproached those who criticised universities for allegedly failing to live up to some ideal or arbitrary metric. Medley urged practical solutions to problems. Universities were simultaneously the keepers of technical knowledge and the training grounds of the learned professions, yet they were also protectors of knowledge, interested only in truth.

Medley welcomed the Commonwealth student financial assistance scheme, but warned against simplistic solutions to the challenge of 'wastage' of Australian talent. Much more needed to be done outside universities, including raising the school leaving age, and wider social recognition of the benefits of higher education. He also warned that not all who came to universities were 'well placed', either with intellectual capacity or the resources and networks necessary, to establish themselves in professions such as medicine and law, and care must be taken against over-supply.

On research, Medley urged massive increases in funding 'up to one million pounds per annum'.[60] Such unprecedented funding was necessary, he argued, to protect researchers from the pressure of achieving 'immediate utilitarian results', and also to allow it to be distributed across an ecosystem of 'interacting and cooperating centres of research' across Australia, engaged in interchanges with similar bodies internationally.[61] A smaller fund with stricter controls would stifle the development of this ecosystem.

This latter comment took particular aim at the proposed Australian National University (ANU), which threatened the existing order with a new model of university funded by the Commonwealth. While Medley would not oppose the plans, he argued that it would

> be a catastrophe if this Federal Child is allowed to wax fat at the expense of existing Universities, if it receives the favourite's share of moneys available for research whilst others put up with the crumbs that fall from the table.[62]

Rather than wait on the good graces of government, Medley urged action: 'can we do nothing but live precariously on a diet of hope? I do not advocate so pusillanimous a policy'.[63]

Research remained a contentious issue. Although Medley had called boldly for up to a million pounds annually, universities found it difficult to achieve consensus. Not all universities were prepared to accept large increases in postgraduate students. Those with more generous state government support, such as the University of Sydney with an annual research allocation of £30 000 from the New South Wales Government, were concerned about the conditions that might be applied to Commonwealth funding. Lacking a united front, universities agreed to request only £100 000 for scientific research, plus an additional £25 000 for social sciences.[64] The Commonwealth provided grants of £40 000 in the sciences, and £12 000 for social sciences.[65]

The need to develop research across the other universities was given impetus partly because of the impending ANU, which threatened to draw away the best postgraduate researchers from the older universities. Determined to move first, and clearly frustrated by trying to move the other universities, the University of Melbourne announced its intention in 1944 to introduce a PhD. This, the premier research degree, differed from the existing doctorates, particularly in the requirement that candidates be given regular supervision, embedded formally into their local faculties as postgraduate students. The degree had been introduced in Germany, the United States, Canada and Scotland in the nineteenth century, and in England in 1917, at which time Melbourne had first sought to establish the degree. However, the other universities were not prepared to introduce it then and the University of Melbourne had shelved its plans.[66]

The revived plan was not announced out of the blue. The University's Dean of Science, the botanist John Turner, made 'informal communications' with his counterparts in advance of the next AVCC meeting in August 1944, but the proposal clearly caught the other universities by surprise. By the next meeting, six months later, only some of the universities had a policy: Tasmania was favourable, Adelaide and Queensland were opposed, while Western Australia and Sydney were still unsure. The reasons for the opposition were largely concerned with resources. The supervision required for the PhD was much more onerous than for the existing doctorates, which were awarded for work undertaken independently of the university, and some of the universities had no capacity to provide it.[67] The University of Melbourne went ahead without the others in the following year.

The fears of the older universities about the ANU initially proved misplaced as the creation of a new institution in Canberra proved to be an effective lever for expanding Commonwealth research support across the sector. The ANU's foundation Vice-Chancellor, Douglas Copland, also proved to be a particularly effective lobbyist. The research grant to state universities was increased to £67 000 in 1946–47, with £52 000 earmarked for 'the training of research workers' and £15 000 for 'original research' projects, the latter allocated by an AVCC research grants committee.[68] The new funding also protected the existing state government research grants, requiring the states to agree not to reduce their research funding as a result. As well as securing additional research funding, ANU benefited from national research scholarships, many of which were undertaken in Canberra.

The Commonwealth Government also announced its intention to lift the research grant from £67 000 to £82 000 in the following two years, offering this rolling triennial funding as a deliberate measure to enable universities to plan. In future, funding negotiations would focus on the third year of each triennium, with the amounts available in the first two already confirmed.

These continuing negotiations gave universities greater security than under the previous five-year allocations, which had required universities to make urgent appeals in the final year, often to different ministers.

Universities decided that half of the research money would be shared between the Universities of Sydney and Melbourne. Of the remainder, 18 per cent went to Adelaide, 14 per cent to Queensland, 10 per cent to Western Australia and 8 per cent to Tasmania. The following year, a less arbitrary formulation was developed, with 40 per cent shared equally among universities and the remainder allocated on the basis of student population, although this made little difference to the amounts allocated.[69]

The research funding covered scholarships and equipment, but it also supported the salaries of academic staff who supervised postgraduates. It thereby supported the development of postgraduate work, which in turn fostered a more sophisticated research culture. Universities determined new classifications of Junior and Senior Student, and Junior and Senior Fellow, on a pay scale rising up to that of a Reader, who received £750 per annum.[70] Universities were also determined to share this research funding by confirming a broader definition of 'social science' that included not just Law, Economics and Anthropology, but Psychology, History, and 'aspects of Philosophy and Agriculture'. The AVCC argued that 'in any long-term policy, all the humanities should be included'.[71]

Triennial research funding also enabled universities to press for regular augmentation, their ratcheting up of requests helped by the pattern of regular negotiations. Universities did not obtain the full amounts they sought, but they were able to secure generous annual increases of roughly 25 per cent. In 1948 universities sought an increase to £145 000 and made their case by explaining what more could be achieved than under the proposed allocation of £82 000. In 1949 they justified increases on the principle that postgraduate researchers 'should be trained by University staff rather than by [other] research fellows', which required academic staff to have relief from their teaching duties. Accordingly, universities requested a 'block grant of an amount equal to half the salary bill' of the respective universities.[72] The government lifted the allocation to £100 000. In 1950 universities pushed for an increase to £160 000 to account for inflation, and the 'normal expansion of research programmes'.[73]

This Commonwealth funding was increasingly integrated into operational budgets. Research funding supported salaries, while the funding from the CRTS and associated grants allowed the expansion of university facilities. This approach arose gradually, but it did include financial risk, particularly if the Commonwealth decided to reduce its funding in any year. Here the impending cessation of the CRTS, as the returned soldiers completed their degrees, loomed as a potential catastrophe.

There was also concern about the encroachment of other institutions. Along with the new Canberra research institutions, in 1948 the New South Wales Government announced an intention to convert its Institute of Technology into a full university, and requested Commonwealth research funding for it.[74] Hugh Ward, the University of Sydney's Professor of Bacteriology, urged the Commonwealth to appoint a royal commission to examine the Australian university system to ensure the needs of the older institutions and their capacity for research were not overshadowed by the generous funding provided to new institutions.[75]

Change was also coming to the AVCC. In 1949, Medley announced he would be ending his term as Vice-Chancellor of Melbourne and accordingly would be resigning as chair of the AVCC. Instead of a direct replacement, Medley proposed a 'rotating chairmanship' to relieve any one individual of the burden, and also to move the chair away from Melbourne. With the arrival of air travel, it was no longer necessary for the meeting to take place at the point of greatest convenience for sea and rail transport links. Canberra, moreover, was the centre of federal government with which the AVCC increasingly engaged, though there was no intention that the ANU should provide a permanent chair in the way Melbourne had done over the previous decades. The University of Western Australia's Vice-Chancellor, George Currie, agreed to take the chair for 1950–51, with Copland assuming a new position of deputy chair. From this moment the AVCC chair would be a biennial post and no individual vice-chancellor would again have the same longevity in steering the organisation as had Medley.

It was agreed, however, that the organisation should have a 'central coordinating office' to assist interaction with the Universities Commission and Commonwealth Government, and to provide support to the chair. Foster had already resigned as secretary to take up a position with the Universities' Bureau of the British Empire, promising to do much more to support universities outside Britain.[76] The new secretariat would have two officers, one to maintain the office and the other to gather information from the universities, thus allowing them to prepare more effectively for meetings and negotiations. Copland agreed to approach the ANU Council to provide 40 per cent of the anticipated annual cost of £2000, with the positions to begin from 1950.[77] John Ford, an economics graduate from Sydney, would be appointed secretary in 1950.[78]

The changes in the AVCC also responded to the growing complexity of university sector, and the need for more robust structures to give the universities greater national influence. The establishment of ANU had taken place with limited consultation with the other universities, the AVCC minutes recording that it was 'too late' to raise its concerns. Universities were not consulted either in the establishment of the new University of Technology. Events were moving faster, and the AVCC's detached and aloof structures were in urgent need of reform.

In 1949 the vice-chancellors were invited to Canberra to attend a ceremony laying the foundation stones of the ANU and the John Curtin School of Medical Research. They were joined by the Prime Minister, Ben Chifley, as well as Mills and Dedman, and were invited back to a private afternoon tea by Chifley, at which he handed around a press statement he planned to release. The statement announced that he would appoint a committee, chaired by Mills as head of the Universities Commission, with representation from Treasury, to 'examine the finances of universities, including their sources of income, existing and forecasted future commitments, their staffing position and the relationships of expenditure on research to teaching costs'. The committee would co-opt university representatives 'as required'.[79] Dedman had previously announced in the House of Representatives the government's intention to replace the CRTS in 1951 with 3000 Commonwealth scholarships, with selection based on competitive examination and awarded in state universities in proportion to their student number.[80]

These announcements were greeted with much relief by universities. Copland had made representations on their behalf in February for such a committee to be appointed. The presence of Mills as the chair offered assurance, and conformed with Copland's request that the chair be 'well acquainted with the Australian University problems and conditions'. Typically, universities had not got all they asked for: Copland had urged against the inclusion of a representative from Treasury, whom he believed would 'round down the sums requested'.[81]

Universities had reason to be hopeful. Thanking Medley for his service, they trusted that 'the difficult war years and the post-war period of re-adjustment' that Medley had toiled to manage would at last be behind them.[82] With the Mills Committee of Inquiry, it seemed they and their AVCC might reclaim the initiative to define the structure and direction of Australian higher education.

4
COMMONWEALTH AND STATES

In an address marking the University of Sydney's centenary in 1950, the newly elected Prime Minister, Robert Menzies, told the assembled audience that 'it should never be forgotten that the University's function was to educate individuals in culture and learning and not to create technical experts'. Menzies, a celebrated champion of university education, continued:

> This is an age of increasing cleverness, but not of increasing learning or wisdom. The contest of our time is between true values and an easy shoddy substitute. The true function of the University is to get its values right, and those of the public.
>
> There are some who believe that aeroplanes and scientific gadgets are the proof of civilisation. Civilisation exists in none of these things; they are mere instruments. True civilisation lies in the heart and spirit of man.[1]

The Prime Minister's emphasis on higher purposes served the celebrations well with its strong message to the assembled luminaries from Australia's universities. They were also beliefs Menzies had long held, repeating them often.[2] Yet the speech signalled that the politics of universities would be very different under the new government. Australia was benefiting from the postwar economic boom and grappling with the Cold War, and universities' mission went beyond their role in driving technological advancement and reconstruction after the Second World War.

Australia was becoming wealthier and enjoying the benefits of an economy where the unemployment rate averaged 2 per cent.[3] There were, as the Minister for National Development, Richard Casey, argued in 1951, 'signs of a nation caught up in the full throes of national development'.[4] Although the fruits of the postwar expansion were not universally shared, improved living standards helped drive ever greater demand for education. The states undertook a large program of building and staffing schools to accommodate more children reaching school age. This strained state education budgets and their capacity to fund universities, and also increased the number of students eligible to attend university. The student populations in universities had more than doubled since the introduction of government scholarships, and many students came to the university with the expectation that they could obtain financial support during their studies. The postwar expansion, and most particularly the previous Commonwealth Government's decision to meet the full cost of study for many students, including the provision of equipment and construction of new buildings, had restored universities that had languished since the Depression. The Menzies government inherited a university sector still adjusting to the temporary surge of enrolments brought on by the Commonwealth Reconstruction Training Scheme (CRTS).

The Commonwealth had committed to supporting universities, yet the extent of that commitment was not clear. The CRTS had opened entry to university to many more students from different backgrounds, and in so doing, universities had come to rely on the money the Commonwealth provided. The reduced number of war veterans enrolling through the CRTS brought universities and the Commonwealth to a crossroads. One path continued the closer relationship with the Commonwealth, another led back to the earlier reliance on the states. This was more than a question of who was responsible for providing funds, for it went to the growing national mission of universities and the role of the Commonwealth Government in the federal system.

By the late 1940s, the Cold War and the threat of nuclear conflict loomed over international and local politics. Fears that decolonised countries in Asia, such as Vietnam, would fall like 'dominoes' to communism, and the determination of Western powers to 'contain' communism, turned attention to Southeast Asia.[5] Universities had a manifest role here, being at the forefront of Australia's engagement with Asia, and eventually critical to Australia's contribution to the Colombo Plan.[6] No one listening to the Prime Minister at the University of Sydney centenary could miss the reference to the government's strident opposition to communism and what it asked of universities.[7] Menzies' description of a contest between 'true values' and 'a shoddy substitute' was a pointed allusion to the government's pledge to defend parliamentary democracy.[8] The government's bill to outlaw communism was front of mind for Australian universities, all of which had professors who had been accused by rogue parliamentarians of having communist sympathies. The charge was that these 'pink professors' were corrupting the minds of impressionable university students.[9] The new government also imposed Australian Security Intelligence Organisation (ASIO) security checks on Commonwealth public servants, including staff at the New South Wales University of Technology and the Commonwealth Scientific and Industrial Research Organisation (CSIRO), which had replaced the CSIR in 1949.

Nevertheless, the Prime Minister's characterisation of universities' proper place in teaching civic 'values' elevated their traditional role as part of each state's system of education. The issue went beyond the emphasis that should be placed on a liberal or a technical education, for it raised questions about the constitutional validity of the Commonwealth Government's contribution to education, which was a state responsibility. In effect Menzies argued that the Chifley Government had overextended in supporting universities through the provision of infrastructure, which went beyond the scope of the 'benefits to students' power and revealed the extent to which the constitutionality of Commonwealth support for higher education had still to be settled. Menzies had been elected prime minister on a platform that included upholding states' rights against encroachment from the Commonwealth.[10] The High Court's decision against Chifley's attempt to nationalise the banks had invigorated the Liberal Party. Suddenly, the advances made by universities in the previous decade, such as the generous grants for new buildings and equipment and the steady increases in research funding, appeared more tenuous.

STATES' RESPONSIBILITIES

An immediate casualty of the election of the new government was the Mills Committee of Inquiry, which had been appointed by the previous government in its final year to define the relationship between the Commonwealth and universities as well as to develop a new funding model. Menzies curtailed the committee's large remit and instead directed Mills to produce an 'interim report' with advice only on funding needs for 1950 and 1951. He offered universities a seat on this committee and appointed ANU Vice-Chancellor Douglas Copland as a member.[11] Despite Copland's close relationship with Menzies, this change pitted universities against Commonwealth bureaucrats, and in so doing transformed the committee from a 'trustee' role into a 'delegate' model. This completed the evolution away from a committee that universities had assumed would be a forerunner to an independent statutory grants committee in the British mould.

With its role dramatically altered, the Mills Committee became dysfunctional, and this contributed to a muddled interim report. Copland clashed with the Treasury representative, FJ Goodes, and criticised the process. Mills resisted the change in the committee's purpose, aspiring to a more comprehensive analysis than the time allowed. In particular, he wanted greater precision than reliance on enrolment figures permitted. However, obtaining consistent data for all universities proved impossible since inconsistent accounting methods created discrepancies between government and university figures. Nevertheless, the committee developed its own algorithm that claimed to model accurately the amount of teaching by considering the average subject load per student, with weighting to account for part-time students. The short interim report that emerged from the committee's process was overloaded with this kind of detail, lacked definitive guidance on the data, and amounted to little more than tables listing the amounts to be granted to each university down to the individual pound. The government accepted the recommendations, but left Mills' and universities' hope for a permanent committee unfulfilled.[12]

Vice-chancellors greeted with relief the news that emergency funds had been made available for 1950 and 1951, but this left all but the near future uncertain. It was equally alarming that the government had treated the interim report as an internal Commonwealth Office of Education document and declined to publish it. Lacking clarity on the basis on which the money had been allocated, universities through the AVCC requested a 'summary of the principles' upon which the Mills Committee had drawn its conclusions.

The government replied with a list of nine points explaining its attitude to university funding. The first and most important of these was that the states should have 'primary interest for and have the primary interest in' universities.[13] However, given the 'national importance of the development of the Universities', the Commonwealth allowed that it was 'justified, in association with the states, in accepting further responsibilities'. Commonwealth grants were styled as 'supplementary' and used to allow universities to 'develop beyond existing levels of activities', rather than underwriting their operational costs. To facilitate the payment and to clarify the constitutional issues a *States Grants (Universities) Act* was passed in 1951, establishing a formal process by which Commonwealth funds would be allocated to universities through the states.[14]

The relationship between Commonwealth and state support was based on a guiding principle that the state grant, together with student fees, should amount to 'a figure three times the size of the recommended Commonwealth grant'. This forced the states to continue their contributions even as federal funding increased.[15] Menzies had reconciled Commonwealth support for universities with his desire to support states' rights, even if this meant the Commonwealth had little direct say over universities' governance, as would be recognised by his Cabinet colleagues in later years.[16] Recognising that this affected smaller universities disproportionately, a secondary allocation would be determined based on the number of students, to account for the higher cost per student in smaller universities.[17] With this weighting, the University of Western Australia received 25 per cent more per student, while the University of Tasmania, New South Wales University of Technology and the New England University College each received 100 per cent more per student than the larger institutions. Through this increased allocation, the system explicitly benefited the smaller universities.

The new arrangements altered Commonwealth research support, with all university funding now combined in a single block grant. While this left universities to determine where the funds would be applied and conduct research as they saw fit, it muddied how the Commonwealth was supporting research.[18]

Under this new system, agreed data on student numbers became critical, and university registrars committed to working with the Commonwealth Statistician and Treasury representatives to ensure accuracy in calculating the secondary allocation. The states' role in supporting universities had been reasserted by the Commonwealth, although this would now be on the federal government's terms because the states did not have the same capacity to fund expansion following their loss of power to levy income taxes after 1942. This put universities in an invidious position with the Commonwealth Government as they taught more and more students supported by Commonwealth scholarships.

The new funding model had the unintended effect of driving up university fees at larger universities, as they sought to ensure the funding they obtained from state grants and student fees cleared the threshold for Commonwealth funding. The University of Melbourne increased fees by 50 per cent, and the University of Sydney made similar plans.[19] The overall result of the new model, however, was a dramatic reduction in the proportion of funding universities obtained from the Commonwealth Government, which had risen steadily through the 1940s and was now abruptly clawed back.

Although the Menzies government reduced the overall Commonwealth support for universities, it continued to provide financial support for students. It honoured the previous government's commitment to award 3000 Commonwealth scholarships each year, allocated to universities in proportion to its equivalent full-time students based on Mills' formula. The scholarships covered university fees and provided a means-tested living allowance proportional to family income, reducing for every pound over £400, and with a higher rate for students living away from home.[20] The scholarships were necessary because, although the 1950s postwar boom raised living standards, the benefits for those in low-wage employment were limited.[21]

The Commonwealth also directed Mills to advise on the funding of residential facilities at universities as a response to acute housing shortages in the postwar period. Universities, and sometimes student groups, had taken steps to open new student hostels following concerns that, as the student population grew, an even smaller proportion would be able to live anywhere close to campus.[22] The hostels were concerned less with providing students with a rich cultural environment and educational support than the residential colleges on campus, and much more with secure and cost-effective lodgings.

The scheme was administered by the Universities Commission, which retained tight control over Commonwealth student financial support and refused universities' request, through the AVCC, for control over the selection of candidates, the distribution of scholarships among faculties, and the terms on which scholarships could be terminated. Instead, the commission insisted that the single criterion on which the scholarships were awarded would be the marks obtained in matriculation.[23]

The risk that this simple method of selection could influence student behaviour troubled universities. In particular, they were concerned that students seeking these scholarships might choose less challenging subjects to secure the required grades. As many of the more difficult subjects were prerequisites for some university courses, this had implications for the distribution of scholarships across the university. Plans to recommend that weighting be granted to correct for the difficulty of subjects were abandoned, however, over fears that such a weighting might itself distort subject choice, and the difficulty of administering it.[24]

Universities were eager to ensure that 'new Australians' arriving under postwar assisted-immigration schemes could apply for Commonwealth scholarships. The Commonwealth Office of Education initially resisted this expansion of support to immigrants, imposing a requirement of prior residence as well as an age limit on applicants, the combination of which excluded almost all new Australians. In response, universities adopted uncommonly direct language, arguing that prior residence was 'irrelevant', and they succeeded in obtaining an 'alleviation' that earmarked places for 'mature aged students'.[25] For universities the scholarships were about opening their doors and providing access to the best candidates, regardless of where a prospective student originated.

INTERNATIONAL STUDENTS

During postwar decolonisation and Cold War build-up, universities proved useful in the Commonwealth Government's external affairs ambitions. Universities were well placed to assist in the Colombo Plan for Cooperative Economic Development in South and Southeast Asia, motivated at least in part by the desire to counter the conditions in which communism could take root.[26] The plan emerged from a British Commonwealth of Nations foreign ministers' conference in Ceylon in January 1950 and commenced from July 1951, providing state aid to Asian countries, including those that were not part of the British Commonwealth. Initial modest provision of professional training to visiting students at Australian universities grew rapidly as it proved highly popular and successful.

Students had been arriving at Australian universities from countries in Asia in increasing numbers since the Second World

War, and universities had long supported their presence. George Currie had reported to the 1944 Universities Conference on the desirability of an orderly process for admitting students from Asia, and for programs of exchange between Australian and Asian universities, and urged his fellow university leaders to bring this to the government.[27] Between 1951 and 1965, some 5500 students, most of them pursuing university studies, were supported under the plan.[28] During this time, universities enrolled almost 5000 students from Asian countries each year, meaning the Colombo Plan students comprised only a minority of the Asian students undertaking study in Australian universities, but the government sponsorship of students from the Asia–Pacific region opened conversations about the best way to support them.[29]

While the terms of the Colombo Plan were being thrashed out at international discussions, universities were already engaging with countries and universities across Southeast Asia. Ivor Jennings, Vice-Chancellor of the University of Ceylon, offered to support up to four Australian professors with first-class fares to teach in Colombo over the Australian universities' long vacation. Jennings' counterpart at the University of Malaya made a similar offer. Australia's universities replied through the AVCC that they were 'generally sympathetic' to these requests, leading to discussions on interchange between separate universities.[30]

Universities were now better equipped to support the admission of students from Asia, and they welcomed them. As University of Adelaide Vice-Chancellor Albert Rowe acknowledged:

> the students were proving an asset to universities. The
> mere presence of people of different cultures broadened the
> University outlook and most of the South-East Asian students
> were very talented in many ways.[31]

However, two new issues arose from the government's interest in sponsoring international students to attend Australian universities. First, the problem of determining which of these students had met entrance requirements, given that they had not matriculated; and second, how to assist them once they arrived.

The University of Sydney was quick to rule out accepting block enrolments of groups of international students, requiring their eligibility to stand on their individual merits. The University of Western Australia proposed that other universities follow its example and adopt the standards of the University of London. The idea of introducing preparatory courses in English or mathematics, following the model of the CRTS tutorials, was proposed and adopted for some courses.

Concerns about the academic preparedness of international students led universities to commission a national survey, which found the failure rates of overseas students were higher than for domestic students at the time, but that this largely stemmed from their lower numeracy and English literacy skills.[32] A similar survey of domestic students supported by Commonwealth scholarships was conducted, although this found no measurable difference from students without scholarships.

The survey drove efforts to expand support for international students. Universities engaged with the Department of External Affairs to coordinate with the work of overseas diplomatic missions. The minister, Richard Casey, agreed to sponsor a proposed fact-finding mission to report on the standard of preparatory courses. The fact-finding mission would eventually be taken by the Western Australia Registrar, Col Sanders, who reported on the standards of university education in Pakistan, India, Ceylon, Burma, Thailand, Malaya and Indonesia.[33] Most of these countries were members of the British Commonwealth and had adopted the essential characteristics of the British university system, and even the others, Thailand and Indonesia, were similar enough to enable Sanders to make detailed 'suggestions' for how best to prepare students from these countries to matriculate in Australia. For some countries, such as Ceylon and Burma, Sanders recommended students undertake preliminary years at local universities before coming to Australia; with others, such as Malaya and Hong Kong, he recommended two or more years of Australian secondary education leading to matriculation. For non-English-speaking students, Sanders proposed an 'intensive course in English (written, spoken and technical)' of at least three months' duration to prepare students for university.[34] While not all recommendations were adopted, they showed the diversity in the preparation of students from different countries.

THE COLD WAR

As Australia's universities reached out to Asia, they were drawn into the domestic politics of the Cold War. Several professors were denounced as communists amid concern about the influence of the far left in industry and public institutions. The 1949 revelations of a disgruntled communist, Cecil Sharpley, led to a Victorian royal commission into the 'origins, aims, objects and funds of the Communist Party in Victoria', chaired by the University of Melbourne Chancellor, Sir Charles Lowe. His report would find that most of Sharpley's allegations were groundless. The issue became national after Menzies' election on a vocal anti-communist platform, introducing legislation to ban the Communist Party. However, the government's anti-communism proposals were stymied when the legislation was subsequently disallowed by the High Court. Numerous professors spoke in opposition to Menzies' proposals during the ensuing referendum, which was ultimately defeated.[35]

The issue was also personal for some academics, since ASIO, established in 1949, conducted security assessments of staff at universities. The ASIO assessment of the University of Melbourne named 63 members of staff as constituting a security risk, based on tenuous and in some cases demonstrably false evidence.[36] There were prominent cases, such as the University of Sydney's Richard Makinson, who was passed over for the chair of Physics as the result of security information, and the threat was held over all.[37]

Universities declined to take any common position on the communist issue, even though it was raised repeatedly between them in private. The parliamentary attacks on individual professors were considered too scatter-gun and went to individuals' private beliefs rather than their academic work, and universities did not suffer the purges that happened in the United States. The prospect of government 'security checks' for new Commonwealth public servants raised the concerns of Joe Burton, Principal at Canberra University College, in particular because it was a Commonwealth institution. Burton urged universities to agree to a statement of principle and formal steps to curtail the political activities of professors, but vice-chancellors found the idea of such a public statement an objectionable capitulation that would diminish their academic independence.[38]

The Cold War had other direct effects on universities beyond security checks. The imposition of compulsory national service for the Korean War in 1951 forced universities to accommodate military authorities. Universities obtained concessions from the Navy and Air Force, but the Army was unable to change the period of its training camps, which were held from the beginning of the calendar year until mid-April. This effectively forced universities to delay commencement by six weeks to allow the trainees to return, disrupting the entire academic year. It was not until 1954 that the

Army finally agreed to compromise, allowing the university calendar to return to normal from 1955.[39]

A PUBLIC INTERVENTION

By the mid-1950s, universities were already contending with much larger predicaments than disruption to their calendars. Unresolved problems of Commonwealth support came to a head in 1952, when the funding recommended by the Mills Committee expired. Despite his oft-expressed affection for Australian universities, Menzies' refusal to appoint a standing committee or new inquiry left future Commonwealth support and funding uncertain.[40] The government's practice of delaying the passage of the *States Grants (Universities) Act* until just in time for the following year tested universities' nerve.

Coupled with this uncertainty was the problem of inflation, which had soared after the previous Labor Government's wage controls were lifted. This meant the Commonwealth allocations so precisely calibrated in the middle of 1950 were increasingly inadequate. By 1952, inflation had reduced the effective Commonwealth allocation by 'up to 40 per cent'.[41]

In October 1951 universities used the opportunity of the ceremony installing the first ANU Chancellor, Stanley Melbourne Bruce, to send a deputation to the Prime Minister to urge him to initiate a 'coordinated plan of development'.[42] Menzies was unavailable, and the visiting vice-chancellors had to be content with Paul Hasluck, Minister for Territories, as the Prime Minister's representative. Currie later confessed to other universities that he 'was not optimistic regarding the result'. Hasluck, who held a university post before entering Parliament in 1949, indicated that the Commonwealth had limited interest in establishing a new committee that might bind it to increasing funding.

Universities could not afford to let the matter rest. They formed a second deputation of vice-chancellors with a renewed request for 'urgent action'. The new deputation sought an immediate review of the Commonwealth grant, and the appointment of an inquiry to determine the 'long-term needs of universities'. Vice-chancellors argued that considerable increases in Commonwealth funding were necessary in light of the 'growing demands for trained personnel from both governments and private enterprise', which had led to expansions in the number of students. Funding was also necessary, they argued, to help to develop graduate research training. These themes would become a common refrain as the key to unlocking Commonwealth funding.[43]

Again, Menzies proved elusive, and the lack of effective connection with the government limited the influence of universities.[44] Copland, who by this point was outwardly frustrated by the dealings, took a posting as High Commissioner to Canada in 1952. The AVCC elected Torleiv Hytten, the University of Tasmania's Vice-Chancellor, to replace him as deputy chair, thus dispensing with the custom of the deputy chair being based in Canberra.[45]

Their discreet appeals having failed, universities were compelled to adopt a more public stance. This meant a degree of coordinated public action universities had only infrequently practised. Stephen Roberts, who succeeded Currie as chairman of the AVCC at the end of his two-year term in 1952, announced that the University of Sydney had appointed communications professionals to develop the public case. They were not alone, though, in public advocacy. During a speech on the responsibility of science in the modern world, Ian Clunies Ross, head of the CSIRO and former Sydney professor, 'turned an elegant celebration on the traditional role of the university into an urgent appeal for help'.[46]

Facing a pressing funding shortfall, universities took the unprecedented step of preparing a booklet, *A Crisis in the Finances and Development of the Australian Universities*, signed by vice-chancellors, to set out a reasoned case on university finances.[47] The publication shed the previous restraint of the AVCC's public statements and presented the situation facing universities as a 'crisis'. It explained the funding shortfalls that had become acute as the end of the CRTS meant that enrolments had declined. The combination of the loss of Commonwealth funding, and rising inflation, meant universities were worse off in real terms than they had been in 1939.

The booklet presented concerns to the public, and made the case that the public should value universities' contribution:

> Universities are destined to play an increasingly important role in Australian development. Their future is a matter of grave concern to you and to every other member of the community. Yet there is an alarming degree of public apathy regarding their affairs. While they are accepted as an integral part of our educational system, there is little public appreciation of the wide nature of their responsibilities to the community.[48]

Since student numbers had declined, the customary appeal for funding based on increased student numbers was unavailable. Instead, they argued their role had expanded in the years after the Second World War, and that they now performed many functions of vital national significance.

Their tasks of transmitting knowledge to students, along with the training of professionals with technical expertise, such as 'architects, engineers, scientists, doctors, dentists, lawyers, teachers, economists', were now undertaken to meet national priorities.[49] These priorities included 'the preservation of our cultural heritage and of our democratic traditions of freedom of thought and speech and the development and exchange of new ideas', thus identifying universities with the government's platform.[50]

Another role was in Commonwealth-supported research. Universities distinguished their contribution from that of the CSIRO, with its mission-oriented investigation of specified problems. Universities had the freedom to advance knowledge and make discoveries where the end result was unknown. Moreover, they were the primary source of 'specialist training in professions and science' essential for the national research enterprise. All these benefits crossed state boundaries and had wide public utility. Research, for example, was not the private work of individuals, but rather provided a 'threefold advantage': in 'advancing knowledge', training research workers for government and industrial employment, and 'indirectly maintaining the interest and vigour of the staff with a benefit to teaching standards'.[51] Acknowledging that research did not always produce immediate economic benefits, they argued that their research training provided an essential prerequisite for growth of the economy.

The booklet called for the appointment of a 'long-term inquiry' to 'prepare an overall plan for University development to meet future needs'. The sector must aspire to attain a comparable level of activity, both in teaching and research, to that of the 'universities of the United Kingdom'.[52] This would help to overcome the crippling 'uncertainty', over the future of Australian higher education 'over three to five years'. It was no accident that this accorded with the practice of the British University Grants Committee, the model favoured by universities.[53]

Two thousand copies of the *Crisis* booklet were distributed to politicians, university governing bodies, professors, and others 'interested in increasing government support'.[54] A media statement was drafted emphasising the problem of inflation, and journalists were encouraged to quote from the booklet as the official position of Australian universities.[55]

As the booklet signalled, universities had become aware of the need for them to take the initiative in making their case. Without the same ministerial intervention that had dominated the 1940s, it was up to them to speak more directly for themselves. The AVCC began the practice of generating media statements from its meetings and being more strategic and coherent in their release to journalists.[56]

In the wake of the publication of the booklet, Menzies reiterated his support for Australian universities and agreed to receive a deputation. More promisingly, he indicated broad support for an immediate 20 per cent increase in 'second level' Commonwealth assistance, which benefited the smaller universities, and the establishment of a committee to respond to immediate needs and prepare a long-term plan for university development.[57] Yet by the following February the process had slowed and universities became increasingly frustrated.

The 1953 Premiers' Conference was scheduled for the day after an AVCC meeting, and the vice-chancellors telegraphed the Secretary of the Prime Minister's Department, Allen Brown: 'would it be possible to obtain the Prime Minister's views on additional assistance for universities in current year'. Brown telephoned in reply that the Premiers' Conference would be dealing with 'weighty problems' and unfortunately would not have time to consider universities' appeal. The plight of universities was discussed at the conference, and in response to appeals from Victoria for more support, Menzies replied that they had done well 'without a Commonwealth grant'.[58] Left with little recourse, the vice-chancellors again wrote to the Prime Minister, reiterating their requests.[59]

While universities moved to adopt a public position, there were limits. Looking ahead to the impending introduction of television in Australia, the University of Adelaide Vice-Chancellor Albert Rowe urged universities to seek to reach a wider audience through the joint purchase of a university licence, and thus become a national broadcaster. The issue was live because the University of Melbourne Vice-Chancellor George Paton was chairing the Commonwealth's royal commission into television.[60] This proposal was seriously considered as it presented an obvious opportunity to extend universities' public reach. There was precedent, with individual professors, such as Walter Murdoch, W Macmahon Ball and Hermann Black, presenting regular talks on radio stations, but universities had so far missed the opportunity to use wireless to deliver their extension programs, despite a long-running aspiration to do so.[61] Rowe now criticised universities for failing to harness radio more effectively. Television presented a fresh chance, particularly because of the stronger coordination between universities. Vice-chancellors agreed that universities had 'a duty to safeguard the cultural interests of the community', but ultimately the quotidian challenges of producing sufficient content deterred universities from seeking a television licence. Instead, they urged that the Australian Broadcasting Commission (ABC) be properly resourced to make use of universities' capacity.[62] During the 1960s the ABC produced the series 'University of the Air', drawing inspiration from a British initiative of the same name, broadcasting lectures from professors, and in 1965 'Design in Australia', a series hosted by erstwhile University of Melbourne research fellow, Robin Boyd.[63] The British scheme developed into the Open University, a degree-granting institution delivered via television, a model later introduced in Australia.[64]

COMMONWEALTH AND STATES

THE CAMPAIGN FOR SUPPORT

Support for the Colombo Plan in Australia and its universities reflected the wider interest in the development of the British Commonwealth during the 1950s. It was a period when many of the pan-British organisations grew livelier, supported by greatly improved transport links as air travel became more common and commercial airlines expanded rapidly. Means of exchange grew through the postwar years. The Association of the Universities of the British Commonwealth (AUBC), which succeeded the Universities' Bureau after 1948, continued to provide scholarships for travel, alongside the Nuffield scholarships at Oxford.[65] The United States established the Fulbright Scholarships, with the AVCC allowing universities to determine recipients themselves. Other American engagement continued with the growing relationship between universities and the Carnegie Corporation, which funded infrastructure as well as scholarships.[66] In 1951 universities requested that Commonwealth scholarships also support students from British Commonwealth countries to study in Australia, a proposal that ultimately rested on the Australian Government's willingness to support these scholars.

Sabbatical travel for university staff was supported from 1950 by Australian National Airways, which provided up to fifteen concession flights between Australia and Britain each year, with the beneficiaries again determined by universities.[67] The shipping companies managed to resume their free passages, offering 25 for postgraduate students in 1953, again allocated by universities.[68] In 1953 all of Australia's vice-chancellors travelled to Britain to attend the seventh Quinquennial Congress of the AUBC. At the meeting, delegates raised many issues on which Australian universities could speak with particular expertise, including the provision of Commonwealth scholarships, and the teaching of international students.[69] While the vice-chancellors were away, they took the opportunity to hold meetings and brought the AVCC Secretary, John Ford, with them. This meant that, for the first time, a woman would run the AVCC secretariat and Deputy Secretary Ruth Rolph was made Acting Secretary.[70]

The British connection proved valuable for the vice-chancellors' campaign to move the Menzies government, since it established closer relations with senior university administrators in both countries. These new allies improved the vice-chancellors' grasp of the critical issues in Britain. Vice-chancellors also saw their British counterparts as allies who would have authority in Australia, and whose arguments for university development were more likely to be heard at the highest levels of the Commonwealth Government. Where public advocacy had left the government unmoved, networking might bring about change.

The AVCC invited Sir Arthur Trueman, the immediate past chairman of the British University Grants Committee, to visit Australia in 1954 to speak on university development, as the first of a planned series of prominent visitors.[71] Bringing these senior British figures was an effective tool in building a case for the expansion of the Commonwealth role in supporting universities by contrasting the British experience with that of Australia. Following Trueman, the next guest was Sir Charles Morris, the noted philosopher and Vice-Chancellor of the University of Leeds.[72]

As universities sought to build a case for federal funds and called on their British counterparts for support, they faced growing internal pressures to raise academic salaries. These had declined in real terms as inflation eroded their value, and some disciplines struggled to attract quality candidates. In response, in 1952 staff formed a Federal Council of University Staff Associations of Australia (FCUSAA) and, in 1953, it pressed universities to support its campaign for wage increases.[73] In this, universities were hamstrung by their separate relationships with their respective state governments. While some universities, such as Sydney and Melbourne, had independently granted wage increases, others, such as Adelaide and Western Australia, were not in a financial position to do so. Nevertheless, universities supported the proposal with a statement of principle that academic salaries were 'inadequate in view of changed economic conditions'.[74]

While the funding impasse continued between the government and universities, the weight of the number of enrolments that had grown since the Second World War squeezed operations, leaving little capacity to expand universities' activities in line with international trends. In response to the deteriorating state of affairs, the AVCC conducted its own survey of the needs of universities to prepare for the appointment of a full government inquiry and to provide greater specificity to universities' requests for funding in the meantime. The task of compiling a 'Survey of University Needs' proved challenging and there was no certainty that the members would agree to what emerged.

The first draft was based on reports from the Universities of Sydney, Melbourne, Adelaide and Canberra, but Melbourne characterised its submission as 'only a first look at the problem'. What emerged was a familiar list of deficiencies, including in the support for postgraduate work, how to accommodate increased numbers of students and the associated needs for buildings and equipment. To these were added shortfalls in the numbers of schoolteachers, which was a state issue and unlikely to motivate the Commonwealth Government, and the 'recognition of the need for producing graduates with a sense of responsibility to society, i.e. as future leaders'. This amorphous concept was an attempt to provide a rationale for reducing staff–student ratios, as well as make 'more adequate provision for active student life'.[75]

As the 'Survey of University Needs' was being compiled, the

AVCC established a subcommittee that included representatives from smaller universities to prepare a public statement on the absolute minimum requirements of Australian universities. On the subcommittee were Rowe from the University of Adelaide, Burton from the Canberra University College, and Robert Madgwick, the Vice-Chancellor of the University of New England, which attained university status in 1954.[76] The timing was significant. Rowe had repeatedly corresponded with Menzies since taking the chair of the AVCC to outline the growing consequences of government inaction. On the eve of the 29 May 1954 federal election, Menzies responded that he was 'anxious not to involve the Commonwealth government in the internal affairs of universities'.[77]

Tasked with developing a public statement, the AVCC subcommittee sought to answer profound questions about the shape and character of the whole system, such as the 'optimum size of a university', the 'essential' facilities, what 'special types of university' were necessary, considerations in determining the location of these universities, what residential component was important, what departments were 'too expensive to be duplicated', and where new facilities and departments were needed to overcome 'over crowding'.[78] It concluded that each should commence with Arts and Science, plus 'at least one other faculty reflecting the needs of the district where the university or college is located'. These departments should be headed by professors and as 'adequately staffed as possible'. Staff–student ratios should be as low as possible, with 2500 to 3000 students considered optimal, even though the Universities of Sydney and Melbourne had already grown to twice this size. However, the report also acknowledged that larger universities, with more extensive offerings and a broad range of departments, had stronger reputations. The tension between good education and reputation was difficult to resolve.[79]

The 1955 Inter-University Conference of the AUBC, held

in Australia, afforded another important opportunity to make the case publicly for universities. It took visiting delegates to all institutions. Arriving in Sydney, the visiting party divided between the Universities of Queensland and New England, before travelling to the Universities of Melbourne, Western Australia and Tasmania, and finally reconvening at the University of Adelaide. Delegates then travelled to Canberra to visit ANU and the Canberra University College, before returning to the University of Sydney and the New South Wales University of Technology.[80] This tour was an unprecedented opportunity to exhibit all the different Australian institutions, and to harness the associated media coverage to raise the national profile of smaller universities.

During the visit, universities convened a symposium to discuss 'The Place of the Australian University in the Community' and 'Post-Graduate Studies in the Australian Universities'. The presentations showed a remarkable cohesion of views about the contemporary role of universities. Universities, one participant summarised, were 'on the side of science, by increasing welfare; on the side of the arts, by silently raising the standards of discussion and entertainment'.[81] To reach a wider audience, the collection was published by the AVCC and circulated widely.

THE MURRAY COMMITTEE AND THE SECOND AUSTRALIAN UNIVERSITIES COMMISSION

After the AUBC tour, preparation of a national policy document continued. The secretary of the AVCC collated a list of post-graduate awards offered at each Australian institution. However, consensus about the advantage of pursuing an AVCC policy declaration evaporated. In October 1955 some vice-chancellors came to argue that 'university finance was a state responsibility and that the preparation of a document of the type suggested may adversely affect the relationship of the state universities with their respective state treasuries'. Others urged caution about creating the appearance that universities, in seeking to expand, would duplicate one another's activities.[82]

Instead, in the wake of the 1955 conference, the vice-chancellors adopted a new approach. At the March 1956 meeting, the AVCC chair, George Paton, announced the plans for university coordination would be shelved. He considered them no longer 'desirable at the present stage' and went on to explain that Menzies had joined him for a private dinner at the Melbourne staff club, University House, at which he agreed to appoint a new inquiry, subject to approval from the states. Menzies asked universities for a list of names of potential 'persons in the United Kingdom who would be suitable for appointment as chairman of such a committee'.[83]

This breakthrough was greeted with acclamation by universities, which drew up a list at the top of which was the chair of the University Grants Committee, Sir Keith Murray. Others included Dr James Cook, Principal, University College of South West England, Exeter; and Sir Phillip Morris, Vice-Chancellor of the University of Bristol. The vice-chancellors then prepared a list of potential Australian members, including the chair of the CSIRO, Sir Ian Clunies Ross; Melbourne's Professor of Agriculture, Sir Samuel Wadham; the Wood Professor of Accounting at the University of Melbourne, Sir Alexander Fitzgerald; the Sydney barrister, Major-General Victor Windeyer; the Managing Director of Metal Manufacturers Ltd, Sir Daniel McVey; the retired engineer and industrialist, Sir John P Tivey; and the company director and Secretary of the Collins House group, Hugh Brain.[84] Murray would be appointed to chair the committee of inquiry, with Ross a member. These two men were joined by Sir Charles R Morris, Vice-Chancellor of Leeds, whose Australian speaking tour universities had sponsored in 1954, Alex J Reid, a Treasury representative, and Jack C Richards, Assistant General Manager of BHP.

The appointment of Murray was greeted with more than relief by universities. It was the culmination of more than six years of advocacy, and Menzies' decision to choose a British chair was also welcomed as an acknowledgment of universities' strategy of deepening connections with Britain. Universities hoped the inquiry would recommend government funding on a comparative level to their British counterparts.

Vice-chancellors had been instrumental in the appointment of Murray, and Murray sought guidance from them upon his arrival. Universities set out a template for the 'ideal conditions' for a visit to an Australian university, including the time for a tour of the facilities and the order in which to speak to interest groups. Each visit began with an official exposition of the university's submission, followed by informal talks with professorial and then non-professorial staff, then a meeting with student representatives. Finally, a formal meeting would be held with a university's governing body, with subsequent informal conversations to 'clear up points of doubt'. Receiving this advice with gratitude, Murray agreed in a way that gave comfort to vice-chancellors that 'the problems appeared to be immediate and large'. 'Was anybody thinking in revolutionary terms?' he asked.[85]

The planning work that went into formulating a coordinated approach was not wasted, and it formed the basis of the AVCC submission to the Murray Committee. Drafted by Paton, the report emphasised the need for 'long-range' planning, so universities were not 'faced with a similar problem in two years' time', as they had been after the Mills Inquiry. Although constitutional impediments prevented the 'translating' of the University Grants Committee into Australia directly, the AVCC submission urged

Murray to investigate the creation of an equivalent body.[86] To clarify this for the British members of the committee, Paton explained that

> if the Universities are to develop as they should, we must of necessity depend more on the Commonwealth for our financial requirements, while the Commonwealth has the superior power over taxation. But we are equally anxious that anything the Commonwealth might contribute should not merely ease the financial responsibilities of the States towards the Universities.[87]

The Murray Committee considered the vice-chancellors' submission alongside those of student groups and industry representatives, and undertook the review at remarkable speed with the support of Menzies.[88] The final report drew particular attention to the vice-chancellors' request for a similar organisation to the British University Grants Committee. Menzies adopted the recommendations within three days of the report's release, and the government pledged to establish a permanent body with the support of the state governments.[89] The body would reside in the Prime Minister's Department, separate from the Office of Education, so as to distinguish it from the provision of primary and secondary education. It would have its own secretariat, and although Murray recommended that it act informally, at least at the beginning, it would be established as a statutory authority in 1959. Along with the state universities, its remit should also include ANU and the Canberra University College.[90] This went much of the way to meeting the vice-chancellors' request, although they might have preferred the body to have a more public role.

The AVCC was not universally praised by the Murray Committee, however. It was urged to 'find a way of taking more responsibility and initiative than it has done in the past', to move to provide 'concerted advice' on matters of general applicability. This was necessary to overcome the structural deficiencies in the system that created confusion. Universities' struggles to act collectively echoed government criticisms that they acted 'parochially'. The AVCC should also improve its 'communications', so as to raise the comprehension at all levels of the university system, including perhaps most importantly, the 'bewilderment among academic staff' about common policy.[91] Murray's recommendations for the AVCC induced an organisational transformation. The AVCC would come to employ new forms of advocacy and public communication, underpinned by its own research.

With the Murray report in hand, Menzies requested a 'reply in general terms' from vice-chancellors and 'a more detailed paper covering the points in the ... report to which the AVCC as a whole should devote attention'. This provoked 'considerable discussion'. It was agreed that the AVCC was a 'necessary part of the new proposals', although it conceived of its primary role to be that of a 'sounding board', 'a place where views can be interchanged and the best common solution be hammered out'. As well as this, it argued that it 'must protect and advance the principles of university administration; become powerful and independent enough to be the source of advice to the Commonwealth on university policy; become the central point for the collection of information and planned development and be the recognised channel of communication and representation between the Universities Grants Committee and university governing bodies'.[92]

However, by August 1958, when universities next met, they expressed concern that although the increases in funding recommended by the Murray Committee had been accepted, none of the other measures had been implemented. In particular, they expressed the 'unanimous' fear 'that further steps by government to establish the permanent Committee were being long delayed, and that time was rapidly becoming all too short ... to be implemented'. Menzies adopted his customary measured approach.[93] Paton wrote to Menzies expressing concern that, although Commonwealth grants to the end of 1961 were in train, if steps were not taken soon, there would be insufficient time for the new body to make adequate preparations: 'In England', he wrote, 'the planning for the quinquennial grant period begins nearly two years before the period opens'.[94]

It was with a measure of relief that in February 1959, vice-chancellors received news of the impending appointment of Sir Leslie Martin as chairman of a newly established Australian Universities Commission (AUC). Martin, a professor of physics, was known for having a practical disposition, but he also had wider experience outside his professorial role, including assisting with lighting for the Melbourne Union Theatre for a number of years. The AVCC expressed its delight at his appointment and committed to assist with the transition to the new role. Vice-chancellors sought an 'audience' with Martin and Menzies before the enacting legislation was introduced.[95]

This meeting was unforthcoming, however, and vice-chancellors discovered that the AVCC was cut out of planning major decisions by the new AUC. Martin delayed meeting the AVCC despite repeated requests until his committee had first visited universities separately. The first available date was not until February 1960.[96] The AVCC's continuing role as the central forum for discussion and advocacy was unclear. This matter was urgent because the AUC's work involved not only assessing the needs and coordinating the expenditure on individual universities, but also the expansion of the system. The Murray report cited Commonwealth estimates that the number of students would almost double over the following decade, following 'rapid' population growth and the increasing numbers remaining in secondary school to matriculation. This, Murray argued, would require existing universities to take more students, as well as a new university in Sydney and Melbourne. Yet this grossly underestimated the demand for higher education that came only a few years later.[97] The AUC immediately found itself grappling with a system growing more rapidly than anybody had imagined. New universities cast from the mould of the old would require unprecedented levels of public investment. In just five years a new Committee of Inquiry would be appointed to determine how this expansion could be supported.

5
SYSTEMATISATION

On her 1969 Australian tour, Robin Harris, Professor of Higher Education at the University of Toronto, encouraged Canadian and Australian universities to learn from one another. 'Sydney and Melbourne', she asserted, 'are the contemporaries of Toronto and McGill; Adelaide of Manitoba; Queensland and Western Australia of Saskatchewan and British Columbia'. Higher education in both countries was undergoing structural reorganisation and 'systematisation', whereby formerly separate universities operating in a loose affiliation were being drawn into a close relationship.[1] In Australia the catalyst was the establishment of the AUC in 1959. It operated on the principle that all universities should be treated alike, and that funding should follow institutional needs. Commonwealth funding grew more essential for the universities to cope with unprecedented numbers of students, and particularly to support the construction of new buildings.

The unprecedented scale of postwar immigration and the 'baby boom' produced a growing demand for higher education during the late 1950s and 1960s that threatened to overwhelm existing facilities.[2] While universities had warned in the 1940s that their expansion might outrun demand for graduates, now students were assured of their future prospects of stable 'white collar' careers in the professions and management.³ Philanthropic gifts, which had underpinned some of their work in previous generations, could not keep up with the expansion, and the Commonwealth, in association with the states, emerged as their de facto 'guarantor'.⁴ Britain and Canada experienced similar growth in demand for university places.⁵ In India, the number of students surged from 200 000 in 1945 to more than a million by 1962.⁶

In the fifteen years after the Murray Review, the Australian university system was transformed. By 1972, nine universities had become fifteen. The number of academics more than tripled: 274 professors became 853 and the number of other academic staff increased from 3716 to 9766, with an additional 7107 part-time staff. The number of students increased from 37 900 to 128 700.⁷ The insistent demand for university study ensured universities received significant government and public attention. Yet the growth in student numbers also spread resources more thinly. The pressure of hiring so many new staff while maintaining educational standards was acute. So too was the need for review of teaching and learning practices now operating at a much larger scale.

The university system grew more complex as staff and student numbers increased. Staff organised to form a national association. Changing expectations and management challenges altered the role of vice-chancellors. The AVCC was re-imagined to respond to the more complex environment, including the emergence of a different type of higher education institution, the College of Advanced Education (CAE). These institutions comprised technical institutes, teachers' colleges, and smaller specialised institutions offering diplomas in health sciences. Like universities, CAEs were funded jointly by state and Commonwealth governments, but they received a smaller outlay per student compared to universities. The Murray Committee's resounding endorsement of universities created uncertainties as to how to achieve its aspiration for well-funded liberal higher education for a much enlarged student body. This raised questions about which characteristics of Australia's universities were essential, and which were not.

THE POSTWAR EXPANSION

To meet the postwar demand for higher education state governments built new institutions. New South Wales established additional university colleges in regional centres to make university study accessible beyond Sydney. Newcastle and Wollongong gained university colleges in 1951, affiliated with the New South Wales University of Technology so that they did not have to start from scratch. But as these institutions expanded, the advantages of the college system were outweighed by administrative duplication and cumbersome arrangements for ensuring the equivalent standing of their degrees. The New England University College had gained independence from Sydney, emerging as a separate university in 1956.[8] Newcastle followed in 1965; Wollongong in 1975.[9] In Queensland, the University College of Townsville, established in 1961 and affiliated with the University of Queensland, followed a similar pattern, gaining independence as James Cook University in 1970.[10]

The same process was not followed in Victoria, which had declined to establish a technical university in the 1940s, or redesignate the existing state technical colleges at Ballarat and Bendigo or the Royal Melbourne Technical College as technical universities. The desire for a technical university led the Victorian Government to request the Murray Committee to conduct a separate inquiry into the prospect of forming a second university in Victoria. The committee's confidential report recommended against a technical university in favour of a comprehensive institution combining the humanities and the sciences. Even so, Monash University, as it became, was expected to provide technical education along the same lines as the New South Wales University of Technology.[11]

Despite the increase of students in professional courses and the projected demand, most of the university growth came in the humanities and social sciences, including at Monash.[12] The New South Wales University of Technology changed its name to the University of New South Wales (UNSW) in 1958 after it introduced a medical school and Faculty of Arts, in parallel to Monash, recognising the same demand for study in the social sciences alongside technical subjects.[13] These new institutions still failed to satisfy the rising demand for university places. The AUC attempted to coordinate development, but the task was monumental.

By 1960, the chair of the AUC, Leslie Martin, was convinced of the need for new universities so that the existing ones did not swell beyond the capacity of their laboratories and lecture rooms. There was also the problem that some programs, notably in the natural and medical sciences, did not have facilities to accommodate growing numbers of students. Quotas had been introduced in medical schools in the 1940s for this reason, and from the late 1950s these were also applied to other disciplines.[14]

The AUC approached the task of constructing new universities with gusto. Applying the lever of Commonwealth funding, the commission extracted promises from each state, even 'play[ing] one off against the other'.[15] This process produced separate outcomes without an overarching vision. The AUC's policy of engaging each state and university individually bypassed the AVCC, for which cooperation was a guiding principle. If the Commonwealth's requirement of matching funding from the states was intended to ensure they continued to support their universities, the AUC now used it for the reverse purpose. Because Commonwealth contributions were pegged to those of the states, any increases at the state level raised the Commonwealth outlay, an effect multiplied across the six jurisdictions. This process won considerable increases for the university system, to the Commonwealth Government's mounting concern.

For Martin, expansion meant the development of new university colleges as an intermediate step towards the creation of fully fledged universities, following the pattern established in New South Wales. This was necessary to ensure that the full cost of the expansion spread over a longer period. When he met the AVCC in 1960, he relayed the existing plans for the University College of Townsville and foreshadowed another in Queensland in 1964, allowing the postponement of a new university for 'about ten years'. As it happened, the Queensland Institute of Technology (Darling Downs), later University of Southern Queensland, would not be established until the next triennium, in 1967. In South Australia, he urged the development of an Institute of Technology in the 1961–63 triennium and a second university by 1966. There was less demand for new universities in Western Australia and Tasmania. In Victoria, Martin called for the development of the Royal Melbourne Technical College to provide additional technical training. The 'heavy cost' of Monash University prevented the development of a third university until at least 1966 or 1967, he announced.[16] This suite of new institutions demanded considerable planning to establish facilities and recruit staff, but their creation was slated to take place at breakneck speed.

AVCC AND AUC

Through its influence on how Commonwealth resources were allocated, the AUC asserted a new authority over Australian higher education. Despite repeatedly calling for the establishment of such a national funding agency, the AVCC soon expressed frustration over the new body's approach. Universities had achieved unprecedented unity of action in the 1950s during the AVCC's campaign to restore Commonwealth funding after the CRTS expired. The vice-chancellors expected the AVCC would continue to provide useful guidance to shape developments. However, Martin preferred to deal with each university separately in strict adherence to his terms of reference. Universities felt that the AVCC was excluded from discussions, limiting their ability to mount a collective argument and be kept informed of the changes across the system.

When the AVCC finally secured a meeting with the AUC in February 1960, the vice-chancellors were 'alert to deal with matters raised by the Commission involving principle, and ... prepared to take the initiative in such cases'.[17] In a preliminary AVCC meeting, the vice-chancellors attempted to establish common ideals to advance to the AUC. The expansion of the sector was the primary subject of discussions. Phillip Baxter, Vice-Chancellor of UNSW, and from 1960 the chair of the AVCC, proposed universities advocate a 'multiple campus system', allowing them to grow beyond 50 000 students. His university was already exploring this form of development by incorporating its university colleges. However, other universities favoured University of Melbourne Vice-Chancellor George Paton's suggestion, that they should not grow 'beyond 12,000 students'.[18] Universities agreed to raise the question of common salary scales across the system, urge changes in the way that part-time and full-time student numbers were counted, and seek improvements in the way in which building applications were approved. The University of Tasmania's Vice-Chancellor, Keith Isles, suggested there should be regular consultation to ensure the 'orderly development' of the system.

Martin listened to the AVCC's proposals, but revealed his preoccupation with the larger problem of accommodating the rate of growth. In this, the cost of 'traditional universities' was debilitating. 'It might not be possible', he confessed, 'to continue to develop tertiary education in Australia in this way and that some alternatives might have to be considered'.[19]

The AVCC emerged from the meeting fearing that the AUC 'would develop unbridled powers and that it was the task of the AVCC to counter this'. New England's Vice-Chancellor, Robert Madgwick, set out the predicament the AVCC faced. The AUC has 'ignore[d] us', he wrote:

> and this is about the worst thing they can do for the prestige of the Universities ... we have not been taken into the confidence of the Commission on a single matter. We know nothing as a Committee about State reactions to the Commission's proposals ... We are not in a position to counter rumours about the Commission's attitude on controversial issues ... We have no knowledge of how the Commission intends to interpret its terms of reference, what information it will need or how it intends to work ... We should be strong enough and have sufficient prestige to make this sort of thing impossible.

To develop 'an identity of basic fundamental interests' informed by a 'frank exchange of views', the AVCC increased the frequency of its meetings to four each year and then to six at the following meeting.[20] Universities requested regular AUC–AVCC meetings, and Martin agreed to two a year.[21]

The AVCC also sought to strengthen its secretariat by appointing a new executive assistant to the chairman 'who should know the universities thoroughly and be available to the Chairman and Committee for advice on matters that were academic and affecting university policy'. This individual would have status 'not less than Reader (or Associate Professor)'.[22] The senior adviser would enable the AVCC to respond promptly as circumstances changed and influence decisions in Canberra. However, the AVCC was unable to fill the post, despite the offer of a generous salary, as the sheer number of academic job openings in Australia gave suitable applicants many other choices.[23]

As well as attempting to formulate more detailed policy, universities came to share their AUC submissions privately and thus coordinate their responses to the AUC, which continued to insist largely on individual dealings with universities.[24] The AVCC also resumed its Conferences of Australian Universities, the last of which had been held in 1937. Conferences were held in 1960, 1964 and 1971, with papers exploring questions arising from the new scale of higher education. The first was on 'the general efficiency of the Australian Universities in the face of rising student numbers', responding to the AUC's first report published in 1960.[25] The second was on student accommodation, and the third looked ahead to future challenges.[26] The AVCC convened the first conference in association with university staff representatives and their increasingly significant academic association.

A PROFESSIONAL ASSOCIATION FOR ACADEMICS

The question of how universities were represented was complicated by the increasing prominence of the FCUSAA after the Murray Review created a new national university structure.[27] Its president, Professor Roland Thorp, and secretary, Dr Ken Buckley, were from the University of Sydney, and its membership was drawn from most Australian universities. The staff association saw itself working for 'concerted action of a sort that will promote the educational work of the universities and welfare of members of the academic staffs'.[28] FCUSAA spoke for the interests of its members, while the AVCC spoke for institutions. The two organisations shared some interests, but held different interpretations of a number of issues, and there was an underlying friction between the two bodies.

A unifying issue motivating the formation of FCUSAA was concern about academic tenure and academic freedom. This subject exposed divisions between academics and university management. Many of the criticisms raised by FCUSAA were directed at vice-chancellors, who found themselves caught between academic interests and institutional imperatives.

The most controversial issue arose from the dismissal in 1956 of the Professor of Philosophy at the University of Tasmania, Sydney Sparkes Orr, by the University Council. While the case involved allegations of sexual misconduct with a student, Orr's earlier criticism of the council was widely held to have been the underlying reason for his dismissal. The process by which the council took its decision, denying Orr legal representation, deliberating in camera, and refusing to publish a report providing its reasoning, was considered unjust by his colleagues. In subsequent national speaking engagements Orr protested against his treatment and raised money to support his failed legal claims of wrongful dismissal in the Tasmanian Supreme Court and High Court of Australia. Tasmania was unable to fill Orr's chair for a number of years and alleged that FCUSAA had black-listed the university, although the staff association denied that there was a formal boycott.[29]

Another concern was the widespread belief that universities were influenced by 'security' checks in making appointments. A decision at the New South Wales University of Technology not to proceed with the appointment of Russel Ward as a lecturer in history in 1956 was particularly controversial. The Dean of the Faculty of Humanities and Social Sciences, Max Hartwell, on leaving the university, alleged the decision was politically motivated because of Ward's past membership of the Communist Party. After the FCUSAA gave national publicity to the incident, the university categorically denied that a 'political ... test has ever been applied to persons within this university', but the staff association considered this evasive.[30] Hartwell regarded the incident an 'unpleasant example of what can happen in a university where power is concentrated, where policies are bad, and where professors are timid'.[31]

The tension between academics and university management was aggravated by the separation of powers in university governance. Ultimate power resided with the council, although in practice academic bodies, comprising the professorial and faculty boards, recommended policy on internal policy, including for teaching and research. The executive and academic arms were at times remote from one another and the Murray Committee had recommended that the vice-chancellor chair the professorial board to improve communication. The vice-chancellor would thus be able to explain the rationale for academic decisions to the lay council more effectively. The Murray Committee's recommendations were implemented at many universities; others found different solutions, such as at UNSW where a Vice-Chancellor's Advisory Committee, drawing together professors and deans, registrars and wardens, kept the vice-chancellor informed.[32] Nevertheless, a growing complexity in the operation and structure of the university increased the distance between vice-chancellors and the professoriate.[33]

A common concern of the AVCC and the new staff association was academic salaries and conditions, which had suffered under the inconsistent funding arrangements since the war. There was a greater use of part-time teachers as a stop-gap during the expansion; by 1963 half of the Arts departments employed part-time teachers, while 95 per cent of science departments used part-time demonstrators. Some of these were postgraduate students, others were secondary schoolteachers. The Universities of Queensland, New South Wales, Western Australia, Sydney and Melbourne had implemented training programs to improve university teaching and to relieve a system under growing strain.[34] The vice-chancellors supported salary rises in order to ensure that universities remained internationally competitive, but were conscious that the increases sought by FCUSAA depended on additional government funding.

The issue tested the funding relationship between Commonwealth and state governments, and exposed differences between the FCUSAA and AVCC. Academic salaries were determined by individual institutions in discussion with their respective state governments, and every university had slightly different salary levels. The Commonwealth Government was unwilling to commit states to increases,[35] yet the AUC's influence over university funding made this position increasingly unsustainable. Repeated AVCC advocacy led the AUC to recommend salary increases of up to 15 per cent. Martin's subsequent creation of an AUC committee to inquire into academic salaries produced disagreement from state governments, universities and FCUSAA, and was quickly abolished.

The unwillingness of the AUC to make decisions about salaries created a period of confusion and led to a series of temporary solutions. In February 1962 the AVCC and FCUSAA agreed jointly to urge the Commonwealth to appoint the president of the Commonwealth Conciliation and Arbitration Court to act as arbitrator, with its findings subject to approval by state and federal governments, university governing bodies and staff associations. Menzies adopted the AVCC–FCUSAA proposal and appointed Richard Eggleston, a judge of the Commonwealth Industrial Court and the ACT Supreme Court, to investigate university salaries. He was assisted by Maurice Timbs, general manager of the Australian Atomic Energy Agency, to represent the interests of the government, and the Monash Dean of Law, David Derham, who was one of three nominees of the AVCC and FCUSAA.[36] Eggleston considered the role of university staff and comparable positions in the public service, and recommended pay increases and 'periodic reviews'.[37]

Without a formal standing body to provide oversight, these recommendations provided only temporary reprieve, and the approach of the AVCC and staff association, now renamed the Federal Association of University Staff Associations (FAUSA),[38] diverged. The AVCC urged the Commonwealth Government to bring academic salaries into the National Wage Case hearings, in line with other sectors and industries. FAUSA engaged the AUC through its new chair, Sir Lenox Hewitt, who succeeded Martin in 1965. The AVCC was not consulted during the AUC's review, producing an 'unhappy' result that overlooked junior staff such as tutors and assistant librarians. A permanent machinery, the Academic Salaries Tribunal, was finally established in 1974 after a series of further short-term inquiries.[39]

STUDYING THE CONSEQUENCES OF GROWTH

As universities contended with their expansion, the academic study of university teaching and operations became a higher priority. This idea was taken up by Percy Partridge, Professor of Social Philosophy at ANU, in an influential 1960 article on 'the university system', which set out the need to think carefully about the implications of ever-increasing scale.[40] There were few sustained academic analyses of the operation of higher education in Australia, with the notable exceptions of studies produced sporadically in the *Forum of Education*, published by the Sydney Teachers College from the 1940s, and ACER's *Australian Journal of Higher*

Education. The University of Melbourne Education Faculty commenced an annual *Melbourne Studies in Education* in 1957.

FAUSA publicised its causes through a journal, *Vestes*, which grew from a newsletter into a leading forum for both analysis and advocacy of the federal association's causes. The AVCC also sought to promote analysis of the challenges facing universities in a growing sector, establishing its own journal, *The Australian University*, which gained Menzies' endorsement.[41] It ran from 1962 until 1976 under an editorial board chaired by the Vice-Chacellor of UWA, Sir Stanley Prescott, and was touted as a 'medium for information and discussion on the many-sided and rapid development of the Australian universities', sensitively framed so it would complement *Vestes*.[42] It published scholarly articles and focused research into universities both in Australia and overseas, but included editorials taking up issues of general concern, such as on administrative structures necessary to preserve academic independence.[43] It was filled with detailed analysis of innovations in small-group teaching and tutorials, and new technologies, including computers and visual aids, to improve student learning.[44] Articles examined ways of expanding facilities such as libraries.[45] Contributors dealt with broader questions too, such as tracing educational history, sketching proposals for universal education and exploring universities' relationship with vocational and technical education.[46]

Perhaps the key concern underpinning this research was the reduction of what was termed the 'failure rate': the proportion of students who failed to complete individual subjects each semester, requiring them to repeat subjects and delay their graduation or abandon their course entirely. In Australia this proportion approached 50 per cent of students undertaking subjects in a given year, and the need for so many students to repeat them came at great cost to both students and universities. The Murray Committee considered this a 'national extravagance' that 'can ill be afforded'.⁴⁷ This problem was more severe in Australia than Britain because of the much larger proportion of school-leavers who chose to attend university. There were also larger numbers of part-time students. The issue opened up the whole question of university support for students, and also the consequences of hiring large numbers of junior teaching staff.

The 'failure rate' was high among first-year students, raising questions about where responsibility lay between universities and secondary schools. It was higher again for part-time and evening students.⁴⁸ Questions about the quality of teaching and whether there was adequate support for students became more frequent. As the University of Adelaide's Albert Rowe observed, 'teaching methods and teaching ability' were previously 'not quite respectable subjects' in university circles, but this was yielding to the magnitude of the challenge.⁴⁹

There were green shoots of work on teaching methods at universities across the country.⁵⁰ The University of Queensland Vice-Chancellor, Fred Schonell, a former Professor of Education, championed further research into the effect of class sizes, the benefits of tutorials, and whether standards of teaching were appropriate.⁵¹ To draw together many separate efforts, in July 1960 the AVCC called a 'conference on university education'. Characterising the issue as a 'university problem', the AVCC placed the onus of improving these conditions on universities themselves, rather than attributing them to external factors, or blaming the students. There was a view that expansion of university enrolments had 'aggravated' existing 'university problems', but that this was not itself a sufficient explanation for the high rate of failure. Debate turned to how failure rates were exacerbated by the fact that only a third of students resided on Australian university campuses, unlike in many other countries (two-thirds did so in the United Kingdom), and many lived in boarding houses ill-suited to academic work. Many students were 'handicapped by financial difficulties', which compelled them to undertake paid employment as well as their studies.[52] This led to calls for the introduction of student and staff surveys to appraise the quality of teaching, and to review the adequacy of the Commonwealth scholarship living allowance for those dependent on it.

After the conference the issue of student progress became a central concern of the AVCC. It funded research into teaching methods led by Professor John Passmore, a philosopher from ANU, which concluded a 'university should not be primarily concerned with instruction; it should be concerned with learning'.[53] At the University of Queensland, Schonell, who chaired the AVCC in 1960–62, identified 'pressure' on students to succeed in crowded curricula, and also external pressures, particularly financial, as contributing to the failure rate.[54] Universities had traditionally focused on their strongest students. Ought they now to prioritise raising the pass rate of the weakest? How should universities recognise teaching skills alongside those in research?

The question of student selection was later tackled in a 1968 report, *The Australian University Student*. It examined the 'problem of getting full value out of the great investment in effort, brains, and money that a university represents', and argued the problem of the 'failure rate' was mostly due to unclear 'objectives'. Universities needed to determine what they were selecting for: students with potential for career success or the likelihood of completing a course. The report asked whether aptitude tests or interviews should be considered. Limited resources gave such questions teeth. Any form of selection other than school-leaving results would impose additional tasks on universities. Raising entry standards also risked excluding those without schooling advantages. 'How generous', it asked, 'is the community prepared to be?'[55]

SYSTEMATISATION

THE DUAL SECTOR

Menzies continued to champion the 'great national importance' of universities, as he wrote in his endorsement of *The Australian University*, but 'the challenge is to our willingness as citizens to accept the growing burdens which will result from the satisfaction of the growing demand'. The excessive cost created the 'danger of lowering our standards; of producing numbers at the expense of quality'.[56]

The government's desire to contain the cost of its support for universities was reflected in the 1962 decision to increase the number of Commonwealth scholarships by only 25 per cent, even though the student population had almost doubled from 31 671, when the scheme was introduced in 1951, to nearly 60 000.[57] As Schonell reflected, in the seven years between 1955 and 1962, the proportion of students receiving either a Commonwealth or a state scholarship in Queensland fell from 90 to 60 per cent.[58] He ruefully pointed out that over the same period the proportion of supported students in British universities had risen to 90 per cent, illustrating the different trajectories of government support.

Responding to the expanding budgetary commitment, Menzies appointed Martin in August 1961 to chair a new committee of inquiry into the whole system of tertiary education. He instructed it to 'consider the pattern of tertiary education in relation to the needs and resources of Australia', in effect directing it to find ways of meeting public demand while preserving standards.[59] The ambitious plan was to create 'a broad comprehensive system of tertiary education, with an emphasis different from but complementary to, tertiary education at present provided by the universities'.[60] Martin's new committee drew together representatives of universities with those from technical colleges and secondary schools, as well as vice-chancellors. Peter Karmel, an economist from the University of Adelaide, was co-opted to bring economic expertise.[61]

The Martin Committee focussed on the 'design' of institutions. Comprehensive universities were considered too costly to cope with the increased demand, and the committee sought ways in which both 'academic universities', which undertook basic research, and 'technological institutions', which would train those able 'to apply research findings in industry', could coexist.[62] The rationale behind this distinction was twofold. It allowed existing universities to pursue pure research and would spare students in technological institutions from the financial burden of a full university course, allowing them to graduate in fewer years. Debate among the committee over nomenclature and form led to the recommendation of a higher education system that combined universities and new Colleges of Advanced Education, which would provide diploma- or certificate-level qualifications for entry into a specific vocation.

The implementation of the Martin Committee recommendations created a complex arrangement tailored to the specific features of the various state systems. The states established separate institutes, with members drawn from industry and higher education, to coordinate programs offered by CAEs and direct funding. The CAE sector combined a range of institutions, including large and multifaceted institutes of technology, teachers' colleges, and small specialised colleges offering training for particular vocational groups, such as musicians and artists, and nurses.[63] Although Martin recommended a clear division between universities and other institutions, the system that emerged included some overlapping coverage in some fields of study.

In those states with fewer colleges, the CAE sector was more coherent than in the larger states. Queensland had three Colleges of Advanced Education in 1965: an Institute of Technology, an Agricultural College and a Conservatorium of Music. The Western Australian Institute of Technology combined a School of Mines, an Agricultural College, and Schools of Occupational Therapy and Physiotherapy. By contrast, New South Wales had eight institutions, while Victoria supported 21 separate instiutions of varying sizes, each concerned with a particular form of training in Forestry, Agriculture, Nursing and Physiotherapy, Pharmacy, and Art. These colleges were eligible for Commonwealth capital grants, and after 1967 received recurrent Commonwealth funding. The system was further complicated by the position of teachers' colleges, which were initially denied Commonwealth funding on the grounds that school education was not a 'national' but rather a state concern. This distinction proved impossible to justify and teachers' colleges became eligible for Commonwealth funding in 1973.[64] This confusing arrangement meant the division between universities and the other institutions in their educational programs was less clear than Martin had recommended.

The advent of CAEs did not directly affect universities, and the AVCC took no formal position on their creation. The Commonwealth Government had established a separate Commonwealth Advisory Committee on Advanced Education for CAEs, rather than incorporating them within the AUC, preserving the administrative separation between universities and colleges. Questions about the interaction between universities and CAEs, and the different approach to teaching in the CAEs, were analysed in *The Australian University* journal but were seldom directly referred to in AVCC deliberations.

Nevertheless, universities and the AVCC were conscious of what distinguished universities in the new 'binary' system. Some courses, Medicine in particular, were offered exclusively by universities. They had public research funding and the CAEs did not. They alone undertook research training to the doctoral level. Research, above everything else, distinguished them from CAEs. Tabling the Martin Report on 24 March 1965, Menzies pledged significant additional research funds to be allocated by a new Australian Research Grants Committee (ARGC), chaired by Sir Bob Robertson, Professor of Botany at the University of Adelaide, with members drawn from across disciplines and the CSIRO. The ARGC awarded grants to individual research proposals judged to 'make a significant contribution to the advancement of science and scientific knowledge in Australia', although projects from the social sciences and the humanities were also supported.[65]

The new ARGC grants replaced the previous Commonwealth block grants given on AUC recommendations, some of which universities applied to research. The ARGC fund was reallocated out of general university funding, which created temporary shortfalls in New South Wales and Victoria because of the way funding was allocated in those states. The more lasting change was a shift to funding individual projects, rather than allowing institutions to distribute research support. It imposed additional costs on them to administer the ARGC grants, disadvantaged younger researchers who were less able to compete, and forced applicants to indicate outcomes at the front end of projects, rather than follow where the research might lead.[66]

The establishment of the ARGC ushered in greater research funding over the ensuing years, reflecting the growing importance of research to universities and their missions. The AUC predicted that the proportion of higher degree students would rise above 10 per cent of total enrolments from 1968.[67] This expansion was made possible in part by the CAEs, which reduced the undergraduate load universities had to carry. While student numbers continued to grow, within ten years the majority of students in higher education would no longer enrol in a university. The number of part-time university students also fell as these students were more likely to enrol in CAEs.

Yet the emergence of CAEs also presented universities with an unanticipated challenge. From the moment of their establishment, CAEs began to offer bachelor-level qualifications to meet growing demand, a move endorsed by the Commonwealth committee that oversaw the introduction of the CAEs in 1967.[68] At first CAEs were required to demonstrate a practical application and perceived need to establish these degrees, and they were introduced under strict oversight from accreditation committees comprised of university experts. If bachelor's degrees could be delivered at lower cost, then universities would need to justify what additional value they offered in these degrees. The AVCC made 'the role of universities in higher education' the theme of the Tenth Commonwealth Universities Congress, held in Sydney in 1968, where Schonell emphasised the importance of universities' independence and the need to continue to fund them at levels necessary to meet their distinctive purpose.[69]

Different views about the place of universities and CAEs fostered confusion about the binary system. Menzies saw the colleges as providing for students 'who, though qualified, do not wish to undertake a full university course, or whose chosen course is not considered appropriate for university, or whose level at passing matriculation indicated a small chance of graduation from a university in minimum time or minimum time plus one year'.[70] This framing emphasised that CAEs were 'equal but different', a common formulation at the time, yet it also acknowledged that one cohort within the CAE population consisted of students demonstrating lower academic ability at the point of matriculation.

Educationists differed on the merits of the colleges. Laurence Short, Professor of Education at the University of Newcastle, observed that they demonstrated a 'vitality', which universities would do well to 'acquire', while CAEs in turn should aspire to 'excellence' by adopting 'methods and functions traditionally associated with the universities'.[71] Critics, such as ANU Education

Professor Don Anderson, argued the decision to create CAEs was counterproductive, and that greater emphasis should have been applied to technical training institutes. In his view the CAEs were 'concerned to become universities in all but name'.[72] Such a transition occurred in many of the British polytechnics, and the expectation of their future conversion into universities affected their natural development.[73] Universities made no comment about the relative value of the new colleges, but the 1969 Australian Universities Conference resolved that staff conditions should be equivalent, affirming 'the principle that the universities, colleges of advanced education and teachers' colleges should be regarded as full partners in the system of higher education. Provision should be made for broadly comparable conditions, salaries and facilities in all institutions of higher education'.[74]

While the creation of the CAEs promised new ways of delivering higher education, universities were also prepared to experiment. Particular interest arose over the prospect of 'cross-disciplinary' approaches to curriculum that worked in the spaces between the existing disciplinary boundaries.[75] This followed initiatives in the United Kingdom at the University of Sussex, established in 1961 and Keele in 1962, and fed into the planning for new Australian universities: Macquarie University, established in Sydney in 1964; La Trobe University, in Melbourne in 1965; Flinders University, in Adelaide in 1965; Griffith University, in Brisbane in 1971; Murdoch, in Perth in 1973; and Deakin, in Geelong in 1974.[76] The vice-chancellors of these institutions were invited to represent their universities at the AVCC, as was the University of Papua and New Guinea, established in 1965.[77]

To capture the changes that had taken place in the Australian university system, the AVCC commissioned University of Sydney Archivist, David Macmillan, to prepare a survey of universities and their development after the war. *Australian Universities:*

SYSTEMATISATION

A Descriptive Sketch was published by Sydney University Press for wider distribution than other AVCC publications, and it associated the older institutions with the structural innovations of the newer. Macmillan conceived of the CAEs as wholly distinct from universities and their affiliated university colleges.[78]

THE AVCC AFTER MARTIN

With the completion of the Martin Committee inquiry, universities turned to define the AVCC's role, realising ambitions formed in response to Murray's recommendations for the organisation. They moved to define its remit more clearly and incorporated it as a company limited by guarantee in the Australian Capital Territory.[79] In September 1968 universities published a formal statement of the AVCC's objectives for the first time. It was to serve as the 'means whereby universities can take counsel together on matters of mutual concern' and 'formulate advice to governing bodies on these matters'; to 'make public pronouncements, or to take other appropriate action, whenever it believes this could be useful', and to 'collect and disseminate' information between universities.[80] The AVCC established a greater range of national activities than previously, although it had no power to direct member institutions.

The AVCC formed subcommittees to shape policy in priority areas of 'development', 'teaching', 'research', 'finance and building', 'students', and 'statistics'. These committees comprised a number of vice-chancellors with interest in the areas. The AVCC appointed Percy Partridge to convene a Steering Committee on Research and Experiment into Education Matters, drawing together the work of various higher education study centres across the country.[81] The committees enabled work to be done across a range of fields simultaneously, allowing meetings of the AVCC to be more focused and less reliant on the particular interests of vice-chancellors. The new structure also allowed the AVCC to commission short reports, and to follow up the extent to which recommendations were implemented.

This work brought in house the research about universities that the AVCC had sponsored through its journal and in reports and ensured that this work was directed and purposeful. It also meant that projects commissioned by the AVCC sat alongside other research work undertaken by the AUC. The emphasis was on identifying solutions to problems. An example was the finance committee's support of a series of inquiries into 'greater utilisation of university facilities'. This aimed to resolve the question of how existing facilities could support larger numbers of students without diminishing standards. One purpose of such projects was to forestall the AUC. They also recognised the growing importance of doing more with less. Even so, the vice-chancellors resisted short-term 'fixes' and were concerned to identify pedagogical issues. An initial report recommended research to consider the introduction of year-round teaching, leading the AVCC to appoint the Monash Professor of Economics, Donald Cochrane, to consider the implications of such an arrangement for Monash University, as a case study for discussion among other universities. The report, printed in January 1970, generated such interest that it was reprinted in July.[82]

Partridge's committee on Research and Experiment into Education Matters allocated $23 000 in grants to support a series of projects on small-group teaching, and on the use of audio and audio-visual aids in teaching.[83] Again, this provided guidance on how best to strengthen university teaching programs and adopt new techniques to serve the interests of all students. To disseminate the work, the AVCC appointed an Information Officer, Dr KH Star, an education psychologist based at UNSW Tertiary

Education Research Centre, who produced a series of working papers and a regular newsletter to ensure the coherence of activities.[84]

These changes allowed the AVCC to respond to the AUC, which continued to deal primarily with universities individually. Despite the AVCC's increasing proactivity, it was criticised for being too passive in response to the AUC, and its discreet lobbying efforts made it appear aloof and without a prominent public voice.[85] Yet the AVCC was able to anticipate government policy changes. It appointed economist Geoffrey Brennan to undertake an inquiry into the prospect of abolishing fees, a long-standing concern of the NUAUS and, by this time, the Opposition Australian Labor Party had adopted the abolition of all university fees in its election platform.[86]

6
FREE AND ACCOUNTABLE

On 27 March 1973 the new Prime Minister, Gough Whitlam, wrote to state premiers explaining his government's intention to abolish fees, assume full Commonwealth responsibility for the funding of universities and CAEs, and introduce a means-tested allowance for full-time students. He informed universities on the same day. While Whitlam confidently asserted his government's intention to make the changes, he allowed some scope for discussion over the details. His rationale, he explained, was that 'education is the key to equality of opportunity', and the government was determined to support it.[1] The letter ushered in a new era for Australian tertiary education.

Whitlam presented higher education as serving social, as well as educational and economic, purposes. This had been one of the criticisms of universities raised by a militant student movement, whose energy Whitlam had harnessed in his election campaign in 1972. He thus imposed a new form of accountability on both universities, and CAEs. Other accountabilities would emerge throughout the 1970s. While the transfer to Commonwealth funding would remove inconsistencies between the states and complex Commonwealth–state interactions, universities were now more exposed to changes of policy made by a single level of government. While tertiary education became 'free' in one sense in 1974, in another it was made more accountable to a new set of internal and external interests.[2] The Commonwealth takeover was announced just before the 1973 'oil shock' that crippled economic growth and produced the new combination of 'stagflation', which was high inflation and stagnant growth. The ensuing economic crisis undermined the economic footing that had supported the expansion of higher education over the preceding decades.

THE STUDENT AND STAFF MOVEMENT

A culture of activism in universities ebbed and flowed in the decades following the Second World War.[3] During the 1960s, staff, graduates and students took up a series of causes, including opposition to the White Australia Policy and greater rights for Indigenous Australians, notably in the 'Freedom Ride', a student bus tour of regional cities and towns in New South Wales to protest and raise awareness of the segregation, exclusion and deprivation experienced by Aboriginal and Torres Strait Islander people. Graduates and students asserted responsibility to act on public causes. This extended beyond local issues to include condemnation of the South African policy of Apartheid.[4] The largest single issue was the Vietnam War, together with conscription. A coalition of students, staff and graduates protested against Australia's involvement in the war, culminating in the national Moratorium marches of 1970 and 1971, which brought hundreds of thousands of protestors into the streets of the capital cities.[5]

These protests drew on the ideas of the New Left, an international movement that set out to dismantle hierarchies of 'authority' and 'power'. The main target was the 'establishment', which included the university leadership.[6] Activists sought wider representation in universities, the content of curriculum, and more inclusive teaching practices. They also argued that university dependence on government and industry to undertake research threatened university autonomy and subordinated it to the 'military-industrial complex'.

Australian activists drew on overseas examples, such as the 'free speech movement' of the University of California, Berkeley. A dispute within the university over the right to raise money for political causes escalated into strident protests, 'sit-ins' disrupting university events. Subsequent protests were often violently suppressed by police, such as at Stanford University in 1966, and in Paris in 1968. A key concern was for a more participatory democracy and improved access to education.[7] Activists wanted a say in what was taught and representation in university administration on the principle that 'students and teachers should manage their own affairs'.[8]

Student protest caught senior administrators in universities off guard, causing disruptions across campus and resulting in disciplinary action against students, such as at Monash University.[9] Apart from their demands on universities, activists raised international issues on which universities had no policy. They were also still grappling with their recent expansion. Indeed, the increasing size of Australian universities became a target in much of the activists' rhetoric, and University of California President Clark Kerr's conception of the 'multiversity' – large institutions with many departments and a wide range of public roles – was widely condemned.[10] Previously, student apathy had been the concern in larger institutions. The University of Sydney Librarian reported his frustration that he had closed down a library staff–student liaison council due to lack of interest the year before his library was disrupted by a week of student 'sit-ins' over increased library fines.[11] As protests became more disruptive, universities' fear of public embarrassment grew. They often proved inept at responding, and expressed frustration that protest organisers were unreasonable and apt to renege on agreements.[12]

FAUSA responded to the criticism of universities by calling a national symposium on university 'autonomy' in 1969 that set out a new challenge:

> Is The University its governing body or its academic staff?
> If the academic staff constitutes the real university, does
> it include lecturers (and teaching fellows? and research
> assistants?), or only full professors? Should the democratic
> one-man-one-vote rule entitle the students to lay claim to be
> The University?[13]

In 1971 it followed this up with a symposium on 'how should universities be governed?'

Contributors to these symposia offered different criticisms: the fact that 'ultimate control of academic policy by an inner group of committee-minded professors' was supported by administrators who 'obey and buttress' this authority; the 'conservatism and apathy of the bulk of the staff; the ignorance and dullness of the bulk of the students'.[14] Monash University's Vice-Chancellor, Louis Matheson, defended the existing structures, arguing universities needed members of the 'establishment' for their connections and experience in managing large instiutions. He accepted that academic staff should have some form of representation on university committees, although professors carried 'special responsibilities', and should therefore have 'special rights'. He also saw the value of some student involvement, as Monash had already initiated, although not 'the one-third membership that one sometimes hears suggested', and with protections to ensure that as 'transient members of the university' they should vote on matters 'which concern them exclusively'. Administrative staff could offer advice, but their role to 'interpret and execute policy' clashed with that of policy-making. Vice-chancellors, he argued, were responsible for implementing policy but also 'present[ing] ideas for the running and development' of universities and were therefore justified in exercising their authority.[15]

A 'Free University' was created by University of Sydney staff and student volunteers in 1968 – free in that it charged no fees and determined its own courses of studies and methods. It ran out of a terrace house in Redfern until 1972.[16] A similar enterprise was launched in Canberra.[17] At the University of Queensland, students gained input into course materials, even if they felt this sometimes amounted to being 'co-opted' and thus contained by departmental committees.[18] Students and staff at the University of Melbourne established a 'University Assembly', in which every university member had equal voice, and meetings were held without an agenda. The University Council agreed to consider its recommendations.[19]

The AVCC was not immune from criticism. The president of FAUSA, Harry Medlin, criticised its reliance on 'subventions from the universities' while not being 'answerable to them'. By this he meant that it consisted of a body of vice-chancellors who nominally represented their universities, but who were not required to consult other members of their institutions. On these grounds, he argued, it lacked 'both authority and collective answerability'.[20]

RESEARCH

One of the criticisms the student movement made of universities was their perceived dependence on the Commonwealth Government and other external research partners. These partnerships were in fact more often marked by co-dependence. Medical research was undertaken in partnerships between universities and hospitals. The CSIRO continued to work closely with universities, often in laboratories it had constructed on university campuses. Australian arrangements for research were distinctive. Although sharing 'essentially the same aims' as the United Kingdom, United States and Canada, they were organised as 'different[ly] as one could imagine'.[21] Half of university research funds in the United States were derived from non-government sources, while in Australia nearly all came from the Commonwealth. The Commonwealth interest in research, through universities and its main science agency, the CSIRO, indicated commitment to public investment in new technologies and processes. This was expected to spur economic development and improve productivity, and also support national security imperatives amid the urgency of the Cold War.[22] Universities adopted a largely pragmatic approach, taking opportunities where they arose while seeking to influence the Commonwealth's priorities.

National research efforts focused on key areas. For example, the Australian Atomic Energy Commission (AAEC) was founded in 1953 for industrial and defence purposes, bringing together activities related to uranium mining in Rum Jungle in the Northern Territory and Marcus Oliphant's work at the ANU.[23] The nuclear research facility at Lucas Heights in Sydney was constructed in 1955. Phillip Baxter, Vice-Chancellor of UNSW from 1955 to 1969, was a member of the AAEC and worked with the other universities to establish the Australian Institute of Nuclear Science and Engineering (AINSE) in 1958. This coordinated research and teaching and was founded jointly by all universities in conjunction with the AAEC.[24]

Medical research was another priority area. Australia had gained new medical schools at the Universities of Western Australia and New South Wales in 1958, Monash in 1961 and the

University of Tasmania in 1965. This expanded the research workforce, along with a number of medical research institutes affiliated with universities, such as the Walter and Eliza Hall Institute of Medical Research affiliated with the University of Melbourne. Through its government endowment, the NHMRC provided funds for medical research and training of medical researchers at universities.[25] This funding grew substantially after 1950, sometimes with large increases year on year. From 1963–64 to 1964–65 the appropriation for the NHMRC rose from £318 500 to £413 000.[26]

Astronomy, which had been supported by state governments and taught at the Universities of Sydney, Melbourne, Tasmania and Adelaide since the nineteenth century, came to be a great national endeavour.[27] The Mount Stromlo Observatory, built in 1924 by the Commonwealth Government, was transferred to the ANU in 1957. In 1962 the ANU established its second observatory complex at Siding Spring, housing the largest optical telescope in Australia.[28] The development of the new technology of radio astronomy led to the building of the large Parkes Radio Telescope (1961), funded by the Carnegie Corporation, and the Culgoora Radio Heliograph (1967) through a Ford Foundation grant awarded in 1962.[29] The 1960s 'space race' ensured Commonwealth support for astrophysics in universities, and Australia's new capacity was broadcast worldwide in 1969 as Australian facilities relayed footage of the first lunar landing.

Australian universities invested in international links from the 1960s, including through developing international research collaborations. In 1962, supported by the governments of Australia and Indonesia, the AVCC established a program of inter-university cooperation in agricultural research. In 1968 universities in Malaysia and Singapore joined the scheme, which became the Australian-Asian Universities' Cooperation Scheme (AAUCS) and was expanded to include technology, forestry, agricultural economics and English.[30]

Its work supporting research and research training was administered by the AVCC offices and jointly funded by the Commonwealth. In 1977 Thailand joined the program, followed by the Philippines in the following year.[31] The AAUCS and other similar projects fostered collaborations across many different countries. In 1980 the AVCC surveyed university research collaborations to produce a 400-page directory of 'academic links'. The report traced 'links' across six continents, and included contact details and short outlines of collaborative projects from all Australian universities.[32]

International collaboration flowed from the growth of the international research enterprise. No longer at the margins, research had become intrinsic to many industry and government undertakings. There were striking examples of success: for instance, geological work undertaken as part of a PhD enabled discovery of one of Australia's largest copper reserves at Roxby Downs in South Australia.[33] The Australian Science, Technology and Engineering Council (ASTEC) was established in April 1977 comprising representatives of universities and industry. Its role was to improve the interface between government, industry and researchers and to advise government on matters relating to science and technology.

NEW MODELS

A similar innovation was apparent in the design of new institutions. Universities built in the 1960s and 1970s distinguished themselves through their structure and ethos. They employed distinct models and broke from their older peers. These 'gumtree' universities, as Simon Marginson and Mark Considine described them after their preference for planting their campuses mainly with native trees, 'were aggressively modern, nationalistic and some were educationally radical'.[34]

They were mostly constructed at the suburban edges of the capital cities. In 1965 La Trobe University was established in Melbourne, following the model of the new English 'plateglass' universities (Warwick, Lancaster, York, Essex, Sussex, East Anglia and Kent), in that each had distinctive approaches to internal governance, residential accommodation, and curriculum and degree structure based in general studies emphasising breadth of learning and collegiality.[35] La Trobe was followed in 1966 by Flinders University in Adelaide, which adopted a similar model, with democratic governance structures and greater informality than the older universities. Its first Vice-Chancellor, Peter Karmel, who would later become the long-serving AUC chair and then ANU Vice-Chancellor, led with an experimental organisational ethos. 'Internal research grants' for example 'were allocated competitively'.[36] The structural experimentation continued with Griffith University in Brisbane, which was planned from 1969 with subjects in Arts, Commerce, Education and Science where 'students could choose subjects from any or all of the four ... to foster the interrelationship of courses'.[37] The Vice-Chancellor, Professor F John Willett, argued that the university should avoid becoming a 'slavish handmaid of the status quo, a factory fitting out men and women to serve the community within present values and organisations'.[38]

Griffith and then Murdoch, established in Perth in 1973, adopted interdisciplinary structures with the expectation of 'long-term public funding [that] eliminated the risk factor, greatly facilitating reinvention'.[39] Responsibility for staffing, courses and research was maintained within non-discipline–based schools. Murdoch had four schools of general studies – Human Communication, Social Inquiry, Environmental and Life Sciences – as well as Schools of Education and Veterinary Sciences. Teaching 'programmes' could reside in more than one school. In 1979 Griffith formed a School of Australian Environmental Studies, of Modern Asian Studies and of Social and Industrial Administration. Deakin was the last of the gumtrees to be established, in 1974. Planned as a regionally located university for Victoria, it brought together the former Geelong Teachers' College and the higher education courses of the Gordon Institute of Technology. Focusing on distance education, it did not fully replicate the organisational experimentation of the other gumtrees, offering established courses alongside interdisciplinary offerings, including Australian Studies.

WIDENING ACCESS TO HIGHER EDUCATION

The organisational experimentation occurred alongside the Commonwealth's broader educational ambitions, centred on greater government funds for school education. The Whitlam government's decision to fund all higher education and abolish student fees was consistent with this aim of widening access, including through a new Tertiary Education Assistance Scheme (TEAS), which provided a stipend.[40] The problems of implementation became apparent in the weeks following the announcement in March 1973. On 22 May Ken Jones, Secretary of the Commonwealth Department of Education, convened a meeting with the AUC and the AVCC to determine what fees students had paid across various universities, how this revenue would be replaced and what other support was needed. Schedules were drawn up to account for all the previous student contributions towards libraries, admissions, deferred examination, field work and residencies, and ensure these were included in Commonwealth contributions. In September the AUC wrote to universities to set out the precise basis on which funds would be provided from the beginning of 1974. This served only to complicate matters.[41] It was not clear whether students taking degree subjects, but not enrolled for a degree or a diploma, would be included. A policy was also needed for whether adult education or 'refresher' course students, those returning to university for single subjects, should be charged fees. This had implications for the spirit of the policy and its objective to promote access for all. It was agreed that such students must continue to pay ancillary charges to support union and other student services to ensure that they were included in the number of enrolled students, but not to charge them tuition fees.[42]

When Karmel, as chair of the AUC, circulated the legislation in November, further uncertainties were revealed.[43] Universities were concerned that the abolition of fees might bring a dramatic expansion in the numbers of students, a situation that 'could well make for chaos and confusion'.[44] This issue was left unresolved, but the government agreed that when it assumed responsibility for financing universities from the beginning of 1974, it would institute arrangements to take account of any escalation of costs through 'Supplementary Grants'.[45]

The final aspect of the Commonwealth's commitment was the introduction of means-tested living and other allowances for all full-time Australian students. Students enrolled in approved tertiary and technical courses were eligible for these payments, but not those in higher degree courses, for which competitive awards were provided, or those paid a stipend by a future employer under a 'bond' arrangement.[46] This living allowance, along with the abolition of fees, removed much of the attraction of the system of bonded places that were offered by different governments and a wide variety of industries. The numbers of bonded places quickly diminished.[47]

The government's commitment to ensure access for all sections of society to higher education set out a new priority for the sector. The previous web of Commonwealth, state and industry scholarships had been introduced to ensure that academically capable students of moderate means were able to continue into university. Now this same support was available to all. Students would be supported through university irrespective of how they intended to make use of their degree. No priority disciplines would be identified. The 'circumstances in which students are admitted to courses and permitted to continue', as Whitlam put it, was left to universities and CAEs.[48]

This was a departure from the rationale that had governed the expansion of higher education over the preceding decades, which was characterised by concern to maximise human capital by producing graduates able to enter the professions. Now the implication was that once students gained entry to university, they would be free to change courses if they wished. This gave students unprecedented autonomy and encouraged the view that they should have greater involvement in the governance of institutions, the design of the curriculum, and teaching and assessment.

Whitlam's interest in promoting social equality through higher education was shared by universities. The challenge was that universities had only very limited knowledge of the socio-economic and demographic composition of the student body. To rectify this situation, the AVCC commissioned the UNSW Tertiary Education Research Centre to undertake a series of inquiries into the socio-economic composition of student communities, and the degree to which people from different disadvantaged groups went to universities.

It was widely acknowledged that working-class students were more likely to study part-time.[49] The vocational degrees offered by CAEs were more popular among this same cohort. Previously universities had not focussed on the socio-economic circumstances of their students upon entry.[50] However, universities had taken up measures to discourage repeating matriculation, a tactic used by wealthier students to boost their marks and gain entry into quota-restricted courses.[51]

Research during the 1970s identified 'four conditions for entry': 'availability', 'accessibility', 'aspiration' and 'achievement'.[52] The first two conditions were the most straightforward. For disadvantaged groups to gain entry they must either live in proximity to a higher education institution or have financial assistance to travel, to remove financial barriers to entry and provide ongoing support with living expenses. The expansion of the tertiary sector, coupled with the abolition of fees and provision of living allowances, had done much to enable these conditions to be met. The other two conditions presented greater difficulty.

'Aspiration' was challenging because the desire to embark on tertiary education was often 'socially determined' and depended on any number of socio-economic and cultural factors. A father's occupation, and to a lesser extent a mother's occupation, was a commonly used proxy to indicate socio-economic status and the likelihood that a family might encourage a student to undertake tertiary education. Other indicators were cultural. New migrants, for instance, were more motivated to enter tertiary education than other groups at equivalent levels of income.[53] The final condition, 'achievement', used matriculation as a baseline requirement and pointed to the need for changes in primary and secondary schooling. Students from poorer backgrounds demonstrating high academic achievement were more likely to be encouraged to take a degree. For these reasons, the abolition of fees alone would not bring greater educational equality.

The socio-economic and cultural makeup of universities was remarkably stable over time and across the country, but there were signs of change. A larger proportion of new migrants would gain access, as did increasing numbers of mature-aged students, many of whom had previously missed out on scholarships and now took the opportunity of going to university. The removal of fees allowed many who previously felt excluded from universities to believe they had a right to be there, and helped to increase numbers of women studying in professional degrees other than teaching, where they had long been present.[54] The main outcome was a clearer understanding of the need to focus efforts on the socio-economic and cultural circumstances that governed the 'aspiration' to come into tertiary education, an objective supported by universities.[55]

AUC TO CTEC

On 30 May 1975 Whitlam announced his intention to amalgamate the Australian Universities Commission and the Commission on Advanced Education to create a single statutory advisory body, a Tertiary Education Commission.[56] Unlike Whitlam's announcement of the abolition of student fees, the AVCC was forewarned of the change and consulted by the government. Concurrently, Peter Karmel, Ken Jones and Thomas Swanson were appointed to review the governance of the tertiary education sector and consult with universities and colleges.[57] Then in February 1975 universities engaged the University of Sydney Vice-Chancellor, Bruce Williams, to examine options for future governance of tertiary education. Williams outlined the complexities of governance of the system and the merging of the AUC and CAE commission.[58]

The Commonwealth's assumption of responsibility meant that universities and the CAEs were now almost entirely dependent on a single source of government support. This funding now became much more publicly visible, which in turn brought political pressure for the government to examine educational outlays. Commonwealth control also amplified an unwanted dynamic in which the CAEs and universities were seen to compete for funding and support. This was compounded by interactions between the AUC and universities, especially around the triennial negotiations. Universities complained that the AUC would 'argue from figures and statistics to which it alone had access'.[59] Universities began to exchange information to avoid 'being played off one against the other', but were not always successful.[60]

The powers of the proposed Tertiary Education Commission risked exacerbating these problems. Universities feared it could entrench 'artificial class distinctions between different types of institutions and the staff and students within them'.[61] At the same time, they feared it could undermine their own research function. They petitioned Karmel and his colleagues that it was in the national interest for their 'special role' to be 'distinct from other forms of tertiary education'.[62] They argued that a 'body of this kind … should not be representative of vested interests' and that it needed commissioners 'who were not members of either the Universities Commission or the Commission on Advanced Education'.[63] This recognised the unresolved tension between the different types of tertiary education institutions. 'Universities, colleges of advanced education and teachers' colleges should be regarded as full partners in the system of higher education', Williams stated, despite their different level of funding and research capacity.[64]

The Commonwealth Tertiary Education Commission (CTEC) was established in 1977 with councils representing universities, CAEs and institutes of Technical and Further Education (TAFE).[65] CTEC advised the Commonwealth on funding and policy for the whole tertiary education sector. Its first chair was Peter Karmel, who transferred from the AUC.

Karmel adopted an approach of tailoring funding to meet the needs of individual institutions, largely alleviating universities' concerns. As he had with the AUC, Karmel received submissions to CTEC from each institution, published and explained its recommendations. By regularly visiting every institution, Karmel argued, CTEC 'built up a knowledge of institutions and an understanding of their aspirations and operations' and was 'sensitive to their ethos and acted to support them'.[66] CTEC served as a buffer between universities and government, and in so doing Karmel saw his role as interpreting policy priorities 'in a way that enable[d] institutions to function as well as possible'.[67] CTEC's funding recommendations to government were informed by its understanding of the needs of individual universities and supported by comprehensive information that extended to the amount of funding they received per student. Through his deft hand in negotiations, Karmel assumed ever-greater authority in managing interactions between universities and government. The effect was to reduce the role of the AVCC as an advocate for universities. That had little consequence while they were reaping the benefits of growth. Once such public beneficence ended, however, the AVCC would have to rediscover its voice.

THE 'STEADY STATE'

The establishment of CTEC in 1977 followed the Whitlam government announcing a freeze of the triennial system of funding that had governed funding since the establishment of the AUC. In that year projections for tertiary education were for a 30 per cent increase at a time when the budgetary deficit and inflation were escaping government control.

The cuts inflicted in the 1975 Budget precipitated an abrupt stalling of growth in the sector. Demand for teacher training plummeted as the number of state-funded bonded places fell. Demographic changes, especially as the postwar baby boomers graduated and the number of school leavers subsequently fell, contributed to reduced demand for university places. That was occurring internationally, including in the United States.[68] In Australia demand had reached a saturation point. While CTEC imposed quotas on student places, many universities failed to fill them. The shortfalls were unevenly spread, being particularly severe in Geology, Metallurgy, Engineering and Education.[69] The CAEs, by contrast, continued to expand despite government directives that they should not enrol additional students, suggesting greater interest in vocational courses.

This set of circumstances brought about what became known as the 'steady state'. Universities had strained to accommodate the previous growth in the number of students. They now found themselves faced with the opposite problem, with too many staff and some under-utilised facilities. Commitment to existing staff also limited universities' capacity to hire new staff to accommodate new patterns of student demand.[70]

This prompted discussions about ways of introducing more 'flexible' conditions of employment. In the decade from 1967 to 1977 the full-time workforce had more than doubled from roughly 5000 to almost 12 000. The numbers in the CAEs increased from only 1200 full-time staff to almost 8500.[71] Now, as all institutions confronted similar challenges, there was an effective hiring freeze across the system, halting the mobility of university staff. The effects of tenure under these conditions meant that the workforce would age. Since many universities had expanded with young staff, this meant that they were 'stuck – for better, for worse – with most of our tenured staff until their retire'.[72] This in turn raised concerns that university staff would become more costly as they were promoted. It also limited universities' and CAEs' capacity to reform their teaching programs in response to new technologies and workforce requirements.

The AVCC commissioned David Myers, La Trobe University's founding Vice-Chancellor, to inquire into the staffing issues. Myers dampened the alarmist rhetoric. There was no impending crisis, but there were limited opportunities to address shifting system-wide staffing needs. He suggested universities consider a range of approaches, including the creation of part-time and fixed-term positions.[73]

The new circumstances prompted Commonwealth and state governments to appoint inquiries into 'post-secondary' education. The Commonwealth was the primary funder for universities and CAEs, although they remained state institutions, while the states provide the majority of the funding for the TAFE sector. To cope with the complexity of division in responsibility for tertiary education, these inquiries all recommended the creation of state authorities to govern tertiary education.[74]

In addition to these reports, the Fraser Liberal government, which assumed office in 1975, appointed Bruce Williams to chair an inquiry into the long-term direction of the tertiary education system under conditions of reduced growth. The Williams Committee identified demographic shifts that would have the effect of reducing the numbers of children in primary and secondary education, but observed that the public commitment from state and Commonwealth governments to education had doubled from 2.9 per cent of GDP in 1961–62 to 5.8 per cent by 1976–77. The proportion of this outlay spent on tertiary education had more than doubled, from 15 to 36 per cent, in part owing to the great expansion in the higher education sector brought by its increasing diversity, and more labour-intensive teaching methodologies such as tutorials.[75]

The Williams Committee forecast that growth would not return for decades, and accordingly identified 'efficiency', 'accountability' and 'flexibility' as guiding values for the tertiary education sector.[76] The committee had been instructed to connect 'post-secondary education', with 'the needs of individuals', and to make 'education and employment' a priority. It recommended that growth in the tertiary sector should be pegged to that of the GDP, and that this growth should be taken up by the CAEs and TAFE. For universities, the committee recommended that the existing geographical coverage should not be expanded further. Instead more teaching should be offered through correspondence. To avoid unsustainable duplication, smaller universities should only broaden their programs by entering into 'contract agreements' with other institutions. It proposed that degrees be awarded for 'work undertaken between institutions'. University entry should be competitive and based on the likelihood of graduation.[77]

Taking up the theme of accountability in the Williams Committee report, Karmel argued that universities had a number of accountabilities. They had financial accountability to ensure that funds were properly spent. They had social accountability to 'meet their broad objectives' and ensure that graduates were produced in 'the right numbers', of 'the right kind'. The third accountability was economic – to ensure that expenditure was justified and allocated as efficiently as possible.[78] Universities retained their independence but were required to act with regard to the broader economic consequences of their policies and ensure their programs were delivered economically. Since the Commonwealth had supplanted all the other sources of funding, this accountability was more overt.

Universities accepted the benefits of such accountability, including its potential to assist internal reform. Yet they also cautioned of the dangers of external oversight. They urged academics to be active in the governance of the university system, following Peter Karmel in CTEC and Bruce Williams chairing the Commonwealth review.[79]

The Williams Committee recommended mergers and closures of a number of institutions, not unlike changes underway in Canada and the United Kingdom, where smaller teachers' colleges in particular were absorbed by larger institutions. Staff wages were guaranteed to prevent 'antagonism'.[80] Mergers offered opportunities for those excluded from senior leadership, including women.[81] In Western Australia the Graylands CAE was closed; mergers took place between CAEs in Ballarat and Bendigo, and two Geelong CAEs merged with Deakin. Other mergers were proposed in Adelaide and Sydney. The Western Australia Government committed to retain Murdoch University against the recommendation of the Williams report.[82] Karmel's recommendation that the University of Tasmania and the local CAEs be 'rationalised' was not implemented, yet in 1980 the university absorbed the Hobart-based institutions.[83]

The impetus for CAEs in particular to find efficiencies was brought into stark relief in 1981 by the report of the Commonwealth Government's 'Razor Gang'. It aimed to curtail the growth in spending and define the boundaries between state and federal responsibilities. Education was highlighted, and the Commonwealth committed to 'reduce significantly its involvement in this area', 'promot[ing] a major rationalisation and re-allocation of resources in higher education'. Smaller CAEs concerned with teacher education would be amalgamated with larger ones or face withdrawal of funding in 1982. Fees would be reintroduced for second and higher degrees, and eligibility for government financial assistance would be tightened, replaced by a 'loans scheme' repayable after graduation. Additional resources would be provided for courses in 'technology and business studies'.[84]

Further mergers followed, including that between James Cook University and the Townsville CAE, the University of Wollongong and the Wollongong Institute of Education.[85] Others, such as a proposed merger between the University of New England and the Armidale CAE, which had been discussed through the 1970s, did not eventuate until later.[86] A Sydney CAE emerged out of five separate smaller teachers' colleges in 1981.[87]

Under these circumstances, universities had no prospect of expansion. The need to find efficiencies was taken up by the AVCC through a series of surveys of university policies on recruitment and staff conditions, to ensure equivalency and guide the adoption of new measures. These included the conditions of employment of 'junior teaching staff', 'fractional appointments', conditions of promotion, the probationary period of employment, 'limited term' appointments, and tenure generally.[88] Another strand of work considered policies to encourage Aboriginal and Torres Strait Islander students and staff to enter universities.[89] Provisions for long-service and maternity leave were also reviewed.[90] A final theme concerned provisions for student unions and the services they provided.[91]

A picture emerged of remarkable consistency in staff conditions across universities, which was hardly surprising given the similar legislative framework in the various states. The review of policies for Aboriginal and Torres Strait Islander staff, however, revealed one difference. Most universities did not collect information on Indigenous students and staff. At the time this was inconsistent with their anti-discrimination policies. Nonetheless, many had policies actively to recruit Indigenous staff and students to redress vast under-representation, with the aim of promoting a larger intake. Another aspect of this benchmarking concerned research policy, including regulations for examination of the PhD.[92]

Government funding cuts left their mark on universities. This was apparent in areas such as research, where cutbacks had deleterious consequences for the scale and quality of research. A 1984 survey conducted by the AVCC, in association with the ARGC and ASTEC, found a considerable 'shortfall in funding'.

Of 2000 projects identified by the ARGC as worthy of funding in 1983, only 514 received funding, mostly at lower rates than requested. The consequences were 'slower progress, reduced expectations, elimination of more difficult, complicated or adventurous studies, reliance on obsolete equipment, difficulty in retaining experienced support staff, and for many a feeling of deep personal discouragement'. The negative effects were not restricted to those whose applications were unsuccessful.[93] There were other consequences for teaching, including larger class sizes in some courses, which strained university facilities, such as laboratories and libraries. Although inquiries such as the Williams review forecast the steady state would persist for decades, it would not. Direct measures to promote access would be introduced by another Labor government at the end of the decade. These measures achieved many of the goals of Whitlam's changes through a set of policies aimed at restoring growth. At the same time universities would be newly accountable to entrepreneurial ideals, and training students in skills over and above those required by traditional degrees.

7
A UNIFIED SYSTEM

In a lecture delivered at the Royal Melbourne Institute of Technology (RMIT) in 1987 the new Commonwealth Minister for Employment, Education and Training, John Dawkins, proclaimed a 'new age' for Australian higher education.[1] It would need to do more to provide skills needed for industry. It would have to be more responsive to public expectations and 'to the emerging needs of the economy', and include a wider range of Australians. It needed to forge connections with industry, particularly in research. He therefore urged older universities to 'shake off' what he regarded as 'their ingrained resistance to change'.

The division of labour between universities and CAEs was also changing. Since their creation in the mid-1960s, CAEs had accommodated most of the growth in student places. Some CAEs were also taking a greater role in research and offering research master's degrees. The 'binary' divide between universities and other higher education institutions was increasingly seen as arbitrary, and there was pressure to convert many of the larger CAEs into universities.[2]

From his appointment as Minister for Education, Dawkins made sweeping changes that reshaped Australian higher education. He brought the colleges and universities together to form a Unified National System (UNS) and encouraged their consolidation.

A UNIFIED SYSTEM

No fewer than twenty new universities emerged in the ensuing scramble, doubling the total number. Growth resumed in the number of higher education places, with additional places made possible by a new government-backed income-contingent student loan scheme, the Higher Education Contribution Scheme (HECS). Dawkins' policy program drew on arguments similar to those that the government had used to float the dollar and restructure the public service, and would later bring to the removal of tariff protection and centralised wage fixation. Australia was falling behind and needed to become more competitive, with a more educated workforce. It had to produce greater numbers of university graduates with the knowledge and expertise to meet the needs of an increasingly deregulated economy created by the Hawke Labor government, and to widen access to higher education in a way that fee abolition alone had not achieved.

The changes challenged universities, inviting them to adapt to widening access, and reshape themselves to foster growth in student numbers as well as forge growing international connections. The creation of new universities posed questions for the enlarged system. Universities' concerns went beyond questions of funding and growth. New information and computing technologies created opportunities to transform the work of universities. This led the AVCC to set up the computer network architecture that became the initial backbone of the internet in Australia. Universities would become in many ways more agile than Dawkins demanded in his 1987 RMIT lecture.

DAWKINS AND AFTER

Gough Whitlam's assumption of federal responsibility for funding tertiary education and the subsequent removal of student fees changed the way higher education was viewed in Australia. Despite the hopes that the removal of fees would widen access, the expansion was limited, hampered by the Commonwealth's iron grip on the number of enrolments. The AVCC began to estimate the number of applicants who had missed out on a university place, which had grown to 20 000 by 1987.[3] CAEs, by contrast, grew at a faster rate during the 1970s and 1980s, quickly becoming the majority tertiary education providers. By 1986 they admitted 25 per cent more students each year than universities.[4] Students with fewer financial means were more likely to attend a CAE, those from more privileged backgrounds were more likely to attend university.[5]

The growth of CAE enrolments went hand in hand with their expansion into new activities. The binary divide became less distinct as both universities and the larger colleges supported research programs and offered research training. As University of Melbourne higher education researcher John Anwyl observed, many people were openly referring to 'the death of the binary system'.[6] The AVCC and the equivalent body representing CAEs, the Australian Committee of Directors and Principals (ACDP), set up working parties in an effort to reconcile the differences. They discussed the possibility of converting large institutes of technology into universities, establishing new universities, or employing a combination of the two strategies.

The tensions were revealed in the dual system of accountabilities for universities and CAEs, which were funded by the Commonwealth, but incorporated under state legislation. 'Few would disagree', stated a 1986 joint AVCC–ACDP working paper, 'that there are signs that proper consultation between state and Federal bodies is faltering'.[7] Such fears were confirmed later that year. Without seeking Commonwealth approval, the Western Australia Government enacted legislation to convert the Western Australian Institute of Technology (WAIT), a CAE, into the Curtin

University of Technology.⁸ By this stage WAIT, with 12 967 students, was almost three times larger than Perth's Murdoch University and it had extensive research programs.⁹ The Act explicitly stated that this was little more than a 'change of name', but it had implications for the way the institution was funded. The expectation was that Curtin would receive Commonwealth funds on the basis that it was a university, rather than a CAE. This was not guaranteed, however, as any change of funding was at the Commonwealth Government's discretion. An AVCC delegation visited Curtin in 1987 and admitted its Vice-Chancellor, Don Watts, as a member.

Pressure was building to end the long hiatus in the establishment of new universities. Curtin prominently demonstrated the possibility of converting CAEs into universities through state government intervention, breaking the thin line that marked the 'binary' divide. This showed once again that inconsistencies could arise in a system where higher education was funded by the Commonwealth but largely governed by state legislation. There was also public debate about creating private universities to meet the demand for alternative institutions.[10] Discussions about a Catholic university had been conducted for many years, to integrate Catholic traditions into higher education alongside the secular public universities.[11]

The centrepiece of Dawkins' policy after he was appointed Minister for Employment, Education and Training in July 1987 was to expand the size of the Australian university system. As he saw it, this would bring three central benefits. First, it would increase the number of university graduates. Second, it would widen university access, in keeping with the government's broader agenda. Third, it would solve the problems of the 'binary' system by removing the distinction between higher education institutions. Expansion required changes in the way funding was allocated to higher education institutions. Dawkins would not meet the AVCC in his first months as minister, although he had represented the prime minister in earlier meetings. In September 1987 he received an AVCC delegation of vice-chancellors, Brian Wilson (Queensland), Michael Birt (New South Wales) and David Caro (Melbourne), and agreed to their request for 'closer consultation'. Yet the speed with which the new minister acted on his plans left little time for detailed negotiation.[12]

In the following week, Dawkins shared a pamphlet he intended to publish, *The Challenge for Higher Education in Australia*, which set out his reasoning. 'The ongoing adjustments required in the structure of our economy', he argued, 'will place a much greater premium on technical knowledge and labour force skills, and likewise on quality, innovation and technology'. Dawkins argued that the role of universities to train people for traditional professions should give way to a new emphasis on the underlying skills inherent within them, which could be applied in a range of future careers. He envisioned 'leaps in participation in higher education', for which the existing budget could not provide. For this reason, the funding base was 'to be considerably broadened'. There would also be a process of 'rationalisation' in the administration of higher education and the use of resources to ensure the most effective use of public money.[13] Dawkins gave the AVCC and ACDP just ten days to prepare a response. The University of Wollongong's Vice-Chancellor, Professor Ken McKinnon, urged the government to 'weigh the evidence coolly' before embarking on radical reform, but Dawkins was determined to keep up the pace of change.[14]

Shortly after issuing *The Challenge*, Dawkins assembled an advisory group that came to be known as the 'purple circle'.[15] This brought senior university and college administrators together with public servants who had not previously been responsible for higher education. Existing higher education experts in the public service were sidelined to ensure that discussion was open to all possibilities.[16] In October Dawkins announced that CTEC would be replaced with a different advisory body, the National Board of Employment, Education and Training (NBEET), which would have four councils, for training, schools, higher education and the Australian Research Council (ARC).[17] This arrangement grouped higher education and training explicitly with employment, imposing a more instrumental framework on the sector. NBEET's Higher Education Council would have a more limited role to advise on funding allocations than had been the case for CTEC, leaving the new body with less influence. CTEC's staffing and other resources were transferred to the department while the Higher Education Council had only a small staff and limited capacity for independent policy work.

The AVCC received little notice of the impending dissolution of CTEC, and the shocks continued.[18] In November 1987 the AVCC hosted a two-day discussion about the current and future role of universities, the third such decennial conference, but the discussion immediately became obsolete after Dawkins released a Green Paper, *Higher Education: A Policy Discussion Paper*, in December.[19] The Green Paper set out the government's plan more fully and promised a 'consultative and collaborative process' before the changes were implemented. The minister embarked on a national tour over the following months, although his audiences were given little chance to engage with the proposals.[20]

The Green Paper proposed to replace the 'binary' system with a 'unified national system' of higher education. Institutions were free to join if they accepted key conditions, but if they did not they would not be eligible for funding incentives. Central to the design was a consolidation of all higher education providers, including universities, colleges, institutes of technology and some TAFEs, into a single system. All participating institutions would have access to research funding and be able to offer research degrees, so long as they met a threshold size of enrolments. A minimum was set at 2000 equivalent full-time students, 5000 were needed to conduct research and 8000 for a 'comprehensive research' program. These thresholds effectively mandated consolidation and ended the support for smaller, specialised institutions. Twenty-one colleges had fewer than 2000 students; eight universities fell short of the 5000-student threshold to be eligible for research funding.[21]

The plan met with a mixed reception. Both universities and CAEs welcomed the prospect of increases in their student places, so long as it came with adequate funding.[22] A number of the larger CAEs in particular voiced their approval, as it promised them access to research funding. However, universities and CAEs protested against the insistence that they comply with all the conditions for membership of the UNS, and its implication for the relationship with government.[23] There was anxiety about the Green Paper's privileging of technical disciplines. Staff associations were concerned by the Green Paper's intention to dispense with collectively bargained salary and conditions. Some colleges worried that mergers would disperse universities across multiple campuses, and that the result could be a new 'binary' divide between institutions with access to different resources.[24]

Many of the changes the Green Paper specified, such as clearer definitions of the role and mission of universities, strategic planning, and efficient use of resources, were adapted from recommendations in CTEC's 1986 *Review of Efficiency and Effectiveness in Higher Education*. Such ideas had already gained wide currency.[25] Institutions were accordingly conscious of the need to raise the 'productivity of their capital resources' by adopting a common academic year and possibly increasing its length. They were alert to the calls for strategic planning with 'strong managerial modes of operation', 'stream-lined decision-making' and new mechanisms of accountability.[26] A deadline for responses to the Green Paper was set for April 1988.

The AVCC was galvanised by the imminent reorganisation of the sector to expand its own internal structures, going so far as to consider adopting a new title. It agreed on 16 November that the AVCC secretariat be expanded to accommodate a full-time communications officer and a policy and planning analyst to 'create more impact' and foster a better 'understanding of the universities' in government and by the general public.[27] Frank Hambly, the AVCC's long-serving Secretary, was asked to adopt a more public role with his title changed to Executive Director. The AVCC reconstituted itself in the mould of other representative bodies, such as business peak bodies and the Australian Council of Social Services. It would eventually move into new offices in the Canberra suburb of Deakin, where many not-for-profit advocacy groups were situated.

The government received over 600 submissions in response to the Green Paper, many from outside the sector.[28] The AVCC submission 'strongly supported' the Green Paper, but rejected its 'arbitrary ruling about size'. It urged amalgamations between institutions be based on geographical and system considerations.[29] The ACTU gave support, as did the Business Council of Australia, although not the Australian Chamber of Commerce.[30]

In July 1988 the government released its White Paper, *Higher Education: A Policy Statement*, clarifying how the UNS would work. Two proposals troubled universities. First, that 'an increasing share' of resources would be 'directed to those fields of study of greatest relevance to the national goals of industrial development and economic restructuring'. Second, that the ARC would determine 'areas of basic research that hold the greatest potential for exploitation in Australia'.[31] By diverting resources in this way, these changes were seen to threaten university autonomy.

The most radical proposal was the transfer of research funds from the operational grant to the new ARC. The justification for this change was to direct more research activity into project grants awarded on a competitive basis, and also to encourage universities to do more to solicit research funding from industry. The Green Paper had stated that $50 million might be reallocated from operating grants 'over time', but the White Paper announced that this 'clawback', as it became known, would amount to $125 million over three years.[32] The cuts amounted to 4.5 per cent of universities' operating grants. The University of Queensland Vice-Chancellor, Brian Wilson, worried it was a 'blue-print for over-regulation' and University of Sydney Vice-Chancellor John Ward wanted the AVCC to consider a challenge to the constitutional validity of the powers the minister proposed to exercise, a proposal independently taken up but subsequently abandoned, by student unions.[33]

Despite these concerns, the Commonwealth proceeded with its plans. It invited universities and colleges to join the UNS, requiring each to commit to a management review and establish and implement plans for management of staff and research. They would need to adopt a system of credit transfer from TAFE and incorporate equity considerations into all aspects of planning and management.

In September 1988 Dawkins met an AVCC delegation of vice-chancellors to seek to allay their concerns. Since universities were worried that HECS might deter students from embarking on research higher degrees, Dawkins promised additional scholarships for honours and postgraduate students. He agreed to ask NBEET to reconsider the size of the research 'clawback' and to consult universities further to determine research priorities. To allow time to consider these proposals, he delayed the date for joining the UNS until the end of October 1988.[34]

The transfer of operational funding to the ARC remained the outstanding issue. The University of Melbourne Vice-Chancellor,

A UNIFIED SYSTEM

David Penington, raised concerns that even with the additional consultation the research 'clawback' would remain largely unchanged. Don Aitkin, the chair of the ARC, had already dismissed such concerns at a meeting with Monash academics.[35] The AVCC informed Dawkins three weeks later that it could not recommend joining the UNS unless universities were explicitly party to the reconsideration of the research funding and the setting of priorities. Dawkins obliged, asking Penington to participate in his review of research policy.[36] By this time, many CAEs and universities were beginning negotiations to amalgamate, often with an eye to meeting the enrolment threshold for research activity.

NEW UNIVERSITIES

The removal of the binary divide between universities and colleges was premised on the creation of larger institutions through consolidation. This was achieved through an intricate process of merger between institutions of different sizes. Detailed negotiation involved the particular qualities of the organisations that would be established, how these would fit within the wider university system, and how they would be funded.[37] For mergers to be approved, the Commonwealth required a single governing board, a chief executive, one educational profile, one funding allocation and one set of academic awards.[38] Since the Commonwealth had no legal power to control the process, it created joint planning committees comprised of Commonwealth and state representatives, which would assess the 'educational benefits' of proposed mergers. It also provided incentives, eligibility for which guided the types of organisation able to be established. These included capital works needed to accommodate larger student numbers, increases in student quotas, and assistance with transitional arrangements. Research funding mandated universities have a certain number of students, further encouraging institutions to seek partners.[39]

The mergers reshaped the higher education landscape, with new institutions emerging from three main processes. The first of these was for smaller institutions or individual campuses to be drawn into new conglomerates with larger institutions. Between 1988 and 1992 many of the smaller technical and specialist colleges and institutes joined established universities, such as the merger between several Brisbane CAE campuses and Griffith.[40] Some mergers were large and complex, such as Monash's acquisitions of the Victorian College of Pharmacy, Chisholm Institute of Technology and Gippsland Institute of Advanced Education.

The second process was the conversion of larger CAEs and institutes of technology into universities. The institutes of technology were well-established organisations, the oldest in Brisbane and Melbourne growing out of the technical schools established in the nineteenth century. By 1986, they were large, with the largest having around 13 000 enrolments. They offered a wide array of professional courses and had built a growing research effort despite being barred from access to the national research schemes; all had extensive relationships with industry.[41]

At various times since the Martin Committee there had been proposals that the state institutes, including the RMIT, the Queensland Institute of Technology (QIT) and the South Australian Institute of Technology (SAIT), should become technical universities, with full access to Commonwealth research funding. This followed the precedent established by WAIT and the New South Wales Institute of Technology, which became the University of Technology, Sydney (UTS) in January 1988.[42] During 1990 and 1991, the newly created UTS merged with Kuring-gai CAE and the Sydney CAE, which itself had been formed from a merger of the Institute of Technical and Adult Teacher Education, and several smaller colleges.⁴³ QIT also converted into a university, merging with those Brisbane CAE campuses that did not become part of Griffith University to become the Queensland University of Technology, which was later joined by the Queensland Conservatorium of Music.⁴⁴ In South Australia the Institute of Technology initially planned to join Flinders, while the South Australia CAE would join the University of Adelaide. However, after a staff revolt in the institute and at Flinders University, the CAE was split and most of its parts combined with the Institute of Technology to form the University of South Australia.⁴⁵ In Victoria, RMIT absorbed the Phillip Institute of Technology, a large college in its own right with undergraduate and graduate programs.⁴⁶

A third avenue into university status was the amalgamation of groups of similarly sized institutions. Western Sydney University was first established in January 1989 as the University of Western Sydney through mergers between the Hawkesbury Agricultural College, Nepean CAE and, in October 1989, the Macarthur Institute of Higher Education.⁴⁷ It became the largest institution in Sydney's growing western suburbs. In regional New South Wales, Charles Sturt University was established in July 1989 through the merger of the Mitchell College of Advanced Education and the Riverina-Murray Institute of Higher Education, creating a university with campuses across regional New South Wales. A similar pattern occurred in Queensland, where Central Queensland University (later called CQUniversity) was established in 1992 from the Queensland Institute of Technology (Capricornia). CQUniversity came to have campuses and study centres in most states. The University of Southern Queensland was formed in 1990 from the Darling Downs Institute of Advanced Education, which was the biggest regional higher education college in Queensland.

In Victoria, the Footscray Institute of Technology combined with the Western Institute of Technology (and TAFE) to become the Victoria University of Technology, while the Swinburne Institute merged with two smaller TAFE colleges to become the Swinburne University of Technology.[48] The Ballarat University College became the University of Ballarat in 1994, incorporating the School of Mines & Industries, in Ballarat, and the Wimmera Institute of TAFE. Later, in 2014, it became Federation University, incorporating the former Monash campus at Churchill, and the Berwick Institute of TAFE. Across the other side of the country, Edith Cowan University was formed in 1991 from the former Western Australia CAE. It remained small at first but grew in subsequent years. In the Northern Territory, Charles Darwin University was originally established as the Northern Territory University in January 1989 through a merger of the Northern Territory University College and Darwin Institute of Technology, the first university in that territory.

As well as the main approaches, there were a number of special cases. The University of Canberra was established in 1990 out of the Canberra CAE. This occurred after the Commonwealth Senate refused to pass the Dawkins' bill for merger between ANU and Canberra CAE, which both operated under Commonwealth legislation.[49] Consolidation of universities and colleges in northern New South Wales proved difficult. Initially, The Network University of New England was established in July 1989 when the University of New England was joined by Armidale CAE and Northern Rivers CAE. Orange Agricultural College joined on 1 January 1990. When geography and organisational differences brought this amalgamation to an end in December 1993, Northern Rivers became Southern Cross University, while the other partners either remained with the University of New England or joined the new Charles Sturt University. The University of the Sunshine Coast opened with only 524 students in 1996 as the Sunshine Coast University College; it was redesignated as a full university in 1999.

The changes also offered more scope for not-for-profit private universities. The University of Notre Dame Australia opened in 1990 as a private university associated with the Catholic Church under Western Australian legislation passed on 21 December 1989.[50] Bond University opened on 15 May 1989 after Queensland passed its Act of Incorporation in 1987. It was named after its original benefactor, the high-profile business figure Alan Bond. It opened with 322 students at a newly built campus at Robina on Queensland's Gold Coast. The Australian Catholic University (ACU) was formed in 1991 following the amalgamation of four Catholic tertiary institutions in eastern Australia, which coordinated groups of smaller colleges: the Catholic College of Education Sydney in New South Wales; the Institute of Catholic Education in Victoria; McAuley College of Queensland; and Signadou College of Education in Canberra. ACU came to have campuses across Australia and was initially sponsored by La Trobe University for university status, a common practice for public university colleges as they transformed into full universities. The AVCC welcomed the 'important contribution' of not-for-profit private universities as helping to 'relieve pressure on the public purse' in some courses of study, such as 'Law and Commerce'. There were 'good equity grounds' it argued, for also allowing students in private universities access to AUSTUDY (which had replaced the Tertiary Education Assistance Scheme in 1987).[51]

All this took place over a concentrated period, redrawing Australia's tertiary education map in only a few years. Although membership of the UNS was voluntary, in the end no public institution remained outside the system. The universities that emerged all came to have strong identities. The mergers did not result in a geographical consolidation within the capital cities; rather they created several new universities based in regional centres. The creation of the new universities also brought other changes.

It stimulated the establishment in 1993 of the National Tertiary Education Union (NTEU), amalgamating FAUSA, which represented predominantly university academic staff, with the Union of Australian College Academics, representing CAE academic staff, the Australian Colleges and Universities Staff Association, which represented professional staff in higher education, and the two staff organisations at ANU and Adelaide.[52] The emergence of so many institutions with the title of 'university' posed a thorny question for the AVCC. Would it admit the vice-chancellors of new universities?

THE MEANING OF 'UNIVERSITY'

The right to adopt the designation 'university' was bestowed by state government legislation, and once an institution was admitted to the UNS it enjoyed parity of treatment by the Commonwealth. Despite the historical differences between CAEs and universities, in practice they had long collaborated. Academic links had already been established in areas such as teacher training. Given the diversity among older universities, and the overlapping functions of universities and CAEs under the 'binary' system, there were few inherent distinctions between old and new institutions. In the period immediately after the mergers, some universities had benefited disproportionately from greater student numbers and associated economies of scale. The new universities quickly began teaching some of the professional disciplines hitherto largely the preserve of the old ones. Law schools proliferated, as did Engineering and Science faculties. Yet many older universities, through the process of merging with other institutions, also broadened their offering to include teachers' colleges, Physiotherapy and Health Sciences.

A UNIFIED SYSTEM

In 1989 the AVCC prepared a statement with guidelines on 'the nature of a university', laying out a process to admit new members into the organisation.[53] This process aimed to overcome the challenges of considering on a case by case basis so many new institutions that were settling after a period of change. The statement approached the problem by setting out a series of 'indicators', thresholds that institutions had to meet in order to claim university standing. The statement defined two tiers, one as a minimum for university status and the other setting a standard for the status of 'well-established university'.[54]

Under this standard a 'university' was required to have at least 500 'effective full-time student units' in at least four distinct fields, and 7 per cent of its students needed to be engaged in postgraduate research. At least three research grants were needed for every twenty academics, 60 to 80 per cent of whom would hold doctorates and must produce between two and five research 'publications' each year. Not all the existing universities satisfied the criteria for well-established status. A number of the new universities exceeded the proportion of postgraduate research, but none met the publication standard and only the science disciplines came close to the quota for competitive research grants. Almost all university staff held doctoral qualifications, although this was less marked in professional disciplines, where only 70 per cent of all academic staff held the qualification.[55]

At the end of 1989 the AVCC dispensed with these metrics and admitted new universities as 'associate' members. The associate category was abolished from 1 January 1991, when all institutions within the UNS were eligible for full membership. The ACDP was absorbed into the AVCC at the end of 1990 as its membership dwindled. The AVCC thus retained its position as the central forum at which all universities across Australia met. As the number of voices grew, so consensus became harder to achieve on some issues, but the AVCC retained the mode of operation that had developed over preceding decades, with a smaller board reporting to a plenary meeting of all vice-chancellors. To cope with enlarged membership, the AVCC made other changes, extending its operations and capacity to undertake research and analysis on higher education policy and funding. In addition, it expanded the subscription information services it provided to members and other organisations.

THE HIGHER EDUCATION CONTRIBUTION SCHEME

The expansion of university places was predicated on introducing a new student contribution, which came to be known as the Higher Education Contribution Scheme, or by its acronym HECS. Universities had anticipated the reintroduction of tuition fees after Prime Minister Bob Hawke had John Dawkins, who was at that time Minister for Finance, test the idea with vice-chancellors at an AVCC meeting in 1983. The proposal was greeted with little enthusiasm because of concerns about equity and the disruption that administering the change would create.[56] Moves to reintroduce student fees began in 1985, with the introduction of an annual $250 Higher Education Administrative Charge, collected by universities on behalf of the government.[57]

The government recognised the political difficulties of introducing a more substantial student contribution. However, the argument that higher education conferred private as well as public benefit was generally accepted across the political spectrum. A return to up-front student fees was rejected as that would set back the government's goal of increasing the participation of disadvantaged students, and the cost of reintroducing means-tested Commonwealth scholarships would make it difficult for the government to expand the number of places. A long-discussed solution was for student contributions to be deferred until after graduation, but this could be problematic as students provided no collateral, and overseas experience, such as in the United States, had shown high rates of default on student loans.[58]

The Commonwealth appointed a panel, chaired by the former premier of New South Wales, Neville Wran, to design a deferred payment scheme that would be efficient, equitable and administratively feasible.[59] The committee proposed that the student contribution be recovered from graduates through the tax system.[60] The AVCC had commissioned research on options for a student contribution so when it was privy to an early draft of Wran's report, and in light of the government's determination to increase the student contribution, it measured its response. In public statements the AVCC stressed the need to establish the actuarial details of the scheme and model its likely effects on student demand.[61]

Staff and student organisations vehemently rejected the Wran Committee's recommendations, prompting the government to write to all currently enrolled students explaining the changes and how they would affect them.[62] The AVCC criticised the proposal, publicly querying the revenue calculations provided by the Wran Committee, which fell short of the amount needed to meet the enrolment targets. It urged the Commonwealth to commit to an industry levy to broaden the funding base and, as a condition of the new arrangements, called on the government to restore its spending on higher education, which had fallen to 0.83 per cent of GDP in 1988. Dawkins dismissed the call as an 'unrealistic and fanciful hope'. Sensing a fait accompli, the AVCC wrote to the minister later in May 1988 to say that 'of the options raised so far, the proposals of the Wran committee appear to us to be both feasible and the least inequitable'. Dawkins had appointed an ANU economist, Bruce Chapman, to work on the financial aspects of the Green

Paper. Chapman now turned to HECS, modelling interest rates and repayment thresholds to inform the implementation of the innovative scheme, which was introduced from the beginning of 1989.[63]

GROWING PARTICIPATION

The Commonwealth implemented HECS without modelling to show whether it would create a significant barrier to university entry, at a time when the government was already concerned about increasing the participation of proportionally under-represented groups. The government repeatedly contended that the social composition of those attending university remained stubbornly unchanged despite Whitlam's abolition of student fees.[64] Although by 1987 women were the majority of undergraduate enrolments, they remained strikingly under-represented in many disciplines.[65] The government classified other groups as under-represented, including Aboriginal and Torres Strait Islander people and people with a disability.[66]

The National Economic Summit, called by the Hawke government when it won office in 1983, had discussed the need for broader participation of under-represented groups in the higher education system as part of a strategy to enhance social justice.[67] This aspiration fed into the Green and White Papers' intention to overcome the 'substantial inequities in access to higher education'.[68] 'Growth and Equity' were linked in these policy documents, and the rationale for expansion was partly 'to ensure that Australians from all groups in society have the opportunity to participate successfully'.[69] Previous attempts to broaden access to higher education had relied on the provision of financial support; the new policy declared that this could be achieved only by dramatically expanding the system.[70] Through the White Paper, the government made equity objectives central to 'higher education management, planning and review', rather than a subsidiary concern.

Universities were thus drawn into the Hawke government's wide-ranging 'Access and Equity Strategy', which was first introduced to overcome the disadvantage suffered by immigrants.[71] 'Access implies', it argued, 'that all who are entitled to a public service should be able to have access to it on a comparably equitable basis to all others so entitled', and it viewed higher education as a public service.[72] There were few international models from which to draw guidance.[73]

A discussion paper, *A Fair Chance for All: Higher Education that's within Everyone's Reach*, was released in 1990.[74] The paper classified those living with a disability, Aboriginal and Torres Strait Islander people and women in some disciplinary areas as under-represented groups in higher education. So too were people from financially disadvantaged backgrounds, those from rural and isolated areas, and some migrant groups. Unlike the common practice of many United States universities of looking at individual family circumstances, the government pursued a policy of lifting aggregate levels of participation by these groups. This approach was deemed to be more appropriate since it allowed comparison of the relative composition of universities.[75] It required them to collect statistics for specific groups: people from 'socio-economically disadvantaged backgrounds', Aboriginal and Torres Strait Islander people, women, people from non-English–speaking backgrounds, and people with disabilities. The policy sought to identify their particular needs, devise strategies for improvement and monitor the outcomes.

Universities gave their 'unequivocal support' to the government's policy, and most institutions set about reviewing their internal programs to see how they could meet the new targets.[76]

It became evident that numerical targets would be hard to reach within the short timeframe the Commonwealth proposed. It called, for example, for universities to double the number of students with disabilities enrolled within four years. This necessarily involved the construction of new infrastructure and widespread recruitment, and that would take some time. Universities accordingly devised longer-term strategies, which included programs of capital works to build new facilities and establishing central administrative officers responsible for improving equity.[77]

One goal seen as particularly challenging was reducing the under-representation of students from regional areas.[78] The Commonwealth established Distance Education Centres to provide classrooms and other facilities to students in rural areas, and other measures included a review of agricultural and related education.[79] The creation of a number of new universities with regional and rural campuses, such as Ballarat, Charles Sturt, Central Queensland, Southern Queensland and Southern Cross, increased the presence of universities in regional areas.

AARNET AND THE BIRTH OF THE INTERNET IN AUSTRALIA

Meanwhile, the AVCC was involved in a new project that would extend the virtual reach of universities throughout the country and internationally, by establishing the internet in Australia.

As Dawkins urged universities to become more flexible, they were actively engaged in a project that would connect them globally and transform the way in which knowledge was shared. The Australian universities, in partnership with the CSIRO, were responsible for the infrastructure and operation of the network that connected Australia to the internet. Despite the ubiquity it would achieve, in the 1980s the thought of a universal network of computers connected internationally was viewed by most people as an esoteric academic aspiration. It was dismissed as too expensive, technically difficult and a low investment priority. Although the internet's promise of rapid transfer of large amounts of data was a vast advance on existing telephone communication, its material benefits were not immediately evident, and efforts to convince the national telephony provider, Telecom, to build the network stalled. Yet many individuals in universities saw the possibilities and from the mid-1980s began to advocate for Australia to join a growing global network.[80]

Development of the network was driven by the universities through the AVCC and eventually with additional financial backing from the ARC. When they established the Australian Academic Research Network (AARNet) in 1990, universities collectively took a risk with an eye to the future. The pivotal role of the nation's universities in connecting Australia to global computer networks that were the forerunners of the internet is in many ways unsurprising, given their long-standing use of computers to support their research and guide their operations. The first computer built by an Australian university was Sydney University's SILLIAC, completed in 1956 with £50 000 donated by philanthropist Adolph Basser after his horse won the 1951 Melbourne Cup.[81] The University of Melbourne had gained CSIRAC in 1955 from the CSIR.[82] During the 1960s and 1970s the AUC funded the purchase of computers by most Australian universities, each a significant piece of infrastructure. By the 1970s, these computers were linked together by telephone, using tailored infrastructure and protocols. The first and largest of the international networks was ARPANET, created by the United States Department of Defence's Advanced Research Projects Agency as part of a developing distributed system of computer control for the nuclear arsenal that could function in the event of a nuclear strike.[83] Australia had several small fledgling networks in the 1970s and early 1980s, the largest of which was CSIRONET, connecting 50 computers in 1976. The only international connection was at the University of Melbourne. The need for a national network was taken up at an AVCC meeting in July 1988, when universities agreed to develop it themselves.[84]

AARNet was established between April and May 1990. This feat was achieved in just six weeks by a team of two who installed nodes across Australia. It was connected to the rest of the world through a linkage sponsored by the National Aeronautics and Space Administration (NASA). The potential of the new network was recognised immediately and it attracted interest from government and business alike. So clear was its commercial potential that in 1990 the United States Boeing company's computing venture, Boeing Computer Services, attempted to buy the network. The fact that AARNet was established outside government meant it remained controlled by its members.[85]

Although initially conceived as a research tool, AARNet services were available to government departments and quasi-government organisations so long as they were willing to contribute to the cost of expanding and running the network. By 1992, organisations using AARNet included all 37 universities, 30 out of 36 CSIRO departments and another 42 fully connected members, including the Anglo-Australian Observatory, the Australian Nuclear Science and Technology Organisation, BHP Research Laboratories and the National Library of Australia. There were also 141 members accessing the email service, ranging from 'one person systems to entire government departments'.[86]

The cost of running and maintaining such a large and complicated network tempered the growing enthusiasm for the internet.[87] In 1992 the AARNet board decided to expand the affiliate membership program to bring in more commercial users and the first 'internet service providers', and by 1994 AARNet connected 40 000 computers across Australia. The dramatic growth in its first two years led the AVCC to employ a general manager.[88] In 1995 AARNet had become so extensive that it outgrew the AVCC's capacity, and it asked Telecom to take over the network it had earlier declined to finance.[89] Telecom's early scepticism was understandable, yet also unfounded. Former AARNet manager Brenda Aynsley noted: 'there was nothing at the end of it. You had these boxes terminating. But for what? Information to do what? It was a great leap of faith'.[90]

COMPREHENSIVE UNIVERSITIES

The university sector that emerged after 1988 was both similar to and profoundly different from that of only a few years earlier. The UNS had not dramatically increased the geographical coverage of higher education and, while many more student places had been made available across the system, there were few new campuses. The older universities continued to claim the lion's share of research funding and the overwhelming majority of students continued to attend public universities. However, the UNS set in motion many changes that turned Australian higher education into something new. The distinctive organisational structures at universities such as Griffith and Flinders disappeared as their multidisciplinary faculties were reorganised along the lines of their peers. Australia's universities all came to offer comprehensive programs across a large range of disciplines. In a few short years, all taught Law or Legal Studies, and although the number of medical faculties remained limited, all offered courses in Health Sciences.[91] All taught Arts, Education and Commerce courses. As they grew, universities brought many more students into bachelor's degrees, as well as embracing international students who were coming to Australia in increasing numbers.

The desire for stability after a period of great change informed the 1994 AVCC policy statement. This was a product of the AVCC's new administrative machinery and the elevation of secretary to executive director, as well as the need for a public statement following the abolition of CTEC.[92] The AVCC lamented the difficulty in forming a consistent position, as three separate ministers with responsibility for higher education had already served after Dawkins. The AVCC framed interactions between universities and the government as a 'partnership' of 'mutual interests' and defined the responsibilities of the two parties. Universities had responsibility to demonstrate public accountability and to work within budgetary 'constraints'; they had accepted the need for quality assurance. Government must recognise university autonomy, and assure universities with 'continuity in broad policy planning', including for 'long-term activities'. Such language belied concerns that the government might not continue to support the growth in the number of university places allowed by the introduction of HECS. These fears proved unfounded, as the system would come to educate many more students each year.[93]

8
INTERNATIONAL UNIVERSITIES

In the three decades following the creation of the Unified National System of higher education, Australian universities were increasingly well regarded internationally. They performed strongly compared to those in similar countries. They had high graduation rates, produced 3 per cent of world research output, and rose in international rankings.[1] Total student enrolments more than tripled from 300 000 to 1.4 million between 1989 and 2017. More than a quarter of the total were international students. Australia's universities became large by global comparison: Monash enrolled 78 000 students in 2017. Larger institutions meant new efforts were required to maintain the quality of students' educational experience. As they embraced growth, Australia's universities came to offer a broad and more diverse range of disciplines and courses, and supported research programs with specialisations across the country. Most higher education students enrolled in one broad type of institution, the comprehensive Australian university.[2]

The ability of Australia's universities to educate significantly more students reflected major changes to their operations and characteristics. They internationalised rapidly after 1990, both in outlook and in the number of international students enrolled. Universities embraced the information age and developed international partnerships in research. They harnessed information technology to deliver teaching programs and facilitate administration, and brought about the most significant pedagogical changes in more than a century. Universities welcomed a more diverse domestic student demographic following the growth in enrolments that brought in many people who were the first in their family to attend. They invested in new buildings and infrastructure, renewing much of those built during the 1960s and 1970s. Universities changed their processes to support the new diversity on campuses. Many regional universities continued to be the largest single employer in their areas. The number of employees at the large universities came to rival that of the automotive companies in the heyday of Australian manufacturing. The idea of a 'public university' came to include a global public as many more international students came to Australia.

By 2017, almost one third of Australia's higher education students came on a student visa. This brought not only a more global character to campuses themselves, as universities catered for much higher proportions of students living away from their home country, but also led to changes in the suburbs and towns around universities. Many international students lived closer to their university than was usual for domestic students. This shift, and creation of large-scale accommodation in some inner urban areas, altered cityscapes and enlivened these communities with a new cosmopolitanism.[3] As universities grew, they altered the cities and towns around them, making them more global.

The physical campuses were not the only manifestation of this extraordinary growth. Universities now also had a significant footprint in the sharing of knowledge through information and communications technology. Universities had first offered courses through correspondence in the early twentieth century, at the University of Queensland, and continued to adopt new methods of distance education.[4] The new model of online education could now be offered to students around Australia and the world. It became a core, rather than subsidiary, activity for most universities. By 2017, one in three domestic bachelor students at an Australian university completed at least part of their studies online and one in seven undertook their entire course this way.[5]

These developments were supported by growing investment in higher education, by the Commonwealth Government and by students. From 1974, when the Commonwealth assumed sole responsibility for funding higher education places, the fortunes of universities had ebbed and flowed in response to different national priorities. This was no longer the case, for while periods of growth and contraction in government funding became more frequent after the late 1990s, these changes were offset by the increasing diversification of funding sources, primarily student fees. Between 1997 and 2007 universities could also enrol local students who attracted no government subsidy, 'full fee-paying' domestic undergraduate students, as well as those who were supported by Commonwealth subsidy through HECS.

Changing student demography and greater internationalisation altered universities' relationship with the Commonwealth. Fourteen individual ministers held the portfolio between 1989 and 2017, often with responsibilities for higher education shared between more than one minister. Flux in ministerial responsibility meant shifting policy frameworks, and universities became adept at meeting changing policies. New pressures on public finances made unwelcome funding choices apparent, and these were at times exacerbated by contradictory expectations that dominated public policy debates over education. Despite these ups and downs, public investment in public higher education remained relatively stable by world standards, even during the global financial crisis of 2007–08, which precipitated deep cuts in university funding overseas, including for most state university systems in the United

States.[6] Successive Commonwealth Governments supported university growth by encouraging international and postgraduate education, while concentrating public subsidies on undergraduate education and research.

As universities grew in scale and outlook, they sought to advance diversity and governance. Coordinated efforts began to lift the numbers of women in leadership roles and boost the low rates of Aboriginal and Torres Strait Islander participation in education and research, and broader reforms to campus culture and learning environments were initiated. They introduced internal structures to support the additional population of international and domestic students. In the context of these changes, the AVCC needed to adapt to improve its representation of the interests of universities and the communities they serve, now internationalised and more diverse than ever before. When universities first met formally as a group in 1920, they had been creatures of their states. A century later, they had a global outlook.

INTERNATIONALISATION

One in twenty enrolments in 1989 was an international student. Most international students studied at the larger and older universities, but they were present in all. Within two decades, almost one in three students in Australian higher education was an international student, making Australia one of the most internationalised of the major higher-education systems, both in terms of its student makeup and the links its universities had with the rest of the world.[7] Australia's position as the second or third most popular destination for students wishing to study away from their home country, behind only the United States and vying with Britain, was encouraged by government policies, but it had been a deliberate strategy of university leaders since the 1940s to internationalise Australia's universities and build their global reputation, a process now accelerating.[8] The AVCC defined this as broadly 'giving universities an international dimension', including making provision for students from overseas to study in Australia, more international recruitment of staff, and a curriculum tailored for graduates who would work outside Australia.[9]

The growth of international enrolments followed the Commonwealth Government's 1986 decision to allow universities to enrol international students freely and cover the cost of their tuition by charging fees. Despite the withdrawal of Commonwealth subsidies for those students from overseas, demand grew following the removal of full-fee paying international places. A growing Asian middle class, the lack of places in their own country's universities, the opportunity to live in Australia and, later, the high ranking of Australian universities in global league tables, made Australia appealing. The strategy to attract international students was initially viewed by the government as a vehicle for international engagement, overseas aid and an 'export' industry.[10] Backed by the government, and expecting only modest initial demand, universities began to market their courses overseas.[11] Universities undertook promotional tours of different countries supported by Commonwealth Export Market Development Grants, a scheme that subsidised promotional costs to facilitate export growth. The government encouraged universities to apply for support through the scheme instead of seeking direct grants. Rather than intervene, as the government had in other export industries, it left universities largely to their own devices.

From the outset, universities sought students from countries in Asia and the Pacific region, as well as from Europe and the Americas. In each country, student recruitment was facilitated by individual university teams and locally employed agents, and collectively through IDP Education. This organisation's mission evolved from assisting government aid programs to one promoting Australian education overseas and facilitating the recruitment of fee-paying students.[12] IDP was not structured to represent all universities, and most also undertook their own direct recruitment. The AVCC advocated a sector-wide approach to marketing and to set consistent entry standards and support for international education.[13]

Universities also urged the government to become more involved in supporting the recruitment of international students through a presence in diplomatic missions and consulates throughout Asia. This, they argued, was necessary to explain complex immigration procedures. The Department of Employment, Education and Training agreed. It stationed education officers in Beijing, Hong Kong and Kuala Lumpur, and established Australian Education Centres in diplomatic missions in other countries.[14] These centres provided a comprehensive range of services, including student counselling, application processing and verification of information provided by private agents. The choices of China and Malaysia reflected an anticipated growth in demand from both countries, as well as historical educational ties through the Colombo Plan in the case of the latter.

As international student populations flourished, a set of issues emerged that universities had faced in the early days of Australia welcoming proportionally large numbers of international students after the Second World War. Support services expanded and cross-cultural support became crucial. A *Code of Ethical Practice in the Provision of Education to International Students by Australian Universities* was published in 1989 by universities through the AVCC, to cover recruitment, enrolment and support for international students.[15] Universities created new senior leadership positions with a responsibility for the recruitment and well-being of international students. These roles, given the title Deputy Vice-Chancellor (International) or similar, became a fixture across the sector.

The government's decision to allow universities to enrol more international students and the ability to charge them fees meant universities were increasingly competing as well as cooperating in their recruitment efforts. While collective endeavours continued, each university increasingly recruited its own students. In 1997 the AVCC established an International Standing Committee and developed the first international relations strategic plan for the sector, a key objective of which was to maximise the profile of all Australian universities overseas.[16] It recognised that competition made it important to maintain 'brand Australia' and in subsequent years produced research based publications in conjunction with Australian Education International, an initiative of the Department of Education.[17]

By 1998, the numbers of international students had risen to over 70000, prompting a revision of the 1989 *Code of Ethical Practice* to ensure the quality of education and care of students as numbers expanded.[18] Stronger safeguards were needed to ensure academic standards were preserved, and that support services were in place. In August 1998 the AVCC revised the *Code* to tighten procedures for handling breaches and clarify recruitment guidelines. Most importantly, universities pushed to clear out unscrupulous recruiting agents and misleading promotion.[19] This action came as universities courted the largest potential source for recruitment: China. In early 1998, the Commonwealth signed an agreement with Chinese education authorities to strengthen the emerging educational relationship between the two countries.[20]

The international market supported growth and, as it expanded, provided economies of scale that offset shortfalls elsewhere. The speed at which numbers grew outstripped even the most optimistic outlook. In 2002 IDP predicted that international education export earnings to the Australian economy as a whole might be worth '$10 billion a year by 2010, and $38 billion by 2025'. By 2018–19, the Australian Bureau of Statistics estimated that international students and their families contributed $37.7 billion to the Australian economy.[21] Despite the benefits that international education brought them, universities were wary about its stability. International fees should not be viewed as a permanent subsidy for other activities.[22] Australia was not alone in seeking to attract international students. While it led the way in actively recruiting students, other countries soon followed. New Zealand adopted a similar approach, and the United Kingdom was concerned it would fall back from its leading position, coming to realise that it could no longer rely on the prestige of its universities. In 1999 it initiated recruitment targets urging universities to grow international enrolments.[23]

TECHNOLOGIES OF LEARNING AND TEACHING

The expansion in international student recruitment followed growth in Australian student enrolments, requiring innovation in the delivery of high-quality teaching.[24] Universities adopted technology to assist teaching and learning at scale to accommodate these increasing student numbers. Systems including online Learning Management Systems, such as Blackboard, eCollege and Smarthinking, which were introduced in 1998. University-wide enterprise learning systems emerged in the following decade, and it became routine to provide course material digitally, to record all lectures automatically and to require electronic submission of written assignments. These innovations drew on the expertise universities had acquired through their computer and software engineering departments, and also through their early investment in computer labs, which were made widely available to students from the 1990s.[25] Universities had employed large computer enterprise systems and computers for research and management from the 1960s. In the 1990s the AVCC established UniOn to develop common IT systems for all university management.[26] At this time universities routinely incorporated what was originally referred to as 'computer-aided instruction' into many technical and engineering disciplines, as well as multimedia teaching technologies, ranging from playing videos to the three-dimensional simulation of microscopic processes and virtual reality tours of ancient Cairo.

Many universities began offering fully online courses as soon as the internet was widely adopted. Some of the first online courses were provided by the University of New England and Monash University through the Open Learning Agency of Australia, which was established in 1993 as a government-backed initiative. Six other universities joined in 1996, and partnered with the Australian Broadcasting Commission to broadcast lectures on television.[27] Reconstituted as Open Universities Australia (OUA) in 2004, its university members became the largest providers of online education in Australia. By 2017, more than 350 000 students throughout Australia and internationally had undertaken OUA courses.[28] In 2017 the University of New England taught over 80 per cent of its students through online courses, and 42 per cent of Swinburne University students were taking online courses.[29]

Technology changed how students engaged with campuses during the late 2000s, particularly social media and mobile technologies. From 2010, many Australian universities began to redesign their study spaces and libraries to accommodate students using laptops and other mobile devices. Curation and storage of books and other written material, which had consumed significant proportions of university budgets for most of their history, began to be rivalled by digital collections and subscriptions.[30] At the same time universities explored space using social media to engage students, and encourage interaction between them and institutions.[31] While growth in the size of universities risked making campuses impersonal, students and universities came to be more connected digitally.

Australian universities were among the first to offer Massive Open Online Courses (MOOCs), free courses with teaching provided by short pre-recorded videos and online assignments. These courses were arranged in partnership with international consortiums, Coursera, Udacity and edX, which provided the digital platform. They were highly popular from the outset, with many signing up hundreds of thousands of students. These global offerings multiplied after 2006, albeit with mixed student success.[32] MOOCs revived the universities' community access programs in the spirit of the first workers' education and 'extension' programs, and through radio and television, yet the internet gave these programs unprecedented reach.

The interest in MOOCs drew on broader efforts to change teaching and learning in higher education through student tracking and other data-driven techniques that allowed analysis of student learning in an unprecedented way.

THE EVOLVING RELATIONSHIP WITH GOVERNMENT

At the same time as universities made rapid changes in teaching technology, the relationship between universities and government changed.[33] The expansion of university education came at a rising cost to the Commonwealth Budget. This had been offset by the direct student contribution through HECS, but the cost still mounted, increasing the Education Department's outlay.

The Coalition government elected in 1996 had signalled its intention to restrain expenditure across the public sector, including universities, to overcome the Commonwealth budget deficit. Soon after the election of the new government, the AVCC and NTEU undertook a joint public campaign warning of the consequences of university funding cuts.

The government acknowledged the concerns, but was not dissuaded from changing higher education policy. It sought to tie university funding more directly to student enrolments, looking to make it more responsive to competitive forces. Reduced public subsidies were offset by the introduction of fee-paying domestic undergraduate places, which provided universities with no public subsidy. The Commonwealth budget position would also be improved by lowering the HECS income repayment thresholds and increasing the proportion of an individual's income repaid. The Commonwealth also introduced three discipline 'groups', with differing student contribution rates.[34] Summing up much of the media commentary on the changes, AVCC Executive Director Frank Hambly predicted that students would 'go slightly ballistic' at the higher cost.[35] There were protests on several campuses against the proposals and some students made their way into the minister's offices in Adelaide and chained themselves to the furniture, but the overall response was muted and the government proceeded to make the changes.

In September 1996 the AVCC and the NTEU established a broad alliance with the National Union of Students, the Council of Australian Postgraduate Associations, and alumni associations, as well as the four learned academies of science, humanities, social sciences, and technological sciences and engineering.[36] The alliance made a case against the proposed reductions in public funding for higher education through high-profile media advocacy as well as directly to politicians. In response, the Minister for Education,

Amanda Vanstone, put the onus back on the AVCC and universities, arguing they should not rely on 'the vagaries of the economy and the Government of the day'. Rather, she said, they would need to 'show more leadership' in seeking efficiencies.[37]

After the 1996 cuts were implemented, the government pursued a more sweeping change to Australian higher education policy. It appointed a school principal, Roderick West, to chair a review of the sector in January 1997. This was the first major evaluation of higher education since the Dawkins White Paper, and it considered nearly 600 public submissions. The review concluded that existing policies encouraged universities to under-invest in teaching, and that there were insufficient inducements for them to improve their teaching and administrative practices. It recommended the continuation of a universal but limited entitlement to subsidised higher education and HECS loans, but with the introduction of market-based incentives. It also proposed that HECS should support places at both public and private institutions and that there should be no cap on the fees that public universities could charge.[38] These proposals followed the accelerating growth in the numbers of fee-paying international students, which reduced the share of university budgets contributed by Commonwealth grants.

In October 1999 a new Minister for Education, David Kemp, took a proposal to Cabinet to permit universities to increase fees for domestic undergraduates in addition to those already supported through HECS. In addition, the minister proposed the application of an interest rate to HECS debts, which until then had been indexed to inflation.[39] The AVCC viewed the proposals with caution, and government decided not to proceed.[40]

While these proposals were shelved, the increasing numbers of international students achieved some of the government's aim to diversify university finances and make universities less reliant on public funding. Universities had always enjoyed academic autonomy and they were now contending with changes that implied greater financial independence from government, potentially with less predictability. As circumstances changed, they required a renewed peak body.

THE CREATION OF UNIVERSITIES AUSTRALIA

Brendan Nelson was appointed Minister for Education after the 2001 federal election and immediately undertook a review of the system. He learnt from John Dawkins' tactic from a decade earlier, and in April 2002 he released a report, *Higher Education at the Crossroads*, followed by a series of issues papers. These papers advocated tying funding to changes to university governance structures and industrial relations practices, while continuing to link teaching grants to enrolment numbers. Nelson also proposed the government would raise the threshold for repayment of HECS to an annual income of $35 000, up from $21 000. The AVCC commissioned research on the changes to HECS and their potential to affect student demand.[41]

Nelson's changes were implemented with little fanfare in the following year, but questions over whether the AVCC had the right organisational structure to engage with government and whether its lobbying effectiveness was diminished became regular topics of media speculation. As the former Vice-Chancellor of the University of Sydney, Bruce Williams, put it, 'the trouble with the AVCC is that it's got so large and there are so many different interests involved'.[42]

A new university organisation, the Group of Eight (Go8), had been formed in 1999 to represent the interests of the research-intensive universities: the Universities of Adelaide, Melbourne,

Monash, NSW, Queensland, Sydney and Western Australia, and the ANU. In the same year another organisation had formed to represent the interests of the former technical institutes, the Australian Technology Network. It included UTS, RMIT, the University of South Australia, Curtin University and Queensland University of Technology.[43] A third group, the Innovative Research Universities Australia had formed in 2003, with Flinders University, Griffith University, La Trobe University, Macquarie University, Murdoch University and the University of Newcastle.[44] In 2011 these associations would be joined by the Regional Universities Network. It included CQUniversity, Federation University Australia, Southern Cross University, and the Universities of Southern Queensland, New England, and Sunshine Coast.[45]

The AVCC continued alongside these sectional groups with a role that was increasingly challenged. In September 2005 the Go8 released a public statement criticising the AVCC as ill-equipped to respond to the Commonwealth's research priorities. It proposed an overhaul of the AVCC executive structure, which had remained largely unchanged since the 1980s. In its place, it proposed the employment of a full-time president, who would focus on issues common to the 38 members, supported by a small secretariat.

In October 2005 the AVCC board advanced plans to review the organisation's structure and purpose. The new AVCC chair, Gerard Sutton, Vice-Chancellor of the University of Wollongong, said the organisation was committed to evolve in response to a sector characterised by sub-groupings of universities with different priorities. In February 2006 Nelson urged universities to 'have one peak umbrella organisation because otherwise governments will pick the sector off', echoing calls from some media commentators.[46] The AVCC commissioned a review of options.[47] The final report, released to the public in August 2006, concluded that it should be modelled on other industry peak bodies and its counterpart organisations in other countries, such as Universities UK and the German Rectors' Conference.[48] The report stated that dissolution was not a stable long-term option, as

> common interest would soon reinvent some form of body able to act, at least minimally, in the collective interest of Australian universities and to be an interface for the whole sector with government, industry and other organisations nationally and internationally.[49]

Adopting the recommendations, universities announced the AVCC would be renamed Universities Australia (UA) in 2007, a title inspired by Universities UK. It would have a chief executive, who would be a member of a new board of nine directors, including a chair. The new board would represent the geographic reach and diverse character of universities to become a stronger advocate for the whole sector. The organisation's membership would remain all universities, represented by their vice-chancellors. The inclusion of external directors, such as business leaders, was rejected, although a separate council for university chancellors was established to formalise dialogue with the chancellors.[50]

A key aspect of the new entity was the appointment of a CEO. This officer was now more fully empowered to speak on behalf of universities. The subsequent expansion of UA's policy and communications staff also enabled universities to be proactive in formulating policy and to be much more responsive to public issues as they arose. Glenn Withers, an ANU Professor of Economics with previous experience as a senior public servant, took the helm as UA's first chief executive in 2007. This replaced the position of executive director, held by Stuart Hamilton from 1996 and then from 2001 John Mullarvey.[51]

The new organisation had little time to settle in as the government planned to review the *Higher Education Support Act 2003*, the legislation under which most government grants were allocated, which had been enacted only a few years earlier.

MEETING DOMESTIC DEMAND FOR EDUCATION

The Labor government elected in 2007 had promised to phase out the domestic fee-paying places.[52] It also indicated a desire to renegotiate the relationship between government and universities. The Minister for Education, Julia Gillard, appointed former University of South Australia Vice-Chancellor Denise Bradley to chair an inquiry, to which the government responded in the 2009 Commonwealth Budget.[53] Although the recommendation for a 10 per cent increase in base funding for teaching and learning was not implemented, the government accepted most of the review's other recommendations. These included higher student participation and equity targets, increased research infrastructure funding, and greater transparency through agreements with universities called 'compacts', which required them to publish their performance against agreed metrics. It also accepted two recommendations that would have great significance for universities over the next decade: establishing national higher education regulatory arrangements, and introducing what would later become known as the 'demand-driven' system to allow universities to provide government-funded places to qualified applicants. This latter policy allowed universities to enrol as many bachelor's degree students as met the course entry requirements according to demand, removing long-standing government caps and permitting more students to attend university. Endorsing the plans as 'practical' and 'comprehensive', universities cautiously welcomed both a new system that would allow expansion in publicly supported student places and greater protection for standards and quality, even if it meant they would be subject to stricter regulation.[54]

In 2000 the Commonwealth Government had established the Australian Universities Quality Agency (AUQA) to provide independent assessment of a university's performance against its declared goals, ensuring quality and standards were maintained.[55] Such oversight had been anticipated by universities, which developed their own system of quality control through a series of quality panels and internal reviews. The AVCC published a series of reports under the title *Academic Standards in Higher Education*.[56]

The growth and increased diversification of the Australian system had encouraged several overseas-based higher education institutions to establish a local presence during the 1990s. This included interest from 'degree mills', such as the notorious Saint Regis University in the United States, that offered low-quality programs and sought to have them legally recognised as Australian university qualifications. The AVCC had defined what constituted a university based on a generalised teaching and research profile, and 'recognition by an Australian Government', and had asked federal and state governments to legislate to protect the terms 'university' and 'degree'.[57] Most state governments agreed and, in addition to enacting legislation, created procedures and used expert accreditors to establish new universities.

The reason for this concern became apparent after an exposé of the quality of education at the newly established Greenwich University on Norfolk Island.[58] When Brendan Nelson was Minister for Education, he intervened to ensure that it could not continue to offer sub-standard education; it eventually closed. The case for a national regulator with some responsibility for universities became more pronounced. As successive governments granted Australian higher education providers greater autonomy, there was a need for common regulatory oversight of universities as well as other higher education institutions.

The Bradley Review recommended a new national regulator, focused on outcomes as a measure of quality, to replace AUQA and state regulators. This echoed calls to renew regulatory arrangements, with stronger standards for higher education courses delivered by universities and other training organisations, such as state TAFE institutes and for-profit providers.[59] On 2 February 2010 the government announced it would establish the Tertiary Education Quality and Standards Agency (TEQSA) with powers to regulate university and non-university higher education providers.[60] A new Higher Education Standards Framework (HESF) would define the minimum level required of universities and other higher education providers. TEQSA's primary tasks were to regulate existing providers against the HES and to assess application for registration from new providers against the same standards.[61] The new agency replaced regulatory activity undertaken by states and territories and the quality assurance activities formerly undertaken by AUQA. Universities negotiated with government on the establishment of TEQSA, forming a standing group to work with officials on the new governing architecture for the system.[62] The UA working group negotiated with the government the terms on which TEQSA was established, preserving universities' self-accreditation and adopting nationally consistent standards. TEQSA's oversight powers helped to protect universities and their standing by strengthening measures to ensure the high quality of all higher education providers.

The establishment of national regulation of higher education was also a precondition for the introduction of the demand-driven system recommended by the Bradley Review.[63] This change was justified by evidence that despite the growth in university participation facilitated by the creation of the HECS, many more eligible applicants still wanted to enrol than there were places available. The Unified National System had controlled the supply of places offered in different institutions and courses. Enrolment quotas were not always responsive to student demand or the needs of employers. The new demand-driven funding regime allowed a university to enrol into a publicly supported place any qualified domestic bachelor's degree student, except in medical studies. The policy was to commence in 2012, with transitional arrangements in 2010 and 2011 as the cap on enrolments was progressively lifted.[64] The implications were quickly apparent, and universities organised through UA a program of initiatives to examine the likely needs of students, how universities could respond, what it would mean for facilities and infrastructure, as well as equity and workforce implications.[65]

Demand for university study was higher than anticipated, partly because of a higher rate of unemployment following the onset of the global financial crisis. Before the introduction of the policy, domestic government-supported bachelor enrolments increased from 397 000 in 2002 to 409 000 equivalent full-time students in 2008.[66] This number grew to 546 000 equivalent full-time students by 2015. The rate of growth was highest in the first few years of the demand-driven system and fell away after 2013. From 2016, annual growth has been below the rate of population growth. Science and Health degrees proved popular during this period, with enrolments growing by 38 per cent, while the humanities, social sciences and many professional disciplines grew by a quarter. In only a few years, the large unmet student demand diminished, especially for prospective students who had recently completed secondary school. By 2016, the proportion of 25- to 34-year-olds with a bachelor's degree approached 50 per cent in many major city postcodes.[67]

The introduction of more flexible funding structures was not without risk, and a reduction in enrolments could have implications that were not lost on universities. A downturn in the international market occurred when the number of Indian students almost halved, falling from 26 000 in 2009 to near 10 000 in 2012 following claims in the Indian press that Australia was not doing enough to protect students following several high-profile assaults.[68] Aided by a 2010 delegation of vice-chancellors and government officials to India, student confidence was restored after 2012 and Indian students returned.[69] Despite the temporary downturn in Indian enrolments, overall growth continued, especially from China, which by 2017 came to represent nearly 35 per cent of international students in Australia's higher education sector.[70] Along with the growth that came with the demand-driven system of domestic students, the increasing number of international students made universities much bigger than a decade before.

Alongside the increase in student numbers, Australian universities invested in their research efforts, producing journal papers and other publications at a higher rate per capita than other countries with advanced research systems including that of the United States, United Kingdom, Canada, Japan, China and Germany.[71] By the 2000s, Australian research and science matched and often outperformed many similar countries in its number of 'highly cited' research papers, and performed well on other measures of the success of a national research effort, such as Fields Medals for Mathematics and Nobel laureates.[72] Buoyed by growth across the university system, Australia enrolled one of the highest per capita rates of doctoral students each year by international measure. In 2017 there were almost 11 000 higher degree by research students graduated from Australian universities. Australia emerged as an international destination of choice for many postgraduate research students, with their number reaching 21 700 of the 66 100 students undertaking a higher degree in Australia in 2017.[73]

INTERNATIONAL UNIVERSITIES

The increase in research student numbers and some publicly subsidised master's by coursework students, along with the increasing number of domestic undergraduate students, required commensurate public funding. Since the government subsidy was based on the number of student enrolments, it was difficult to forecast funding. The Commonwealth Government underestimated growth in the number of domestic students wishing to enrol in university education for each year between 2010 and 2013.[74] In November 2013 the new Coalition government initiated a review of the demand-driven system.[75] The government signalled its determination to increase direct student contributions and reduce its own outlay.[76] In May 2014 the Commonwealth indicated its intention to cut the government subsidy for teaching by 20 per cent.[77] To compensate universities, it would allow them to set the student contributions at a level determined by universities through the Higher Education Loan Program (HELP), which had replaced HECS in 2003. It also proposed applying a higher interest rate to HELP loans to offset the cost of running the student loan scheme. Following the Budget announcement, universities accepted the government's aspiration to implement a system of financing that it viewed as sustainable, while calling for careful reflection on proposals.[78]

UA joined students in calling for 'a rethink of key measures' and in particular the proposed changes to the HELP interest rate. By the end of May 2014, heated public debate took place over the merits of the proposals, and, by June, a student and staff campaign against them was underway. The enabling legislation was rejected several times by the Senate, and when it became clear that the proposals would not pass, the measures were dropped.[79]

CHANGING INSTITUTIONS

Growth in the number of domestic and international students gave Australia's universities a new character. They were also undergoing other fundamental changes. Some of these were long overdue, such as the belated emergence of many more women in leadership roles, though their under-representation remained a key issue UA sought to address. By 2017 women held 38 per cent of the senior leadership positions in Australian universities.[80] From the 1980s universities sought to promote more women to leadership positions and, in 1999 the AVCC had issued an *Action Plan for Women Employed in Australian Universities*. It asked all universities to report on equity strategies and performance indicators and integrate them into their institutional planning. Universities also agreed to monitor patterns of entry of women into academic employment and respond to identified barriers. They established a joint research program on gender equity, which would disseminate guidelines for best practice, including employment and promotion procedures. Dianne Yerbury, an industrial relations scholar, was Australia's first female vice-chancellor and was also the longest serving Vice-Chancellor of Macquarie University, from 1987 to 2005. Fay Gale, Vice-Chancellor of the University of Western Australia, was the first woman to chair the AVCC in 1996–97, after which time a number of women have held the chair: Yerbury from 2004 to 2005, Sandra Harding from 2013 to 2015, Margaret Gardner from 2017 to 2019, and Deborah Terry from 2019. UA has also appointed women as CEO, including Belinda Robinson from 2011, and Catriona Jackson from 2018.

Another issue with which universities were increasingly concerned from the 1990s was Indigenous participation and advancement. There was notable progress in areas such as undergraduate participation, with Indigenous student enrolments growing by 103 per cent in the decade from 2008, which brought the number of Indigenous student enrolments to 19 237 in 2017. There was also strong sector collaboration on initiatives such as the National Best Practice Framework for Indigenous Cultural Competency. In 2017 UA launched the UA Indigenous Strategy in partnership with the peak body for the Indigenous academy, the National Aboriginal and Torres Strait Islander Higher Education Consortium. All 39 UA member universities signed up to ambitious targets on Aboriginal and Torres Strait Islander student participation, success and employment in universities. Under the strategy, this became a core goal of the sector, with Indigenous representation embedded throughout UA. The initiative required universities to work in close partnership with Indigenous academics, researchers and communities to embed Indigenous perspectives and knowledge in teaching and research throughout the Australian higher education system.

As part of the widening of access, universities enhanced policies and support to enrol more Australians from sections of the community who had historically been under-represented in higher education. These included students who had faced socio-economic disadvantage throughout their lives. Although such students remained under-represented as a proportion of all students in 2017, their share of enrolments had grown through the decade of uncapped student places. This concern had been an abiding priority for universities and government since the 1990 *A Fair Chance for All* policy statement defined new 'national equity objectives … to increase participation by disadvantaged groups', setting out the 'responsibilities of the Federal Government and universities and colleges in achieving' them.[81]

Such programs reflect universities' desire to embrace a wider range of students with different points of view and from all walks of life. Today, Australian universities are more diverse than they have ever been. In 1920, if a thousand Australian adults were asked at random whether they had studied at university, only five or six would have said they had. Almost a hundred years later, 270 could have a bachelor's degree. Among those under 34 years of age, it would be closer to 400. One third of the students studying in Australia now come from overseas. From the late 1980s, more than half of students were women and Australian universities enrolled adult students of all ages in significant numbers; at some universities the majority of commencing students had completed their high school certificate long ago.

In adapting themselves to serve their communities, local and national, universities have collectively been the partners of government and have worked in the service of the nation. This was most explicit as they served Australia during the Second World War, although it informed many of their actions before and since. They have shaped, and been shaped, by Australia's school education systems, and worked with the professions and professional accreditation bodies in the education and preparation of graduates. They have been the foundation of the research system in Australia, from agricultural innovation to the space race to biotechnology. They have been simultaneously places of abstraction and highly applied technical institutions, both 'blue sky' research as well as research innovations for immediate application.

The modes of interaction between Australian universities changed significantly as their number grew. They were once institutions separate from one other but this is no longer the case. While the Commonwealth has increasingly sought to shape the terms on which universities interact, universities have also defended their own common cause. The partnership with government has helped universities support high-quality education and research. In 2020 Australia's 39 universities form a tight network. As their number has grown, they have embraced their diversity and intersecting histories. With the increasing competition that internationalisation has brought, the resilience of the Australian university system has never been more vital.

NOTES

INTRODUCTION

1. Roger L Geiger, *The History of American Higher Education: Learning and Culture from the Founding to World War II* (Princeton, NJ: Princeton University Press, 2015); Roger L Geiger, *American Higher Education since World War II: A History* (Princeton, NJ: Princeton University Press, 2019); Walter Rüegg (ed.), *A History of the University in Europe: Vol. 3, Universities in the Nineteenth and Early Twentieth Centuries (1800–1945)* (Cambridge: Cambridge University Press, 1992); Walter Rüegg (ed.), *A History of the University in Europe: Vol. 4, Universities since 1945* (Cambridge: Cambridge University Press, 2011); Lester Goodchild and Harold Wechsler (eds), *The History of Higher Education*, 2nd ed. (Needham Heights, MA: Simon & Schuster, 1997); Ralph D Christy and Lionel Williamson (eds), *A Century of Service: Land-Grant Colleges and Universities, 1980–1990* (New Brunswick, NJ: Transaction Publishers, 1992); Robert O Berdahl, *British Universities and the State* (Berkeley: University of California Press, 1959); Michael Shattock, *The UGC and the Management of British Universities* (Buckingham: Open University Press, 1994); Deryck M Schreuder (ed.), *Universities for a New World* (Thousand Oaks, Cal.: SAGE Publications, 2013).
2. Simon Marginson, *Educating Australia: Government, Economy and Citizen since 1960* (Cambridge: Cambridge University Press, 1997); Simon Marginson, *Education and Public Policy in Australia* (Cambridge: Cambridge University Press, 1993); Simon Marginson, *Markets in Education* (Sydney: Allen & Unwin, 1997); Simon Marginson and Mark Considine, *The Enterprise University: Power, Governance and Reinvention in Australia* (Cambridge: Cambridge University Press, 2000); Peter Coaldrake and Lawrence Stedman. *Raising the Stakes: Gambling with the Future of Universities* (St Lucia: University of Queensland Press, 2013).
3. Julia Horne, 'Looking from the Inside Out: Rethinking University History' *Journal of Educational Administration and History* 46, no. 2 (2014), pp. 174–89; Julia Horne and Geoffrey Sherington, *Sydney: The Making of a Public University* (Carlton, Vic.: Melbourne University Publishing, 2012); Graeme Davidson and Kate Murphy, *University Unlimited: The Monash Story* (Sydney: Allen & Unwin, 2012); Jenny Gregory and Jean Chetkovich (eds), *Seeking Wisdom: A Centenary*

History of the University of Western Australia (Crawley, WA: UWA Publishing, 2013).
4 Hannah Forsyth, *A History of the Modern Australian University* (Sydney: NewSouth, 2014); Tamson Pietsch, *Empire of Scholars: Universities, Networks and the British Academic World, 1850–1939* (Manchester: Manchester University Press, 2013); Kate Darian-Smith and Edward James Waghorne (eds), *The First World War, the Universities and the Professions in Australia 1914–1939* (Carlton, Vic.: Melbourne University Publishing, 2019).
5 Clark Kerr, *The Uses of the University* (New York: Harper & Row, 1963); Jaroslav Pelikan, *The Idea of the University: A Re-examination* (New Haven, Yale University Press, 1992); Sheldon Rothblatt, *The Modern University and Its Discontents: The Fate of Newman's Legacies in Britain and America* (Cambridge: Cambridge University Press, 1997); Simon Marginson, *The Dream Is Over: The Crisis of Clark Kerr's California Idea of Higher Education* (Oakland: University of California Press, 2016).

CHAPTER 1 - A PRACTICAL FEDERATION

1 JM Bennett, 'Cullen, Sir William Portus (1855–1935)', *Australian Dictionary of Biography*, National Centre of Biography, Australian National University, <adb.anu.edu.au/biography/cullen-sir-william-portus-5838/text9919>, published first in hardcopy 1981, accessed online 23 April 2019.
2 *Conference of Australian Universities: Held in the Senate Room at the University of Sydney, May 26th–29th, 1920* (Sydney: WE Smith, 1920), p. 4.
3 *Conference of Australian Universities: Held in the Senate Room at the University of Sydney, May 26th–29th, 1920* (Sydney: WE Smith, 1920), pp. 4–8.
4 Tamson Pietsch, *Empire of Scholars: Universities, Networks and the British Academic World, 1850–1939* (Manchester: Manchester University Press, 2013).
5 Clifford Turney, Ursula Bygott and Peter Chippendale, *Australia's First: A History of the University of Sydney, Vol. 1, 1850–1939* (Sydney: Hale & Iremonger, 1991); WF Connell, Geoffrey Sherington, BH Fletcher, Clifford Turney and Ursula Bygott, *Australia's First: A History of the University of Sydney, Vol. 2, 1940–1990* (Sydney: Hale & Iremonger, 1995); Julia Horne and Geoffrey Sherington, *Sydney: The Making of a Public University* (Carlton, Vic.: Melbourne University Publishing, 2012); Ernest Scott, *A History of the University of Melbourne* (Melbourne: Melbourne University Press, 1936); Geoffrey Blainey, *A Centenary History of the University of Melbourne* (Carlton, Vic.: Melbourne University Press, 1957); RJW Selleck, *The Shop: The University of Melbourne, 1850–1939* (Carlton, Vic.: Melbourne University Press, 2003); John Poynter and Carolyn Rasmussen, *A Place Apart: The University of Melbourne: Decades of Challenge* (Carlton South, Vic.: Melbourne University Press, 1996); Carolyn Rasmussen, *Shifting the Boundaries: The University of Melbourne, 1975–2015* (Carlton, Vic.: Melbourne University Publishing, 2018); WGK Duncan and Roger Ashley Leonard, *The University of Adelaide, 1874–1974* (Adelaide: Rigby, 1973).
6 Richard Davis, *Open to Talent: The Centenary History of the University of Tasmania, 1890–1990.* (Hobart: University of Tasmania, 1990); Malcolm I Thomis, *A Place of Light and Learning: The University of Queensland's First Seventy-Five Years*

(St Lucia, Qld: University of Queensland Press, 1985); Fred Alexander, *Campus at Crawley: A Narrative and Critical Appreciation of the First Fifty Years of the University of Western Australia* (Melbourne, Vic.: F.W. Cheshire, 1963); Jenny Gregory and Jean Chetkovich (eds), *Seeking Wisdom: A Centenary History of the University of Western Australia* (Crawley, Western Australia: UWA Publishing, 2013).

7   Turney, Bygott and Chippendale, *Australia's First, Vol. 1*; Selleck, *The Shop*.
8   Phillip Raymond, 'The Decline of Melbourne's Affiliated Colleges: The Effect of the Report of the Royal Commission on the University of Melbourne, 1904', *Melbourne Studies in Education* 39, no. 2 (1998), pp. 91–113.
9   *Official Year Book of the Commonwealth of Australia*, no. 15, 1922 (Melbourne: Albert J Mullett, 1922), p. 746.
10 While the University of Western Australia charged no tuition fees it did collect 'Guild fees', which were then supplemented by 'faculty' fees.
11 *Official Year Book of the Commonwealth of Australia*, no. 15, 1922, p. 747.
12 William Connell, *The Foundations of Secondary Education* (Melbourne: Australian Council of Educational Research, 1962).
13 Connell, *The Foundations of Secondary Education*.
14 RJW Selleck, *The Shop: The University of Melbourne, 1850–1939* (Carlton, Vic.: Melbourne University Press, 2003), p. 52.
15 With the exception of Western Australia, and its motto 'Seek wisdom', unconventionally in English.
16 RW Home, 'Origins of the Australian Physics Community', *Historical Studies* 20, no. 80 (1983), pp. 383–400.
17 Tamson Pietsch, '"They Do Not Go as Strangers": Academic Connections between Australia and Britain, 1880–1939', *Australian Studies* 5 (2013), pp. 1–13.
18 Roy M MacLeod (ed.), *The Commonwealth of Science: ANZAAS and the Scientific Enterprise in Australasia, 1888–1988* (Melbourne: Oxford University Press, 1988); RW Home, 'A World-Wide Scientific Network and Patronage System: Australian and Other "Colonial" Fellows of the Royal Society of London', in RW Home and Sally Gregory Kohlstedt (eds), *International Science and National Scientific Identity: Australia between Britain and America* (Dordrecht: Kluwer Academic Publishers, 1991), pp. 151–79.
19 The Rhodes was created in 1902.
20 *West Australian*, 18 June 1909, p. 7.
21 Pieter Dhondt, 'Introduction', in Pieter Dhondt (ed.), *University Jubilees and University History Writing: A Challenging Relationship. Scientific and Learned Cultures and Their Institutions* (Leiden: Brill, 2015).
22 From Sydney the meeting was attend by TT Gurney, Walter Scott and Richard Threlfall, respectively former professors of Mathematics, Greek and Physics. Adelaide was represented by professors Lamb and Beare, and the Reverend Dr Paton.
23 *Maitland Weekly Mercury*, 18 July 1903, p. 2.
24 Tamson Pietsch, 'Out of Empire: The Universities' Bureau and the Congresses of the Universities of the British Empire, 1913–36', in Deryck M Schreuder (ed.), *Universities for a New World: Making a Global Network in International Higher Education, 1913–2013* (Thousand Oaks, Cal.: SAGE Publications, 2013), pp. 11–25.

25 Eric Ashby, *Community of Universities: An Informal Portrait of The Association of Universities of the British Commonwealth, 1913–1963* (Cambridge: Cambridge University Press), 1963, pp. 21–22.
26 Pietsch, 'Out of Empire', pp. 17–18; 'The Universities Bureau of the British Empire', *Nature*, vol. 141, p. 406 (1938), doi.org/10.1038/141406b0.
27 Leonie Foster, *High Hopes: The Men and Motives of the Australian Round Table* (Melbourne: Melbourne University Press, in association with the Australian Institute of International Affairs, 1986).
28 Jenny Baldwin, 'World War I and the Development of Language Study at Australian Universities', in Kate Darian-Smith and James Waghorne (eds), *The First World War, the Universities and the Professions in Australia, 1914–1939* (Carlton, Vic.: Melbourne University Publishing, 2019), pp. 261–68.
29 Joy Damousi, 'Universities and Conscription: The "Yes" Campaigns and the University of Melbourne', in Robin Archer, Joy Damousi, Murray Goot and Sean Scalmer (eds), *The Conscription Conflict and the Great War* (Clayton, Vic.: Monash University Publishing, 2016), pp. 71–100.
30 Jim Hyde, 'The Development of Australian Tertiary Education to 1939', *Critical Studies in Education* 24, no. 1 (1982), pp. 125–27; Stephen Murray-Smith, 'A History of Technical Education in Australia: with Special Reference to the Period before 1914', PhD thesis, University of Melbourne, 1966, p. 731.
31 Debate about the role of universities was the centrepiece of the 1902 Sydney Jubilee with a lecture by Mungo McCallum, Professor of Modern Languages and Dean of the Faculty of Arts. McCallum took up the recommendation of the university's founder, William C Wentworth, that its mission was 'to enlighten the mind, to refine the understanding and to elevate their fellow-men'. Culture was 'knowledge that has life, motion, growth; intelligence that has seriousness, verity, substance', and this could take place anywhere in the university program. Others went further. Edgeworth David argued during his lecture that scientific knowledge was intrinsic to universities' cultural role. Basic research was valuable because it was more robust: 'the tortoise of investigation method and preparation will always catch up and overtake the hare, which leaves everything to the inspiration and effort of the movement'. He did not miss the opportunity to call for increased government funding for pure basic research, even if its benefits were not immediately apparent.
32 *Record of the Jubilee Celebrations of the University of Sydney, September 30th, 1902* (Sydney: William Brooks and Co., 1902).
33 Christopher J Lucas, *American Higher Education: A History* (New York: St. Martin's Press, 1994), p. 195.
34 John Brubacher, *Higher Education in Transition: History of American Colleges and Universities* (New York: Routledge, 2017).
35 Keith Vernon, 'Calling the Tune: British Universities and the State, 1880–1914', *History of Education* 30, no. 3 (2001), pp. 251–71; Robert O Berdahl, *British Universities and the State* (Berkeley: University of California Press, 1959).
36 Geoffrey Searle, *The Quest for National Efficiency: A Study in British Politics and Political Thought, 1899–1914* (Oxford: Blackwell, 1971); HGC Matthew, *The Liberal Imperialists: The Ideas and Politics of a Post-Gladstonian Elite* (London: Oxford University Press, 1973); Bernard Samuel, *Imperialism and Social Reform:*

English Social-Imperial Thought, 1895–1914 (London: George Allen & Unwin, 1960); Roy M MacLeod, 'Science, Progressivism, and "Practical Idealism": Reflections on Efficient Imperialism and Federal Science in Australia, 1895–1915'; *Scientia Canadensis: Canadian Journal of the History of Science, Technology and Medicine* vol. 17, nos 1–3 (1993), pp. 7–25; Walter Rüegg, 'Themes', in Walter Rüegg (ed.), *A History of the University in Europe, Vol. III: Universities in the Nineteenth and Early Twentieth Centuries (1800–1945)* (Cambridge: Cambridge University Press, 2004).

37 RW Home (ed.), *Australian Science in the Making*s (Cambridge: Cambridge University Press, 1988); Ann Moyal, *A Bright and Savage Land: The Science of a New Continent Australia – Where All Things Were 'Queer and Opposite'* (Ringwood, Vic.: Penguin Books, 1986).

38 P Board, *A Report Following Upon Observations of American Education* (Sydney: William Applegate Gullick, 1909), ch. 4

39 *Inauguration of the University of Queensland: Queensland's Jubilee Day, 10th December, 1909* (Brisbane: Anthony James Cumming, Government Printer, 1909).

40 MA Clements, 'Frank Tate and the Politics of Agricultural Education in Victoria, 1895–1905', *Critical Studies in Education* 19, no. 1 (1977), pp. 190–226.

41 Selleck, *The Shop*, pp. 453–56; WGK Duncan and Roger Ashley Leonard, *The University of Adelaide, 1874–1974* (Adelaide: Rigby, 1973), p. 49; Alexander, *Campus at Crawley*, p. 30; Turney, Bygott and Chippendale, *Australia's First, Vol. 1*, pp. 374–75.

42 Milton J Lewis, *The People's Health: Public Health in Australia, 1788–1950* (Westport, Conn.: Praeger, 2003), p. 180; Lori Harloe, 'Anton Breinl and the Australian Institute of Tropical Medicine', in Roy MacLeod and Donald Denoon (eds), *Health and Healing in Tropical Australia and New Guinea* (Townsville, Qld: James Cook University, 1991), pp. 34–46.

43 George Currie and John Graham, *The Origins of CSIRO: Science and the Commonwealth Government, 1901–1926* (Melbourne: Commonwealth Scientific and Industrial Research Organisation, 1966), p. 40.

44 MacLeod, 'Science, Progressivism, and "Practical Idealism"': pp. 7–25; RJW Selleck, *Finding Home: The Masson Family* (North Melbourne: Australian Scholarly Publishing, 2013), pp. 170–73.

45 'Prickly Pear', *The Capricornian*, 4 November 1922, p. 7; Australian Academy of Technological Sciences and Engineering, 'Pest and Disease Control', in *Technology in Australia 1788–1988*, (Australian Academy of Technological Sciences and Engineering), <www.austehc.unimelb.edu.au/tia/043.html#158>.

46 'Government Research Scholarships', *Melbourne University Magazine* 10, no. 3, October 1916.

47 Turney, Bygott and Chippendale, *Australia's First, Vol. 1*, pp. 250–51.

48 *Royal Commission on the University of Melbourne: Minutes of Evidence on Administration, Teaching Work, and Government of the University of Melbourne* (Melbourne: Robt S Brain, Government Printer, 1903), pp. 61–62.

49 HE Barff to JP Bainbridge, 14 May 1917, University of Melbourne Registrar's Correspondence, folder '1917/366 Universities Conference: Correspondence relating to', 1999.0014 UMA, University of Melbourne Archives. Discussed at

the 1917 conference was that each student would be expected to have completed English, a language other than English, Mathematics and 'at least one other subject'. As well as this, various degrees added their own requirements. Medicine required Latin as well as a further language other than English; Arts required a pass at a higher standard of a language other than English; Engineering required a higher standard of mathematics. The universities would allow the free transfer of students between institutions upon demonstration that they had achieved the requisite matriculation requirements.

50   AD Ross, to Barff, 22 June 1917, UM312, University of Melbourne Archives.
51   Thomas Tucker, *The Place of Classics in Education: An Inaugural Address Delivered in the Wilson Hall of the University of Melbourne, 22nd March, 1886* (Melbourne: S Mullen, 1886); *Record of the Jubilee Celebrations of the University of Sydney*, pp. 17–18.
52   The meeting had an impossibly broad agenda, ranging over common arrangements for examination, the 'interchange of teachers', 'mutual recognition' of degrees, diplomas and certificates, formalisation of arrangements for granting *ad eundem* degrees, a proposal to establish an Australian University Press, and the holding of inter-university conferences of students and graduates. No agreement was reached except that the 'occasional interchange of University teachers is desirable' and talk of formal cooperation went no further. University of Melbourne Council Minutes, 1906; Minutes of a Conference of Representatives of the Universities of Australia and New Zealand, Melbourne, 25 April 1906, UM174, UMA, University of Melbourne Archives.
53   NTW Lawson, Minister of Public Instruction Vic., to Chancellor, University of Melbourne, 27 June 1917, UM312, University of Melbourne Archives.
54   Ansell to Bainbridge, 2 August 1917, UM Registrar's Correspondence, folder '1917/366 Universities Conference: Correspondence relating to', 1999.0014 UMA, University of Melbourne Archives; Katrina Dean, 'The Physicist's Homestead: Alexander McAulay, Hydroelectricity and Mathematical Physics in Tasmania', *Tasmanian Historical Studies* 8 (2003); Barff to Bainbridge, 10 July 1917, UM Registrar's Correspondence, folder '1917/366 Universities Conference: Correspondence relating to', 1999.0014 UMA, University of Melbourne Archives.
55   Conference of Universities: Topics Suggested for Discussion, 10 May 1920, Registrar's Correspondence, Folder '1920/119 Conference of Australian Universities', University of Melbourne Archives.
56   'Method and Function of the Proposed Standing Advisory Committee of the Australian Universities', 1920, Folder 1, UM35, University of Melbourne Archives.
57   'History of Rail in Australia', Department of Infrastructure, Regional Development and Cities, <infrastructure.gov.au/rail/trains/history.aspx>, accessed 13 February 2018; Minutes of the Australian Conference of Universities, University of Sydney, 25 August 1932, p. 4, UM35, University of Melbourne Archives.
58   The 1920 Conference of Australian Universities set the pattern for subsequent biennial conferences, with the number of delegates increasing with each iteration. The second conference was held at the University of Melbourne on 31 May

1922, chaired by the Chancellor, Sir John MacFarland. Attending were the vice-chancellors of the University of Adelaide, William Mitchell, and Western Australia, Edward Shann. The conference returned to Melbourne in May 1926 and August 1928 and moved to Sydney in August 1930 and 1932. The last of these conferences took place in Melbourne in 1934. Each was chaired by the senior representative of the host university, although not always the chancellor.
59   Alexander Morgan, *Scottish University Studies* (London: Humphrey Milford, 1933), pp. 85–91.

CHAPTER 2 - AUSTRALIAN UNIVERSITIES

1   'Universities in Conference', *Sydney Morning Herald*, 28 May 1920, p. 8.
2   Conference of Australian Universities, 1920.
3   Minutes, Standing Advisory Committee, 15 November 1920.
4   Robert O Berdahl, *British Universities and the State* (Berkeley: University of California Press, 1959); Michael Shattock, *The UGC and the Management of British Universities* (Buckingham: Open University Press, 1994).
5   Milton J Lewis, *The People's Health: Public Health in Australia, 1788–1950* (Westport, Conn.: Praeger, 2003), p. 180; AH Brogan, *Committed to Saving Lives: A History of the Commonwealth Serum Laboratories* (South Yarra, Vic.: Hyland House, 1990).
6   SAC, 15 November 1920; Conference of Australian Universities, 30–31 May 1922.
7   SAC, 24 November 1921; Conference of Australian Universities, 30–31 May 1922.
8   Conference of Australian Universities, 30–31 May 1922; Carolyn Rasmussen, '"Constructive Work": The Engineering Profession in Australia and World War I', in Kate Darian-Smith and James Waghorne (eds), *The First World War, the Universities and the Professors in Australia, 1914–1939* (Carlton, Vic.: Melbourne University Publishing, 2019), pp. 149–50.
9   Renate Simpson, *The Development of the PhD Degree in Britain, 1917–1959 and Since: An Evolutionary and Statistical History in Higher Education* (Lewiston: The Edwin Mellen Press, 2009).
10 Conference of Australian Universities, 21–22 August 1924.
11 Conference of Australian Universities, 14–15 August 1934.
12 Ian D Rae, 'False Start for the PhD in Australia', *Historical Records of Australian Science* 14, no. 2 (2002), pp. 129–41.
13 Minutes, Standing Advisory Committee, 13 August 1923.
14 Kate Darian-Smith and James Waghorne, 'Introduction', in Darian-Smith and Waghorne (eds), *The First World War, the Universities and the Professions*.
15 Australian University Conference, 15 August 1927; AW Beasley, *The Mantle of Surgery: The First Seventy-Five Years of the Royal Australasian College of Surgeons* (Melbourne: Royal Australasian College of Surgeons, 2002); Julian Ormond Smith, 'The History of the Royal Australasian College of Surgeons, 1920–1935', *Australian & New Zealand Journal of Surgery* 41, no. 1 (1971), pp. 1–19; Andrew Newton, 'The History of the Royal Australasian College of Surgeons from Foundation to 1935', BA (Hons) Thesis, Monash University, 1979; in Patrick Kenny Syme (ed.), *The Founders of the Royal Australasian College of Surgeons* (Melbourne: Royal Australasian College of Surgeons, 1984).

16 Australian Universities Conference, 18–19 August 1930.
17 James Waghorne, 'Growth and Specialisation: The Medical Profession in Interwar Australia' in Darian-Smith and Waghorne (eds), *The First World War, the Universities and the Professions*, pp. 39–40.
18 John Egerton and Hannah Forsyth, 'Veterinary Science, World War I and the Professions', in Darian-Smith and Waghorne (eds), *World War I, the Universities and the Professions*.
19 Warwick Anderson, 'Knowing Natives: Instituting Social Anthropology in Australia after the Great War', in Darian-Smith and Waghorne (eds), *The First World War, the Universities and the Professions*.
20 Melanie Oppenheimer, 'The Professionalisation of Nursing through the 1920s and 1930s: The Impact of War and Volunteerism', in Darian-Smith and Waghorne (eds), *The First World War, the Universities and the Professions*.
21 SAC, 24 November 1921.
22 Conference of Australian Universities, 30–31 May 1922; ER Holme, 'Universities and the State': Paper by ER Holme, to the Third Imperial Congress on Higher Education, Cambridge, July 1926.
23 Conference of Australian Universities, 21–22 August 1924.
24 SAC, 15 August 1927; Conference of Australian Universities, 20–21 August 1928.
25 Conference of Australian Universities, 30–31 May 1922, 21–22 August 1924.
26 Australian Universities Conference, 20–21 August 1928.
27 CB Schedvin, *Shaping Science and Industry: A History of Australia's Council for Scientific and Industrial Research, 1926–49* (Sydney: Allen & Unwin, 1987).
28 George Currie and John Graham, *The Origins of CSIRO: Science and the Commonwealth Government, 1901–1926* (Melbourne: Commonwealth Scientific and Industrial Research Organisation, 1966), ch. 7.
29 Conference of Australian Universities, 31 May–1 June 1926.
30 Stuart Braga, *Anzac Doctor: The Life of Sir Neville Howse, Australia's First VC* (Alexandria, NSW: Hale & Iremonger, 2000), pp. 308–12.
31 Stuart Macintyre, 'Useful Knowledge: The Contribution of Universities to Government between the Wars', in Darian-Smith and Waghorne (eds), *The First World War, the Universities and the Professions in Australia 1914–1939*.
32 Gerald E Caiden, *Career Service: An Introduction to the History of Personnel Administration in the Commonwealth Public Service of Australia 1901–1961* (Carlton, Vic.: Melbourne University Press, 1965), p. 126.
33 Nicholas Brown, *A History of Canberra* (Port Melbourne, Vic.: Cambridge University Press, 2014).
34 Caiden, *Career Service*, p. 178.
35 Minutes of the Australian Conference of Universities, 1932, p. 10, UM35, University of Melbourne Archives.
36 Minutes of the Australian Conference of Universities, 1934, p. 10, UM35, University of Melbourne Archives.
37 ACD Rivett, 'Pan-Pacific Science Congress, Australia, 1923', *Nature* 112 (1923), pp. 378–79.
38 SAC, 1925, UM35, University of Melbourne Archives.
39 *Official Year Book of the Commonwealth of Australia*, 1926.

40 'Gifts to Universities', *The Age*, 18 March 1926, p. 18; 'Gift Taxation', *The Advertiser*, 17 November 1926, p. 8; 'Voice of Parliament', *News*, 10 December 1927, p. 4.
41 Conference of Australian Universities, 20–21 August 1928.
42 Conference of Australian Universities, 31 May–1 June 1926.
43 Standing Advisory Committee, 15 August 1927.
44 Conference of Australian Universities, 18–19 August 1930.
45 Edgar Booth, *New England University College: Decentralisation of University Education* (Armidale: Armidale Express Print, 1943).
46 Commonwealth Year Books, various years.
47 Carl Boris Schedvin, *Australia and the Great Depression* (Sydney: Sydney University Press, 1970), p. 219; William Coleman, Selwyn Cornish and Alf Hagger, *Giblin's Platoon: The Triumphs and Trials of the Economist in Australian Public Life* (Canberra: ANU E Press, 2006).
48 Minutes of the Australian Conference of Universities, 1930, p. 29, UM35, University of Melbourne Archives.
49 Letter to John Foster from Page-Hanify, Registrar University of Queensland, 19 May 1939, 1981.0150, University of Melbourne Archives.
50 *Calendar for the University of Adelaide for the Year 1930* (Adelaide: Advertiser Newspapers, 1930); *Calendar for the University of Adelaide for the Year 1933* (Adelaide: Advertiser Newspapers, 1933); *Calendar for the University of Adelaide for the Year 1935* (Adelaide: Advertiser Newspapers, 1935).
51 M Butlin, R Dixon and P Lloyd, 'Statistical Appendix: Selected data series, 1800–2010', in S Ville and G Withers (eds), *The Cambridge Economic History of Australia* (Cambridge: Cambridge University Press, 2014), doi:10.1017/CHO9781107445222.033, p. 558.
52 Minutes of the meeting of the Standing Advisory Committee of Australian Universities 1931, University of Melbourne, p. 1, UM35, University of Melbourne Archives.
53 Standing Advisory Committee, 21 August 1931.
54 *Royal Commission on the University of Melbourne: Minutes of Evidence on Administration, Teaching Work, and Government of the University of Melbourne* (Parliament of Victoria, Melbourne: Robt S Brain, Government Printer, 1903).
55 Clifford Turney, Ursula Bygott and Peter Chippendale, *Australia's First: A History of the University of Sydney, Vol. 1, 1850–1939* (Sydney: Hale & Iremonger, 1991), pp. 440–43.
56 Minutes of the meeting of the Standing Advisory Committee of Australian Universities, University of Melbourne, 15 November 1920, pp. 4–6, UM35, University of Melbourne Archives.
57 Minutes of the meeting of the Standing Advisory Committee of Australian Universities, University of Melbourne, 15 November 1920, p. 7, UM35, University of Melbourne Archives.
58 University of Melbourne Council minutes.
59 Minutes of the meeting of the Standing Advisory Committee of Australian Universities, University of Melbourne, 15 November 1920, p. 5, UM35, University of Melbourne Archives.

60 Raymond E Priestley, *The Diary of a Vice-Chancellor: University of Melbourne 1935–1938*, edited by Ronald T Ridley (Carlton South, Vic.: Melbourne University Press, 2002).
61 Minutes of the Conference of Australian Universities, University of Adelaide, 21 and 22 August 1924, p. 2, UM35, University of Melbourne Archives.
62 Minutes of the Conference of Australian Universities, University of Sydney, 18 and 19 August 1930, 5A, UM35, University of Melbourne Archives.
63 Minutes, AVCC, 14–15 August 1934.
64 Minutes of the meeting of the Standing Advisory Committee of Australian Universities, University of Melbourne, 22 August 1933, p. 1, UM35, University of Melbourne Archives.
65 Stephen H Stackpole, *Commonwealth Program 1911–1961* (Carnegie Corporation of New York, New York, 1963); Minutes of the meeting of the Standing Advisory Committee of Australian Universities, University of Melbourne, 15 November 1925, UM35, University of Melbourne Archives.
66 AVCC, 3 April, 19–20 August, 28 November 1935; 5 March 1936. *Calendar for the University of Sydney for the Year 1937* (Sydney: David Harold Paisley, 1937), p. 1034.
67 AVCC, 28 November 1935.
68 AVCC, 19–20 August 1935.
69 AVCC, 19–20 August 1935; Anne Rees, 'A War of Card Indexes: From Political Economy to Economic Science', in Darian-Smith and Waghorne (eds), *The First World War, the Universities and the Professions*.
70 The corporations power would in later years become a central justification for federal funding for higher education in Australia.
71 AVCC, 19–20 August 1935.
72 AVCC, 27 October 1936.
73 ACD Rivett, 'Paper on the Relations between the Commonwealth Council for Scientific and Industrial Research and the Universities', in *Australian and New Zealand Universities' Conference, Adelaide 1937: Report of Proceedings* (Adelaide: The Hassell Press, 1937), p. 119.
74 AVCC, 2 March 1938.
75 AVCC, 2 March 1938; 28 February 1939.
76 AVCC, 28 February 1939.
77 Stuart Macintyre, *The Poor Relation: A History of Social Sciences in Australia* (Carlton, Vic.: Melbourne University Publishing, 2010), pp. 46–49.
78 Timothy Dyke and Warwick P Anderson, 'A History of Health and Medical Research in Australia', *Medical Journal of Australia* 201, no. 1 Suppl (2014), S33–S36, p. 7; Peter Hobbins, '"Outside the Institute there Is a Desert": The Tenuous Trajectories of Medical Research in Interwar Australia', *Medical History* 54, no. 1 (2010), pp. 1–28; KF Russell, *The Melbourne Medical School, 1862–1962* (Carlton, Vic.: Melbourne University Press, 1977), p. 157.
79 AVCC, 15–19 February 1937; ACV Melbourne, *Report on a Visit to the Universities of China and Japan* (Brisbane: University of Queensland, 1936); ACV Melbourne, 'The Universities of China and Japan', address to Australia and New Zealand Universities Conference, Adelaide, 1937; Malcolm I Thomis,

'Melbourne, Alexander Clifford Vernon (1888–1943)', *Australian Dictionary of Biography* (National Centre of Biography, Australian National University), <adb.anu.edu.au/biography/melbourne-alexander-clifford-vernon-7552/text13177>, published first in hardcopy 1986, accessed online 23 May 2019.
80   AVCC, 15–19 February 1937.
81   'Dr Wallace's Report: Far-Reaching Recommendations', *The West Australian*, 19 June 1940.
82   RE Priestley, *The Problems of the English-Speaking University World* (Adelaide: The Hassell Press, 1937), p. 1.
83   Fred Alexander, *Campus at Crawley: A Narrative and Critical Appreciation of the First Fifty Years of the University of Western Australia* (Melbourne: FW Cheshire, 1963), pp. 240–41.
84   Robert O Berdahl, *British Universities and the State* (Berkeley: University of California Press, 1959), appendix 3.
85   AVCC, 16 February 1937.
86   AVCC, 28 February 1939.

CHAPTER 3 - CONTROL AND INFLUENCE
1   *Year Book of the Commonwealth of Australia*, 1916, 1941.
2   *National Security Act* (Cth) 1939.
3   Minutes, AVCC, 5 March 1940; AVCC, Second Conference of Medical Deans, Sydney 19 October 1944, 1981.0150, University of Melbourne Archives.
4   Minutes, AVCC, 4 March 1941.
5   Paul Hasluck, *The Government and the People, 1939–41. Australia in the War of 1939–1945* (Canberra: Australian War Memorial, 1952), pp. 408–14.
6   AVCC, Second Conference of Medical Deans, Sydney, 19 October 1944, 1981.0150, University of Melbourne Archives; KF Russell, *The Melbourne Medical School, 1862–1962* (Carlton, Vic.: Melbourne University Press, 1977), p. 178; VA Edgeloe, *The Medical School of the University of Adelaide: A Brief History from an Administrative Viewpoint* (Adelaide: University of Adelaide, 1991), p. 23; RL Doherty, 'The Faculty Resolves to Recommend … The University of Queensland Faculty of Medicine, 1936–1985', in RL Doherty (ed.), *A Medical School for Queensland* (Brisbane: Boolarong Publications, 1986), pp. 30–31.
7   Students had the option to take the final year of the normal degree course after the war, Carolyn Rasmussen, *Increasing Momentum: Engineering at the University of Melbourne, 1861–2004* (Carlton, Vic.: Melbourne University Press, 2004), p. 129.
8   Minutes, AVCC, 1942.
9   Minutes, AVCC, 13 August 1941; Queensland had also argued for scholarships of £150 for students to travel to Sydney to study Aeronautical Engineering, a suggestion similarly rebuffed.
10 A compilation of the universities' respective annual reports.
11 Stuart Macintyre, *Australia's Boldest Experiment: War and Reconstruction in the 1940s* (Sydney: NewSouth, 2015), p. 62.
12 'Universities to Help: Post-war Planning', *Herald* (Melbourne), 5 June 1941, p. 8.
13 'Post-war Tasks: The Need for Research', *West Australian*, 9 June 1941, p. 6.

14 Minutes, AVCC, 13 August 1941.
15 DP Mellor, *The Role of Science and Industry. Australia in the War of 1939–1945*, Series 4, Civil, vol. 5 (Canberra: Australian War Memorial, 1958).
16 Minutes of Conference Between the Department for War Organisation of Industry and the Universities, 19 January 1942.
17 AD Spaull, *John Dedman: A Most Unexpected Labor Man* (South Melbourne: Hyland House, 1998); Gavin Souter, *Acts of Parliament: A Narrative History of the Senate and House of Representatives, Commonwealth of Australia* (Carlton, Vic.: Melbourne University Press, 1988), p. 363; Macintyre, *Australia's Boldest Experiment*, 86.
18 'Opening Statement by the Hon. John J Dedman, MP at the Conference Between the Department for War Organisation of Industry and the Universities', Minutes of Conference Between the Department for War Organisation of Industry and the Universities, 19 January 1942, Minutes AVCC.
19 'Opening Statement by the Hon. John J. Dedman, MP at the Conference Between the Department for War Organisation of Industry and the Universities', 19 January 1942.
20 JDG Medley, 'Memorandum by Chairman, Australian Vice-Chancellor's Committee, 19 January 1942'.
21 AVCC Conference with the Department of War Organisation of Industry (and other interested Departments) Melbourne, 19 January 1942, pp. 2–3.
22 National Security (Manpower) Regulations, No. 34, 21 January 1942; Minutes, AVCC, January 1942.
23 Minutes, AVCC, 17 August 1942.
24 Commonwealth Year Books, 1941, 1944–45, 1946–47.
25 AVCC Reports of Committees of the Universities Conference, 20 January 1942.
26 'Bewildered Medico (Caulfield) to the *Age*', *The Age*, 26 May 1942, p. 2; 'Provision for Education at Universities', *The Age*, 28 May 1942, p. 5; SJ Butlin and CB Shedvin, *War Economy, 1942–1945. Australia in the War of 1939–1945*, Series 4, Civil, vol. 4 (Canberra: Australian War Memorial, 1977), p. 37.
27 'For Production Executive Universities', Inter-Departmental Committee on Universities, October 1942, p. 3, NAA: CP6/2, 92.
28 Annual Report, Universities Commission, 1943, p. 2; Minutes, AVCC, 17 August 1942, p. 2.
29 Minutes, AVCC, 17 August 1942, pp. 11–12.
30 Stephen Holt, *A Veritable Dynamo: Lloyd Ross and Australian Labor 1901–1987* (St Lucia: University of Queensland Press, 1996); Michael Easson, 'Ross, Lloyd Robert Maxwell (1901–1987)', *Australian Dictionary of Biography*, National Centre of Biography, Australian National University, <adb.anu.edu.au/biography/ross-lloyd-robert-maxwell-15927/text27128>, published first in hardcopy 2012, accessed online 4 August 2018.
31 Minutes, AVCC and Universities Commission Meeting, 4 December 1942.
32 Annual Report, Universities Commission, 1943.
33 Annual Report, Universities Commission, 1943.
34 *Year Book of the Commonwealth of Australia*, 1942, pp. 170–71.
35 Notes on Conference of Universities Commission with Vice-Chancellors, 4 December 1942.

36 Notes on Conference of Universities Commission with Vice-Chancellors, 4 December 1942.
37 Minutes, AVCC, 10 May 1943; WF Connell, *The Australian Council of Educational Research* (Hawthorn: Australian Council of Educational Research, 1980), pp. 130–66; Brian Williams, 'A Scholar Goes to War: K.S. Cunningham 1914–18', *Critical Studies in Education* 35, no. 1 (1994), p. 1.
38 'Knowledge is Quota! (but don't quote us)', *Smith's Weekly*, 3 April 1943, p. 2.
39 'New Student Quotas', *Sydney Morning Herald*, 7 April 1943, p. 6.
40 A472, W11142, NAA.
41 Minutes, AVCC, 10 May 1943.
42 'King v. The University of Sydney; ex parte Drummond', *Australian Law Journal* 17 (16 July 1943), pp. 103–106; PD Tannock and IK Birch, 'Defining the Limits of Commonwealth Education Power: The Drummond Case, the Federal Government and the Universities', *Critical Studies in Education* 15, no. 1 (1973), pp. 163–74.
43 Conference AVCC and Universities Commission, 25–27 October 1943; Universities Commission Annual Report, 1943.
44 Minutes, AVCC, 25 October 1943.
45 Macintyre, *Australia's Boldest Experiment*, pp. 217–18.
46 Constitution of Australia, Section 52, xxiiiA; PD Tannock, *The Government of Education in Australia: The Origins of Federal Policy* (Nedlands: UWA Press, 1975), pp. 3–22.
47 *Farrago*, 15 March 1944.
48 Conference of Vice-Chancellors and Universities Commission, 25–27 October 1943.
49 Macintyre, *Australia's Boldest Experiment*, pp. 326–33.
50 *Year Book of the Commonwealth of Australia*, various years.
51 Minutes, AVCC, 21 August 1944.
52 'Universities Commission: Report of Activities of Research Section, 1944 and General Research Report for 1944', Universities Commission, p. 3.
53 Conference of Vice-Chancellors and Universities Commission, 25–27 October 1943.
54 Minutes, AVCC, 21 August 1944.
55 'Premier Will Call Talks on Institute of Technology', *The Argus*, 1948, p. 8.
56 TH Laby, 'A University for the Commonwealth' *The Australian Quarterly* 1, no. 1 (1929), pp. 32–42; Milton J Lewis, 'The Idea of a National University: The Origins and Establishment of the Australian National University' *Journal of the Australian and New Zealand History of Education Society* 8, no. 2 (1979), pp. 40–55; JG Crawford, *The Australian National University: Its Concept and Role* (Melbourne: University of Melbourne, 1968).
57 SG Foster and Margaret M Varghese, *The Making of the Australian National University: 1946–1996* (Canberra: ANU E Press, 2009), pp. 6–19.
58 JDG Medley, *The Present and Future of Australian Universities* (Melbourne: Melbourne University Press, 1945).
59 Medley, *The Present and Future of Australian Universities*, p. 10.
60 Medley, *The Present and Future of Australian Universities*, p. 42.

61 Medley, *The Present and Future of Australian Universities*, p. 41.
62 Medley, *The Present and Future of Australian Universities*, p. 41.
63 Medley, *The Present and Future of Australian Universities*, p. 42.
64 Minutes, AVCC, 21 August 1944.
65 Minutes, AVCC, 19 February 1945.
66 Ian D Rae, 'False Start for the PhD in Australia', *Historical Records of Australian Science* 14, no. 2 (2002), pp. 129–41.
67 Minutes, AVCC 21 August 1945.
68 Minutes, AVCC, 28 January 1947.
69 Minutes, AVCC, 23 September 1947.
70 Minutes, AVCC, 23 September 1947.
71 Minutes, AVCC, 23 September 1947.
72 Minutes, AVCC, 18 February 1948.
73 Minutes, AVCC, 24 October 1949.
74 Minutes, AVCC, 24 October 1949.
75 *The West Australian*, 13 January 1949, p. 15.
76 Minutes, AVCC, 18 February 1948.
77 Minutes, AVCC, 24 October 1949.
78 Minutes, AVCC, 23 February 1950.
79 'PM's statement Universities – Cth Committee 25 October 1949', in Minutes, AVCC, 24 October 1949.
80 'New Federal University Scholarships', *Sydney Morning Herald*, 28 September 1949, p. 5.
81 Minutes, AVCC, 21 February 1949.
82 Minutes, AVCC, 24 October 1949.

CHAPTER 4 - COMMONWEALTH AND STATES

1 'The Centenary of the University of Sydney', *Building and Engineering*, 24 October 1950, pp. 20–22.
2 Bob Bessant, 'Robert Gordon Menzies and Education in Australia', *Critical Studies in Education* 19, no. 1 (1977), pp. 76–80; Allan Martin, *Robert Menzies, A Life*, vol. 2 (Carlton, Vic.: Melbourne University Press, 1999); Judith Brett, *Robert Menzies' Forgotten People* (Chippendale, NSW: Macmillan Australia, 1992).
3 'Labour Force: Australia', ABS Cat. Number 6203.0.
4 Quoted in S Lees and J Senyard, *The 1950s: ... How Australia Became a Modern Society and Everyone got a House and a Car* (Melbourne: Hyland House, 1987), p. 5.
5 D McLean, 'American and Australian Cold Wars in Asia', *Australasian Journal of American Studies*, 9, no. 2 (1990), pp. 33–46; A Winkler, *The Cold War: A History in Documents* (Oxford University Press, 2011); P Edwards, *Australia and the Vietnam War* (NewSouth Publishing, 2014).
6 Nicholas Brown, 'Student, Expert, Peacekeeper: Three Versions of International Engagement', *Australian Journal of Politics and History* 57, no. 1 (2011), pp. 34–52; David Lowe, 'The Colombo Plan', in David Lowe (ed.), *Australia and the End of Empire* (Geelong: Deakin University Press, 1996); David Lowe, *Australia Between Empires: The Life of Percy Spender* (London: Routledge, 2010), pp. 128–32;

Christopher Waters, 'Cold War Liberals: Richard Casey and the Department of the External Affairs, 1951–60', in Joan Beaumont (ed.), *Ministers, Mandarins and Diplomats: Australian Foreign Policy Making, 1941–1969* (Carlton, Vic.: Melbourne University Press, 2003).

7 Murray Goot and Sean Scalmer, 'Party Leaders, the Media, and Political Persuasion: The Campaigns of Evatt and Menzies on the Referendum to Protect Australia from Communism', *Australian Historical Studies* 44, no. 1 (2013), pp. 71–88, doi: 10.1080/1031461X.2012.760635.

8 Troy Bramston, *Robert Menzies: The Art of Politics* (Melbourne: Scribe, 2019), p. 191; Paul Strangio, Paul T Hart and James Walter, *The Pivot of Power: Australian Prime Ministers and Political Leadership, 1949–2016* (Carlton, Vic.: Melbourne University Publishing, 2017).

9 'University's Good Name', *The Age*, 24 February 1951, p. 2; 'Restraint Urged on Government', *The Age* 15 March 1950, p. 5.

10 Robert Menzies, Speech delivered 10 November 1949 in Melbourne, Australian Federal Election Speeches, Museum of Australian Democracy, <electionspeeches.moadoph.gov.au/speeches/1949-robert-menzies>.

11 Minutes, AVCC, 23 February 1950.

12 RC Mills, DB Copland and HJ Goodes, 'Interim Report by Commonwealth Committee on Needs of Universities', 1950.

13 Minutes, AVCC, 8–9 November 1950.

14 *States Grants (Universities) Act* (Cth) 1951.

15 ACER, *Review of Education in Australia 1955 to 1962* (Hawthorne: ACER, 1963), pp. 316–17.

16 Allan Martin, *Robert Menzies: A Life*, vol. 2 (Carlton, Vic.: Melbourne University Press, 1999), p. 396.

17 ACER, *Review of Education in Australia 1955 to 1962* (Hawthorn: ACER, 1963), pp. 316–17.

18 Minutes, AVCC, 8–9 November 1950.

19 Minutes, AVCC, 8–9 November 1950.

20 Terms of the scheme taken from *Year Book of the Commonwealth of Australia*, 1953.

21 John Murphy, *Imagining the Fifties* (Sydney: UNSW Press, 2000), pp. 106–10.

22 ACER, *Review of Education in Australia 1955 to 1962* (Hawthorn: ACER, 1963), p. 348.

23 Minutes, AVCC, 23 February 1950.

24 Conference between AVCC and Universities Commission, 16 March 1951.

25 Minutes, AVCC, 13–14 June, 8–9 November, 1950.

26 David Lowe and Daniel Oakman (eds), *Australia and the Colombo Plan* (Canberra: Department of Foreign Affairs and Trade Documents on Australian Foreign Policy, 2004), pp. xxv–xxxv.

27 George Currie, 'Memo. to Vice-Chancellors' Conference, 8 August 1944, re. Students from the Far East attending Australian Universities', Minutes, AVCC.

28 Daniel Oakman, *Facing Asia: A History of the Colombo Plan* (Canberra: ANU E Press, 2010), p. 180.

29 Lyndon Megarrity, 'Regional Goodwill, Sensibly Priced: Commonwealth Policies Towards Colombo Plan Scholars and Private Overseas Students, 1945–72',

Australian Historical Studies 38, no. 129 (2008), pp. 88–105.
30 Minutes, AVCC, 8–9 November 1950.
31 Conference between AVCC and Universities Commission, 16 March 1951; Kate Darian-Smith and James Waghorne, 'Australian-Asian Sociability, Student Activism, and the University Challenge to White Australia in the 1950s', *Australian Journal of Politics and History* 62, no. 2 (2016), pp. 203–18.
32 C Sanders, *Universities and Educational Institutions in South East Asia: Report on Standards* (Australian Vice-Chancellors' Committee, 1958), pp. 41–42.
33 Sanders, *Universities and Educational Institutions in South East Asia*.
34 Sanders, *Universities and Educational Institutions in South East Asia*, pp. 49–52.
35 James Waghorne and Stuart Macintyre, *Liberty: A History of Civil Liberties in Australia* (Sydney: UNSW Press, 2011), pp. 90–96.
36 Stuart Macintyre and RJW Selleck, *A Short History of the University of Melbourne* (Carlton, Vic.: Melbourne University Press, 2003), pp. 103–105; Fay Anderson, *An Historian's Life: Max Crawford and the Politics of Academic Freedom* (Carlton, Vic.: Melbourne University Publishing, 2005), p. 165.
37 Phillip Deery, 'Scientific Freedom and Post-war Politics: Australia, 1945–55', *Historical Records of Australian Science* 13, no. 1 (2000), pp. 1–18; James Waghorne, 'Civil Liberties and the Referendum' *Australian Historical Studies* 44, no. 1 (2013), pp. 105–16; Phillip Deery, 'Remembering ASIO', *Overland*, no. 203 (2011).
38 Minutes, AVCC, 20–22 October 1952.
39 Minutes, AVCC, 27 July 1951, 28–29 October 1953, 6–8 October 1954.
40 Martin, *Robert Menzies*, vol. 2, pp. 390–98.
41 Minutes, AVCC, 5–7 March 1952.
42 Minutes, AVCC, 18–19 October 1951.
43 Minutes, AVCC, 5–7 March 1952.
44 Martin, *Robert Menzies*, vol. 2, p. 394.
45 Marjorie Harper, *Douglas Copland: Scholar, Economist, Diplomat* (Carlton: The Miegunyah Press, 2013), pp. 363–4.
46 Martin, *Robert Menzies*, vol. 2, p. 394
47 AVCC, *A Crisis in the Finances and Development of the Australian Universities*, (AVCC, 1952).
48 AVCC, *A Crisis in the Finances and Development of the Australian Universities*, p. i.
49 AVCC, *A Crisis in the Finances and Development of the Australian Universities*, p. 2.
50 AVCC, *A Crisis in the Finances and Development of the Australian Universities*, p. ii.
51 AVCC, *A Crisis in the Finances and Development of the Australian Universities*, p. ii.
52 AVCC, *A Crisis in the Finances and Development of the Australian Universities*, p. 17.
53 AVCC, *A Crisis in the Finances and Development of the Australian Universities*, p. 18.
54 Minutes, AVCC, 5–7 March 1952.
55 Minutes, AVCC, 20–22 October 1952.
56 Minutes, AVCC, 20–22 October 1952.
57 Minutes, AVCC, 20–22 October 1952.
58 Quoted in Martin, *Robert Menzies*, vol. 2, p. 394.
59 Minutes, AVCC, 19–20 February 1953.
60 Ann Curthoys, 'Television before Television', *Continuum: Journal of Media & Cultural Studies* 4, no. 2 (1991), pp. 152–70; Jim Welch, 'Shaping the Box: The

Cultural Construction of American Television, 1948–1952', *Continuum: Journal of Media & Cultural Studies* 13, no. 1 (1999), pp. 97–117.
61 Jennifer Bowen, '"A Capable Army of Experts": The Broadcasting Profession between the Wars', in Kate Darian-Smith and James Waghorne (eds), *The First World War, the Universities and the Professions* (Carlton, Vic.: Melbourne University Publishing, 2019), pp. 370–71.
62 AVCC, 18–19 October 1951; Special Session AVCC, 7 March 1952.
63 Richard Boyer to George Paton, 6 June 1960. An inter-university planning committee was formed to oversee the scheme, comprising: Zelman Cowen, Professor of Public Law at the University of Melbourne; Louis Matheson, Vice-Chancellor of Monash; Philip Baxter, Vice-Chancellor of the University of New South Wales; JLJ Wilson, Director of Tutorial Classes, University of Sydney; and a representative of ANU; 25-8-2, UA papers; 'What to Stay Home For …', *Canberra Times*, 1 March 1965, p. 13.
64 *A University of the Air, Presented to Parliament by the Secretary of State for Education and Science by Command of Her Majesty, February 1966* (London: Her Majesty's Stationery Office, 1963).
65 Eric Ashby, *Community of Universities: An Informal Portrait of The Association of Universities of the British Commonwealth, 1913–1963* (Cambridge: Cambridge University Press, 1963).
66 Minutes, AVCC, 23 February 1950.
67 Minutes, AVCC, 23 February 1950.
68 Minutes, AVCC, 6 July 1953.
69 Report of Proceedings, Universities of the British Commonwealth, Seventh Quinquennial Conference, 1953.
70 'Rolph, William Kirby (1919–1954)', *Obituaries Australia*, National Centre of Biography, Australian National University, <oa.anu.edu.au/obituary/rolph-william-kirby-875/text876>, accessed 27 May 2019.
71 Minutes, AVCC, 19–20 February 1953.
72 Minutes, AVCC, 28–29 October 1953.
73 John Michael O'Brien, *The National Tertiary Education Union: A Most Unlikely Union* (Sydney: UNSW Press, 2015), pp. 48–49.
74 Minutes, AVCC, 28–29 October 1953.
75 Minutes, AVCC, 7–9 April 1954.
76 Matthew Jordan, *A Spirit of True Learning: The Jubilee History of the University of New England* (Sydney: UNSW Press, 2004).
77 Quoted in Martin, *Robert Menzies*, vol. 2, p. 395.
78 Minutes, AVCC, 6–8 October 1954.
79 Minutes, AVCC, 15–16 February 1955.
80 Minutes, AVCC, 6–8 October 1954.
81 Boyce Gibson, 'The Australian Universities and Public Opinion', in *A Symposium on 'The Place of the Australian University in the Community' and 'Post-Graduate Studies in the Australian Universities* (Canberra: AVCC 1955), p. 43.
82 Minutes, AVCC, 19–21 Oct 1955.
83 Paton paraphrasing Menzies, AVCC, 7–8 March 1956.
84 Minutes, AVCC, 7–8 March 1956.

85   Secretary's notes, Joint Conference of AVCC and Committee on Australian Universities, no date.
86   Minutes, AVCC, 3 July 1957; AVCC, *Submission by the AVCC to the Committee on Australian Universities, 4 July 1957* (Carlton: Melbourne University Press, 1957).
87   'Remarks of the Chairman when presenting the "Submission" to the Committee on Australian Universities', appended to AVCC, 3 July 1957.
88   John Howard, *The Menzies Era: The Years that Shaped Modern Australia* (Sydney: HarperCollins, 2014), p. 246.
89   'Murray Report Adopted: Millions to Rehabilitate Universities', *Canberra Times*, 29 November 1957; Howard, *The Menzies Era*, p. 246.
90   *Report of the Murray Committee on Australian Universities, September 1957* (Canberra: AJ Arthur, Commonwealth Government Printer, 1957), pp. 104–107.
91   *Report of the Murray Committee on Australian Universities*, pp. 92, 94–5.
92   Minutes, AVCC, February 1958
93   Martin, *Robert Menzies*, vol. 2, p. 390.
94   Minutes, AVCC, 29 August 1958.
95   Minutes, AVCC, 3–4 February 1959.
96   Minutes, AVCC, 28–29 October 1959.
97   *Report of the Murray Committee on Australian Universities*, pp. 12, 81–3.

CHAPTER 5 - SYSTEMATISATION

1   Robin S Harris, 'On Higher Education in Australia and Canada', *The Australian University* 7, no. 3 (1969), pp. 190–203.
2   WD Borrie and Ruth M Dedman, *University Enrolments in Australia 1955–1970: A Projection* (Maryborough, Vic.: Hedges & Bell, 1957).
3   JDG Medley, *The Present and Future of Australian Universities* (Melbourne: Melbourne University Press), 1945, p. 20; Alan Barcan, 'The Australian Student, 1961', *Meanjin Quarterly* 20, no. 2 (1961), pp. 194–208; Brian Fitzpatrick, 'The Arts, and the Upsurge of the PTM Class', *Meanjin Quarterly* 20, no. 1 (1960), pp. 73–79.
4   PD Tannock, 'A Study of the Role of the Government of the Commonwealth of Australia in Education since Federation, 1901–1968', PhD Thesis, The Johns Hopkins University, 1969; PD Tannock, *The Government of Education in Australia: The Origins of Federal Policy* (Nedlands, WA: University of Western Australia Press, 1975).
5   Martin Trow, 'Problems in the Transition from Elite to Mass Higher Education', in OECD, *Policies for Higher Education: Conference on Future Structures of Post-Secondary Education, Paris, 26–29 June 1973, General Report* (Paris: OECD, 1974).
6   Minutes, AUBC–AVCC Meeting, 6 August 1962.
7   *Year Books of the Commonwealth of Australia*, 1959 and 1973.
8   DH Drummond, *A University Is Born: The Story of the Founding of the University College of New England* (Sydney: Angus & Robertson, 1959).
9   DI Wright, *Looking Back, a History of the University of Newcastle* (Callaghan: University of Newcastle, 1992); Josie Castle, *University of Wollongong: An Illustrated History* (Wollongong: University of Wollongong, 1991).

10 Peter Bell, *Our Place in the Sun: A Brief History of James Cook University, 1960–2010* (Townsville: James Cook University, 2010).
11 Graeme Davison and Kate Murphy, *University Unlimited: The Monash Story* (Sydney: Allen & Unwin, 2012), pp. 9–11.
12 RM Crawford, 'Humanities and Social Sciences in Australian Universities: Effects of the Bulge and the Trend', *The Australian University* 6, no. 2 (1968), pp. 122–35; Davison and Murphy, *Monash Unlimited*, pp. 1–39.
13 Patrick O'Farrell, *UNSW: A Portrait, the University of New South Wales, 1949–1999* (Sydney: UNSW Press, 1999).
14 For instance, at Melbourne where a quota of 220 was set for entry into second year in 1948, *University of Melbourne Calendar*, 1949, p. 481; in 1958, Melbourne reluctantly imposed quotas on Commerce, Science, Agricultural Science, Engineering, Dental Science and Medicine. This extended to Arts in 1960 and then Law in 1961. *University of Melbourne Calendar*, 1959, p. 602. *University of Melbourne Calendar*, 1961, p. 618, *University of Melbourne Calendar*, 1962, pp. 659–60.
15 David Dexter, quoted in Susan Davies, *The Martin Committee and the Binary Policy of Higher Education in Australia* (Melbourne: Ashwood House, 1989), p. 25.
16 Minutes, AVCC–AUC Meeting, 4 February 1960; Davison and Murphy, *Monash Unlimited*, 37–8.
17 Minutes, AVCC, 3 February 1960.
18 Minutes, AVCC–AUC Meeting, 4 February 1960; this was an advance on the size advocated by the AVCC in its 1952 *Crisis* booklet, the increased size recognising the growth that had taken place over the intervening decade, refer to ch. 4.
19 Minutes, AVCC–AUC Meeting, 4 February 1960; little from his discussions with the AVCC made it into the first AUC report published in October 1960, allocating funding until 1963.
20 RB Madgwick, 'Australian Vice-Chancellors' Committee, Item 1', AVCC, June–July 1960; AVCC, 5 February, 30 June, 1 July 1960.
21 Minutes, AVCC–AUC Meeting, 4 February 1960.
22 Minutes, AVCC, 30 June, 1 July 1960.
23 Minutes, AVCC, 8 September, 15 December 1960; 15 February, 20 April, 21 June, 16 August 1961.
24 Minutes, AVCC, 30 June, 1 July 1960.
25 *Report of the Australian Universities Commission on Australian Universities, 1958–1963* (Canberra: AJ Arthur, 1960).
26 Minutes, AVCC–FCUSAA Meeting, 5 December 1963; 'The Second Conference of Australian Universities', *Vestes* 7, no. 2 (1964), p. 136.
27 Ted Wheelright, *Vestes* 2, no. 1 (1959): pp. 7–12.
28 FCUSAA Constitution (adopted 1963), printed in *Vestes* 7, no. 2 (1964).
29 WHC Eddy, *Orr* (Brisbane: Jacaranda Press, 1961); Cassandra Jane Pybus, *Gross Moral Turpitude: The Orr Case Reconsidered* (Port Melbourne: William Heinemann, 1993); Richard Davis, 'The Battle for Collegiality in Tasmania: The 1955 Royal Commission and the Orr Aftermath', in John Biggs and Richard Davis (eds), *The Subversion of Australian Universities* (Wollongong: Fund for Intellectual Dissent, 2002); Peter McPhee, *'Pansy': A Life of Roy Douglas Wright*

(Carlton: Melbourne University Press, 1999), pp. 115–129; Brian Fitzpatrick, 'An Injustice Has Been Done', *Meanjin* 20, no. 1 (1961), pp. 107–11; various articles, *Vestes*, vols 1–3, 1958–1960; 'FCUSAA Committee of Inquiry into the Orr Case', *Vestes* 4, no. 1 (1961), pp. 70–88.

30 O'Farrell, *UNSW*, pp. 57–8, 70–72; 'Political Tests for University Appointments: The Russel Ward Case', *Vestes* 4, no. 1 (1961), pp. 51–68.

31 RM Hartwell, letter to *The Times* (London), 13 December 1960, published in *Vestes* 4, no. 1 (1961), pp. 65–66; Hannah Forsyth, 'The Russel Ward Case: Academic Freedom in Australia During the Cold War', *History Australia* 11, no. 3 (2014), pp. 31–52.

32 JP Baxter, 'The Role of the Vice-Chancellor in the University of New South Wales', *The Australian University* 6, no. 1 (1968), pp. 4–13.

33 Bob Bessant, '"A Climate of Fear": From Collegiality to Corporatisation', in Biggs and Davis (eds), *The Subversion of Australian Universities*, pp. 55–56.

34 JA Passmore, SW Cohen, Ernest Roe and LN Short, *Teaching Methods in Australian Universities: Report Based on a Survey Conducted by a Committee on Research into Teaching Methods* (Canberra: Australian Vice-Chancellors' Committee, 1963).

35 See, for instance, correspondence between Menzies and FCUSAA, printed in *Vestes* 1, nos 1–3.

36 Minutes, AVCC–FCUSAA Meeting, 13 February 1962; Minutes, AVCC, 18 April 1962; 19 July, 4–5 December 1963; RM Eggleston, *Report of the Inquiry into Academic Salaries* (Canberra: AJ Arthur, 1964).

37 Commonwealth of Australia, *Report of the Inquiry into Academic Salaries* (Canberra: Commonwealth Government Printer, 1964).

38 'Presidential Letter to Members', *Vestes* 7, no. 1 (1964), pp. 72–74.

39 AP Gallagher, 'One in All In: FAUSA and the Origins of the Academic Salaries Tribunal', *Vestes* 25, no. 2 (1982), pp. 35–41.

40 PH Partridge, 'The University System', *Critical Studies in Education* 4, no. 1 (1960), pp. 49–71.

41 RG Menzies, 'Message from the Prime Minister', *The Australian University* 1, no. 1 (1963), p. 5.

42 SL Prescott, '*The Australian University* an Introduction', *The Australian University* 1, no. 1 (1963).

43 Professorial Board, University of Sydney, 'Academic Administrative Structure', *The Australian University* 1, no. 2 (1963).

44 CE Moorhouse and Barbara Falk, 'The University Teaching Project of the University of Melbourne', *The Australian University* 1, no. 3 (1963), pp. 294–307; P Herbst, 'Honours Courses in Australian Universities', *The Australian University* 2, no. 1 (1964), pp. 42–51; 'Adult Education Programmes for Post-graduate Groups', *The Australian University* 2, no. 2 (1964), pp. 143–51; JP Powell, 'Tutorial Teaching and the University Ideal', *The Australian University* 4, no. 1 (1966), pp. 19–36.

45 Harrison Bryan, 'Australian University Library – A Measure of Success', *The Australian University* 2, no. 1 (1964); RL Cope, 'The Rise of the Library of Congress: Lessons for Australia?', *The Australian University* 2, no. 2 (1964);

DH Borchardt, 'Some Administrative and Professional Issues in Australian University Libraries', *The Australian University* 7, no. 3 (1969); Harrison Bryan, 'Rationalisation of Australian Library Holdings', *The Australian University* 9, no. 3 (1971); KA Lodewycks, 'The Departmental Book Collection in Relation to Library Provision in Institutes of Tertiary Education', *The Australian University* 13, no. 1 (1975).

46   JJ Auchmuty, 'The Idea of the University in its Australian Setting – A Historical Survey', *The Australian University* 1, no. 2 (1963), pp. 146–70; David S Macmillan, 'The University of Sydney –The Pattern and the Public Reaction, 1850–1870', *The Australian University* 1, no. 1 (1963), pp. 27–59; Eric Ashby, 'The Diversity of Universities in the Commonwealth', *The Australian University* 2, no. 1 (1964), pp. 1–16; KJ Cable, 'The University of Sydney and its Affiliated Colleges, 1850–1880', *The Australian University* 2, no. 3 (1964), pp. 183–214; JP Powell, 'The Idea of a Liberal Education', *The Australian University* 3, no. 1 (1965), pp. 1–18; S Encel, 'Science, Education and the Economy', *The Australian University* 3, no. 1 (1965), pp. 54–73; AL Moore, 'The History, Machinery and Scope of Direct Grants by the Commonwealth Government to Australian Universities, 1935–1964', *The Australian University* 3, no. 3 (1965), pp. 225–34; 'Editorial – A New University in New South Wales', *The Australian University* 1, 3 (1963), pp. 235–37; JP Baxter, 'A Short History of the University of New South Wales to 1964', *The Australian University* 3, no. 1 (1965), pp. 74–114; JJ Auchmuty, 'Jubilee Account of the Australian Vice-Chancellors' Committee', *The Australian University* 8, no. 3 (1970), pp. 238–76.

47   *Report of the Murray Committee on Australian Universities, September 1957* (Canberra: AJ Arthur, Commonwealth Government Printer, 1957), pp. 32–41, 121.

48   Merrelyn Butterfield, and L Kane, 'A New Look at the Part-time Student: Academic Performance', *The Australian University* 7, no. 3 (1969), pp. 226–49.

49   AP Rowe, *If the Gown Fits* (Carlton, Vic.: Melbourne University Press, 1960).

50   Summary of work in SB Hammond, 'The Students and the University', *Critical Studies in Education* 4, no. 1 (1960), pp. 95–124, 96–98; Naomi Caiden, 'Student Failure in Australian Universities: A Bibliographical Review', *Vestes* 7, no. 1 (1963), pp. 48–56.

51   Minutes, AVCC, 3–5 February 1960.

52   AVCC, *Conference on University Education, 1960*, revised edn (Carlton, Vic.: AVCC, 1961).

53   Minutes, AVCC, 20 April 1961, 15 November 1961, 14 February 1962.

54   FJ Schonell, 'Student Adaptation and its Bearing on Student Achievement', *The Australian University* 1, no. 1 (1962), pp. 60–88. This explored ways in which students from a wide range of backgrounds could be assisted to 'adapt' to university. Placing the onus on student 'adaptation' rather than on universities to become more inclusive was typical of this time, and Schonell stated that some students lacked the intellectual ability to meet university standards, or chose courses to which they were not suited.

55   AG Mitchell and SW Cohen, *The Australian University Student: Admission, Selection and Progress* (Canberra: AVCC, 1968).

56 Sir Robert Menzies, 'Message from the Prime Minister', *The Australian University* 1, no. 1 (1963), p. 5.
57 *Year Book of the Commonwealth of Australia*, 1963, p. 745.
58 Schonell, 'Student Adaptation and its Bearing on Student Achievement', pp. 60–88.
59 Susan Davies, *The Martin Committee and the Binary Policy of Higher Education in Australia* (Melbourne: Ashwood House, 1989), p. 28; *Tertiary Education in Australia: Report of the Committee on the Future of Tertiary Education in Australia to the Australian Universities Commission, Volume 1, August 1964* (Canberra: Australian Government Printer, 1964), p. iii.
60 *Tertiary Education in Australia, Report*, vol. 1, terms of reference.
61 Davies, *The Martin Committee*, p. 37.
62 Davies, *The Martin Committee*, p. 51.
63 LN Short, 'Universities and Colleges of Advanced Education: Defining the Difference', *The Australian University* 11, no. 1 (1973), pp. 3–25.
64 John Polesel and Richard Teese, *The 'Colleges': Growth and Diversity in the Non-University Tertiary Studies Sector (1965–1974)* (University of Melbourne: Educational Outcomes Research Unit, 1998).
65 Press Statement, 'Grants for Research Projects', 17 October 1965.
66 JJ Auchmuty, *Australian Vice-Chancellors' Committee: Chairman's Report on the Years 1967–1970* (Surry Hills, NSW: The Wentworth Press, 1971), pp. 22–24.
67 *Third Report of the Australian Universities Commission: Australian Universities 1964–1969* (Canberra: AJ Arthur, 1966), p. 38.
68 *Commonwealth Advisory Committee on Advanced Education, First Report: Colleges of Advanced Education, 1967–1969* (Canberra: Commonwealth of Australia, 1966).
69 Fred Schonell, *The University in Contemporary Society: Tenth Commonwealth Universities Congress, Sydney, 17–23 August 1968* (Sydney: Association of Commonwealth Universities, 1968).
70 RG Menzies, speech to House of Representatives, 24 March 1965, *Hansard*, ID: hansard80/hansardr80/1965-03-24/0094.
71 Short, 'Universities and Colleges of Advanced Education', p. 25.
72 DS Anderson, 'Access to Higher Education: The Link between Admissions and Social Class', *Critical Studies in Education* 25, no. 1 (1983), pp. 91–111.
73 AEB Phillips, 'Colleges of Advanced Education: In Search of Identity', *The Australian University* 8, no. 2 (1970), pp. 126–51; Eric E Robinson, *The New Polytechnics* (Harmondsworth: Penguin, 1968).
74 Short, 'Universities and Colleges of Advanced Education', p. 23.
75 P Herbst, 'Honours Courses in Australian Universities', *The Australian University* 2, no. 1 (1964), pp. 42–51.
76 These institutions are covered in greater detail in chapter 6. Bruce Mansfield and Mark Hutchinson, *Liberality of Opportunity: A History of Macquarie University 1964–89* (Sydney: Macquarie University in association with Hale & Iremonger, c1992); William J Breen (ed.), *Building La Trobe University: Reflections on the First 25 Years 1964–1989* (Melbourne: La Trobe University Press, 1989); David Hilliard, *Flinders University: The First 25 Years, 1966–1991* (Adelaide: Flinders University of South Australia, 1991); Noel Quirke, *Preparing for the Future: A History of Griffith University 1971–1996* (Nathan, Qld: Boolarong Press for

Griffith University, 1996); *Murdoch Voices: The First 40 Years at Murdoch University* (Perth: Murdoch University, 2015).
77 AVCC, 15 February 1966.
78 David S Macmillan, *Australian Universities: A Descriptive Sketch* (Sydney: Sydney University Press, 1968).
79 JJ Auchmuty, *Australian Vice-Chancellors' Committee: Chairman's Report on the Years 1967–1970*, p. 70.
80 Auchmuty, *Australian Vice-Chancellors' Committee: Chairman's Report on the Years 1967–1970*, p. 70.
81 Auchmuty, *Australian Vice-Chancellors' Committee: Chairman's Report on the Years 1967–1970*, p. 70.
82 JN Darroch, RA Layton and WH Maze, *Report by the Steering Committee to the Australian Vice-Chancellors' Committee on Greater Utilisation of University Facilities* (Canberra: AVCC, 1968); D Cochrane, *Report to Australian Vice-Chancellors' Committee on Year-Round Teaching* (Canberra: AVCC, 1970).
83 $23,000 grants to (i) JA Powell (UPNG), 'A Study of Small Group Teaching Methods', (ii) AE Wood (UNSW), 'Explorations in Small Group Learning', (iii) JR Hanscomb (UNSW), 'Use of Audio-Visual Methods in Physics', (iv) K Burns (Macquarie), 'Research, Development and Evaluation of Audio-Tutorial Teaching Methods of Introductory Mapping and Structural Geology', (v) WA Simpkins (UNE), 'The Role of Discussion Groups in University Teaching', (vi) JW Nevile (UNSW), 'Development of New Teaching Strategies in Economics'.
84 'Items of Interest from The Australian Vice-Chancellors Committee', *The Australian University* 9, no. 1 (1971), pp. 58–63.
85 FS Hambly, 'Australian Vice-Chancellors' Committee', *Journal of Tertiary Education Administration* 1, no. 1 (1979), pp. 64–71.
86 HG Brennan, 'Fee Abolition: An Appraisal', *The Australian University* 9, no. 2 (1971), pp. 81–149; Jenny Hocking, *Gough Whitlam, His Time*, vol. 2 (Carlton, Vic.: The Miegunyah Press, 2012).

CHAPTER 8 - FREE AND ACCOUNTABLE
1 Prime Minister to the Premier of Queensland, 27 March 1973, Noonan Papers.
2 On state–federal interactions see, for instance, Hugh Philp, 'The Piper and the Tune – from Murray to the Fourth A.U.C. Report', *The Australian University* 8, no. 1 (1970), pp. 3–33.
3 Alan Barcan, *Radical Students: The Old Left at Sydney University* (Carlton, Vic.: Melbourne University Press, 2002).
4 DS Anderson, 'The Prospect of Student Power in Australia', *The Australian University* 6, no. 3 (1968), pp. 207–21; Ann Curthoys, *Freedom Ride: A Freedom Rider Remembers* (Sydney: Allen & Unwin, 2002).
5 Tess Lee Ack, 'Student Politics' in Susan Blackburn (ed.), *Breaking Out: Memories of Melbourne in the 1970s* (Willoughby, NSW: Hale & Iremonger, 2015), p. 61; John Murphy, *A Harvest of Fear: A History of Australia's Vietnam War* (Sydney: Allen & Unwin, 1993); CA Rootes, 'The Development of Radical Student Movements and Their Sequelae', *Australian Journal of Politics and History* 34, no. 2 (1988), pp. 173–85; Jon Piccini, 'Transnational Protest, Australia and the

1960s', Stefan Berger and Holger Nehring (eds), *Palgrave Studies in the History of Social Movements* (London: Palgrave Macmillan, 2016); Kate Murphy, '"In the Backblocks of Capitalism": Australian Student Activism in the Global 1960s', *Australian Historical Studies* 46, no. 2 (2015), pp. 252–68; Kate Murphy, 'Student Activism at the University of New England in Australia's "Long 1960s"', *Journal of Australian Studies* 43, no. 2 (2019), pp. 174–87.
6 Nigel Young, *An Infantile Disorder? The Crisis and Decline of the New Left* (London: Routledge, 1977).
7 C Michael Otten, *University Authority and the Student: The Berkeley Experience* (Berkeley: University of California Press, 1970); reported in Australia by Bruce Bolt, Professor of Seismology at Berkeley who visited Sydney as Professor of Applied Mathematics, Bruce A Bolt, 'The FSM Affair at Berkeley', *Vestes* 8, no. 3 (1965), pp. 155–63.
8 Richard Walsh, 'Australian Protest: Odious International Comparisons', *Vestes* 11, no. 2 (1968), pp 126–30.
9 For instance, ANU Vice-Chancellor Sir John Crawford's 1969 address on universities' public accountability made no mention of internal accountability, JG Crawford, *The University and Government: The Robert Garran Memorial Oration, 24 November 1969* (Canberra: Royal Institute of Public Administration, 1969); cf. JG Crawford, 'The Accountability of Universities', in *Opportunity in Education* (Carlton, Vic.: The Australian College of Education, 1968); Murphy, '"In the Backblocks of Capitalism"', p. 252.
10 Clark Kerr, *The Uses of the University* (Cambridge, MA: Harvard University Press, 1963); JAL Matheson, 'Australian Multiversities?', *The Australian University* 3, no. 3 (1965), pp. 204–24; Graham Little, 'Students' Conceptions of the University', *The Australian University* 7, no. 1 (1969), pp. 22–36.
11 Harrison Bryan, 'The Fisher "Sit-Ins" of April 1967', *Vestes* 11, no. 2 (1968), pp. 153–59.
12 For instance, Zelman Cowen, 'Some Thoughts on the Australian Universities', *The Australian University* 9, no. 3 (1971), pp. 159–74.
13 HJ Cowan, 'University Autonomy', *Vestes* 12, no. 2 (1969), p. 101.
14 Anonymous, 'Letter to the editor', *Vestes* 12, no. 2 (1969), p. 150.
15 JAL Matheson, 'Authority and Responsibility: Who Should Run the Universities?', *Vestes* 14, no. 2 (1971), pp. 110–13; cf. DR Ellis, 'Participation or Tokenism', *Vestes* 14, no. 1, (1971), pp. 25–28.
16 WF Connell, Geoffrey Sherington, BH Fletcher, Clifford Turney and Ursula Bygott, *Australia's First: A History of the University of Sydney, Vol. 2, 1940–1990* (Sydney: Hale & Iremonger, 1995), pp. 360–61.
17 Hannah Forsyth, 'Expanding Higher Education: Institutional Responses in Australia from the Post-War Era to the 1970s', *Paedagogica Historica* 51, no. 3 (2015), pp. 365–80, 376.
18 *Up the Right Channels* (St Lucia, Qld: University of Queensland, 1970), p. 119, quoted in Stuart Macintyre, 'Looking up the Right Channels', *Farrago* 48, no. 22, (1970), pp. 12–13.
19 Pam Stavropoulos, *Short Circuit: The Melbourne University Assembly, 1974–1989* (Parkville, Vic.: The Assembly, 1989).

20 EH Medlin, 'A Case for an Association of Australian Universities', *Vestes* 19, no. 1 (1976).
21 WM O'Neil, 'Government Support for University Research in Australia, Canada, the United Kingdom and the United States of America', *Vestes* 13, no. 1 (1970), p. 11.
22 Hannah Forsyth, 'Post-War Political Economics and the Growth of Australian University Research, c.1945–1965', *History of Education Review* 46, no. 1 (2017), pp. 27–28; O'Neil, 'Government Support for University Research in Australia, Canada, the United Kingdom and the United States of America': p. 19.
23 AE Binnie, *From Atomic Energy to Nuclear Science: A History of the Australian Atomic Energy Commission* (Sydney: Macquarie University, 2003).
24 B O'Connor, A Chivas, D Mather, J Studdert and A Binnie, *AINSE – An Institute for Research and Training Excellence in Nuclear Science: The First 50 years* (NSW: AINSE, 2008).
25 *Medical Research Endowment Act* (Cth) 1937.
26 *Year Book of the Commonwealth of Australia*, 1965, p. 667.
27 Ragbir Bhathal and Graeme White, *Under the Southern Cross: A Brief History of Astronomy in Australia* (Kenthurst: Kangaroo Press, 1991).
28 Raymond Haynes, *Explorers of the Southern Sky: A History of Australian Astronomy* (Cambridge University Press, 1996), pp. 152–64.
29 Haynes, *Explorers of the Southern Sky*, p. 158.
30 AVCC, *AAUCS Second Report, 1970–72* (Canberra: AVCC, 1972); FS Hambly, 'Australian Vice-Chancellors' Committee', *Journal of Tertiary Education Administration* 1, no. 1 (1979), pp. 64–71.
31 AVCC, *AAUCS Eight Report 1977–78* (Canberra: AVCC, 1978).
32 AVCC, *Survey of Academic Links Between Australian and Overseas Institutions*, Occasional Papers, no. 3 (Canberra: AVCC, 1980).
33 Inter-University Research Committee, *University Research 1982* (Canberra: AVCC, 1982), p. 6.
34 Simon Marginson and Mark Considine, *The Enterprise University: Power, Governance and Reinvention in Australia* (Cambridge: Cambridge University Press, 2000), p. 198.
35 Michael Beloff, *The Plateglass Universities* (London: Secker & Warburg, 1968); John A Salmond, 'The Academic Structure', in William J Breen (ed.), *Building La Trobe University: Reflections on the First 25 Years 1964–1989* (Melbourne: La Trobe University Press, 1989).
36 Marginson and Considine, *The Enterprise University*, p. 144.
37 The University of Queensland Vice-Chancellor, Sir Fred Schonell, Council Minutes 11/82–12/82, 2/84, GU archives. Quoted in Terry Hogan, *Coming of Age* (Carlton, Vic.: Melbourne University Publishing, 2016).
38 Quoted in Noel Quirke, *Preparing for the Future: A History of Griffith University 1971–1996* (Nathan, Qld: Boolarong Press for Griffith University, 1996), p. 17.
39 Marginson and Considine, *The Enterprise University*, p. 199.
40 Simon Marginson, *Education and Public Policy in Australia* (Cambridge: Cambridge University Press, 1993), p. 183.
41 Peter Karmel to AVCC Chair, 4 September 1973.

42 Minutes, Joint meeting Universities Commission and AVCC: 'Meeting to Discuss Abolition of Fees in Tertiary Education and New Student Assistance Programme', 22 May 1973, AVCC 21–5–2.
43 Peter Karmel to David Derham, 9 November 1973, AVCC 21–5–2.
44 David Derham to Peter Karmel, 19 November 1973, AVCC 21–5–2.
45 AVCC 1/74, 19 February 1974, 5–1–10.
46 AVCC, Assistance for Tertiary and Post-Secondary study 1974, AVCC 21–5–2.
47 *Report of the Murray Committee on Australian Universities, September 1957*, pp. 64–65; DS Anderson, 'The Prospect of Student Power in Australia', *The Australian University* 6, no. 3 (1968), pp. 207–21, 212–13; Gerald Burke, 'The Politics of Bonded Service: The Case of Graduate Secondary Teachers in Victoria, Australia', *Higher Education* 5 (1976), pp. 35–47.
48 EG Whitlam to Premier, Qld, 27 March 1973, Noonan Papers.
49 Merrelyn Butterfield, 'Towards Equality through Inequality in Educational Opportunities at the Tertiary Level', *The Australian University* 8, no. 2 (1970), pp. 169–92.
50 'The Social Composition of Tertiary Students in Australia and the Effect of the Abolition of Fees: Review of Progress and Prospects for Next Stage, 30 October 1975', 'Abolition of Fees, 1974–1979', UA collection.
51 DS Anderson, 'Access to Higher Education: The Link between Admissions and Social Class', *Critical Studies in Education* 25, no. 1 (1983), pp. 91–111.
52 Carmen Moran, *Student Opinions on the Influence of Tuition Fee Abolition Upon Their Choice of Course* (Kensington, NSW: Tertiary Education Research Centre, UNSW, 1975); Clift Barnard and Denis Kelly, *Socio-Economic Background and Enrolment Characteristics of Commencing Students in 1974* (Kensington, NSW: Tertiary Education Research Centre, 1976); Carmen Moran and Denis Kelly, *The Effect of the Abolition of Fees on Commencing Students in 1974* (Kensington, NSW: Tertiary Education Research Centre, UNSW, 1976); Clift Barnard, *Profile of a Student: College and University Students* (Kensington, NSW: Tertiary Education Research Centre, 1976); DS Anderson, R Boven, PJ Fensham and JP Powell, *Students in Australian Higher Education: A Study of Their Social Composition since the Abolition of Fees* (Canberra: AGPS, 1980).
53 R Taft, Patricia Strong and PJ Fensham, 'National Background and Choice of Tertiary Education in Victoria', *International Migration* 9, nos 1–2 (1971), pp. 36–54.
54 Christina Twomey and Jodie Boyd, 'Class, Social Equity and Higher Education in Postwar Australia', *Australian Historical Studies* 47, no. 1 (2016), pp. 8–24.
55 DS Anderson and AE Vervoorn, *Access to Privilege: Patterns of Participation in Australian Post-Secondary Education* (Canberra: Australian National University Press, 1983).
56 Lynn Meek and Leo Goedegebuure, *Higher Education: A Report* (Armidale: Department of Administrative and Higher Education Studies, UNE, 1989), p. 44.
57 Press Release, Prime Minister, 30 May 1975, AVCC 5–11–1.
58 BR Williams, *A Tertiary Education Commission?* (AVCC, 27 February 1975).
59 AVCC 1974, 5–1–10.
60 AVCC 1974, 5–1–10.

61 BR Williams, *A Tertiary Education Commission?*, p. 1.
62 AVCC, Notes on discussion between Government panel and AVCC representatives held on 8 July 1975, p. 3, AVCC 5–11–1.
63 AVCC, Notes on discussion between Government Panel and AVCC representatives held on 8 July 1975, p. 5.
64 Roger Page to Frank Hambly, 24 March 1975, AVCC 5–11–1.
65 *Commonwealth Tertiary Education Commission Act* (Cth) 1977.
66 Peter Karmel, *Reflections on a Revolution*, AVCC Papers, no. 1 (Canberra: AVCC, 1989).
67 Peter Karmel, interviewed by Jamie Button, November 1987, Karmel Papers, Box 8, folder 48, quoted in: Stuart Macintyre, André Brett and Gwilym Croucher, *No End of a Lesson: Australia's Unified National System of Higher Education* (Carlton, Vic.: University of Melbourne Publishing, 2017), p. 26.
68 Martin Trow, 'The Implications of Low Growth Rates for Higher Education', *Higher Education* 5 (1976), pp. 377–96; Clark Kerr, 'Higher Education: Paradise Lost?', *Higher Education* 7 (1978), pp. 261–78.
69 Alex M Clarke and L Michael Birt, 'Some Current Issues in the Administration of Australian Universities', *Higher Education* 8 (1979), pp. 493–94.
70 Grant Harman, 'Introduction', in GS Harman, AH Miller, DJ Bennett and BI Anderson (eds), *Academia Becalmed: Australian Tertiary Education in the Aftermath of Expansion* (Canberra: Australian National University Press, 2000).
71 Grant Harman, 'Academic Staff and Academic Drift in Australian Colleges of Advanced Education', *Higher Education* 6 (1977), pp. 313–35.
72 Richard Campbell, 'Flexibility in a Steady State University', *Vestes* 20, no. 3 (1977), p. 9; Terry Hore, 'Implications for Academic Staff of the "Steady State"', *Vestes* 20, no. 3 (1977), p. 21.
73 DM Myers, *University Staffing in a Static Situation: An Inquiry for the Australian Vice-Chancellors' Committee*, AVCC Occasional Papers, no. 1 (Canberra: La Trobe University for AVCC, 1979).
74 *Post-Secondary Education in Western Australia: Report of the Committee on Post-Secondary Education, appointed by the Minister for Education in Western Australia under the Chairmanship of Professor P.H. Partridge* (Perth: Government Printer, 1976); *Report of the Committee of Inquiry into Post-Secondary Education* (Melbourne: Government Printer, 1978); *Post-Secondary Education in South Australia* (Adelaide: Government Printer, 1979); and *Report of the Ministerial Working Party on Tertiary Education, Tasmania* (Hobart: University of Tasmania Printer, 1978).
75 *Education, Training and Employment: Report of the Committee of Inquiry into Education and Training*, vol. 1 (Canberra: AGPS, 1979), p. 34
76 Alex M Clarke and Lynn M Edwards, 'The Williams Committee of Inquiry into Education and Training in Australia: Recommendations for Universities', *Higher Education* 9, no. 5 (1980), pp. 495–528.
77 *Education, Training and Employment*, vol. 1, pp. iii–iv; J Maxwell Collins, 'Review Article: The Williams Report', *Higher Education* 9, no. 5 (1980), pp. 633–37.
78 Peter Karmel, 'Tertiary Education in a Steady State', in GS Harman, AH Miller, DJ Bennett and BI Anderson (eds), *Academia Becalmed: Australian Tertiary*

Education in the Aftermath of Expansion (Canberra: Australian National University Press, 1980), pp. 38–39.
79   PH Partridge, 'Accountability and Evaluation', in *Australian Universities to the Year 2000: Conference of University Governing Bodies*, AVCC Occasional Papers, no. 2, (Canberra, ANU, 1979).
80   R Selby-Smith, 'The Amalgamation and Closure of Tertiary Institutions', in GS Harman, AH Miller, DJ Bennett and BI Anderson (eds), *Academia Becalmed: Australian Tertiary Education in the Aftermath of Expansion* (Canberra: Australian National University Press, 1980).
81   Jillian Maling, 'The Impact of an Amalgamation on the Career Prospects of Women Staff in a Newly Amalgamated College of Advanced Education', in Grant Harman and V Lynn Meek (eds), *Institutional Amalgamations in Higher Education: Process and Outcomes in Five Countries* (Armidale: Department of Administrative and Higher Education Studies, University of New England, 1988).
82   Alex M Clarke and L Michael Birt, 'Australian Universities in the Post-Williams Period: The Impact of Public Policy on the Small Universities', *Higher Education* 10 (1981), pp. 181–97.
83   KF Collis, P Hughes and P Byers, 'Institutional Rationalization in Tasmania in the Late 1970s Early 1980s: College and University', in Harman and Meek (eds), *Institutional Amalgamations in Higher Education*.
84   *Ministerial Statement: Review of Commonwealth Functions* (Canberra: Australian Government Publishing Service, 1981), pp. 21–25; Grant Harman, 'The "Razor Gang" Decisions, the Guidelines to the Commissions and Commonwealth Education Policy', *Vestes* 24, no. 1 (1981), pp. 28–40.
85   KR McKinnon, 'United We Stand … the Process of Amalgamation at Wollongong University', in Harman and Meek (eds), *Institutional Amalgamations in Higher Education*.
86   Paul Lamb, 'The Merger That Never Was', and Bernard Rechter and John Scott, 'The Proposed Merger between La Trobe University and Lincoln Institute of Health Sciences', in Harman and Meek (eds), *Institutional Amalgamations in Higher Education*; DT Gamage, 'La Trobe and Lincoln Merger: The Process and Outcome', *Journal of Educational Administration* 30, no. 4 (1992).
87   LM Koder and R McLintock, 'The Sydney College of Advanced Education Amalgamation', in Harman and Meek (eds), *Institutional Amalgamations in Higher Education*.
88   AVCC, *Junior Teaching Staff: Conditions of Employment*, Canberra, 9 February 1979; AVCC, *Promotion of Academic Staff*, Canberra, November 1981; AVCC, *Academic Tenure*, Canberra, November 1981; AVCC, *Limited Term Appointments: Academic Staff*, Canberra, November 1981; AVCC, *Junior Teaching Staff: Conditions of Employment*, Canberra, November 1981; AVCC, *Probationary Period of Employment*, Canberra, November 1981; AVCC, *Appointment of Staff: Fractional Appointments*, Canberra, November 1981.
89   AVCC, *Aboriginal Education*, Canberra, 24 July 1981.
90   AVCC, *Maternity Leave*, Canberra, October 1979; AVCC, *Long Service Leave: Academic and General Staff*, Canberra, June 1981.
91   AVCC, *University Unions: Subsidies*, Canberra, April 1981.

92 AVCC, *Aboriginal Education*, Canberra, July 1981; AVCC, *Examination for PhD Degree*, Braddon, ACT, March 1980; AVCC, *Universities' Post-Graduate Scholarships*, Canberra, June 1981.
93 Australian Research Grants Committee, Australian Science and Technology Council, AVCC, *Australian Research Grants Scheme: Research Funding Survey*, Adelaide, 1984.

CHAPTER 7 - A UNIFIED SYSTEM

1 John Dawkins, Francis Ormond Lecture, RMIT, 7 October 1987, University of Melbourne Registry 18–6–27.
2 Stuart Macintyre, André Brett and Gwilym Croucher, *No End of a Lesson: Australia's Unified National System of Higher Education* (Carlton, Vic.: University of Melbourne Publishing, 2017), pp. 36–80.
3 Jane Southward, '20,000 To Miss Places at Unis', *Sun Herald*, 15 November 1987; Anne Susskind, 'More Places, But Tighter Rein on Funds', *Sydney Morning Herald*, 15 September 1987; AVCC Media Release, 'AVCC Reacts to Budget', 16 September 1987.
4 *Year Books of the Commonwealth of Australia*, various years.
5 Don Anderson, 'Access to University Education in Australia 1852–1990: Changes in the Undergraduate Social Mix', *Australian Universities Review* 33, nos. 1 & 2 (1990), p. 41.
6 AVCC 1–30–15; John Anwyl, *Adjusting to the Post-Binary Era*, edited address to the Annual General Meeting of the Federated Council of Academics, 27–28 August 1987; Gregor Ramsay, 'Future Directions for Tertiary Education: the Next Decade', in JE Anwyl and GS Harman (eds), *Setting the Agenda for Australian Tertiary Education: Planning Mechanisms, Policy Issues and Government Guidelines for the 1985–87 Triennium: Papers from a National Conference held at the University of Melbourne, 13–14 August 1984* (Parkville: Centre for the Study of Higher Education, University of Melbourne, 1984); V Lynn Meek and Grant Harman (eds), *The Binary Experiment for Higher Education: An Australian Perspective* (Armidale: Department of Administrative, Higher and Adult Education Studies, University of New England, 1993).
7 AVCC 1–30–15.
8 Michael White, *WAIT to Curtin: A History of the Western Australian Institute of Technology* (Perth: Paradigm Books, 1996), pp. 281–88; *An Act to Amend the Western Australian Institute of Technology Act 1966: Change of Name from WAIT to The Curtin University of Technology* (WA) 1986.
9 Commonwealth Tertiary Education Commission *Advanced Education Statistics*, 1986.
10 'Private Uni Academics Jeer but Libs Cheer', *Herald*, 27 November 1987; White, *WAIT to Curtin*, p. 289.
11 AVCC 1–30–15.
12 AVCC, 23 July 1987, AVCC 11–5–130; Brian Wilson to John Dawkins, 22 September 1987, Noonan papers; Helen Trinca, 'Dawkins Gives a Lesson to the Professors', *The Australian*, 18 September 1987.

13 JS Dawkins, *The Challenge for Higher Education in Australia* (Canberra: AGPS, 1987).
14 Anne Susskind, 'Business Hails Uni Proposals', *Sydney Morning Herald*, 11 December 1987; 'More Radical Changes to Education on the Way', *Australian Financial Review*, 13 October 1987; 'Unions Are Wary of Education Shake-up', *Australian Financial Review*, 16 October 1987.
15 The Purple Circle comprised: Vice-Chancellor of Curtin University, Don Watts; Vice-Chancellor of UWA, Bob Smith; Monash Vice-Chancellor, Mal Logan; Director of RMIT, Brian Smith; former Director of the Ballarat CAE, Jack Barker; economist at ANU, Helen Hughes; and the chair of the ARGC, Don Aitkin.
16 Vince FitzGerald, 'Minute to Divisional and Branch Heads', 12 October 1987, NAA: A1642, 87/7556.
17 Media Release, John Dawkins, October 1987.
18 AVCC Media Release, 'New Higher Education Advisory Arrangements', 15 October 1987.
19 AVCC, 5/87, 16 November 1987; JS Dawkins, *Higher Education: A Policy Discussion Paper* (Canberra: AGPS, 1987).
20 Dawkins, *Higher Education: A Policy Discussion Paper*, p. iv.
21 JS Dawkins, *Higher Education: A Policy Statement* (Canberra: AGPS, 1988).
22 'Govt. Plan Attacked', *Australian Financial Review*, 19 December 1987; 'Shake-Up: Unis May Lose Status', *Sydney Morning Herald*, 8 December 1987; 'The Deregulation of Higher Education', *Sydney Morning Herald*, 11 December 1987; 'Dawkins' Leap in the Dark', *Sydney Morning Herald*, 15 December 1987; 'Academics Left Out of Reform', *Sydney Morning Herald*, 17 December 1987; 'ACTU Back Tuition Tax on Tertiary Graduates', *Sydney Morning Herald*, 17 December 1987; 'Major Move on Tertiary Education', *Herald Sun*, 10 December 1987; 'Unions Fear Tertiary Proposals', *Herald Sun*, 10 December 1987.
23 Anne Susskind, 'Business Hails Uni Proposals', *Sydney Morning Herald*, 11 December 1987.
24 For instance, Grant Harman and V Lynn Meek (eds), *Australian Higher Education Reconstructed?: Analysis of the Proposals and Assumptions of the Dawkins Green Paper* (Armidale: Department of Administrative and Higher Education Studies, University of New England, 1988).
25 *Review of Efficiency and Effectiveness in Higher Education: Report of the Committee of Enquiry* (Canberra: Commonwealth Tertiary Education Commission, 1986).
26 AVCC 1/88, March 1988.
27 AVCC 5/87, 16 November 1987.
28 Dawkins, *Higher Education: A Policy Statement*, p. 3.
29 AVCC Media Release, 'Excellence and Efficiency: The Vice-Chancellors' Response to the Green Paper', 6 April 1988.
30 ACTU submission, NAA: CP 28, 88/15707; Wayne Burns, 'Halloa – Hallooing in the Hallowed Halls', *Australian Financial Review*, 18 March 1988; BCA submission, March 1988, NAA: A1642, 88/16852; Australian Chamber of Commerce Media Release, 5 May 1988, Noonan papers.

31　Dawkins, *Higher Education: A Policy Statement*, pp. 8, 91. The White Paper proposed growth in Engineering and Science and Technology, as well as Business and Management places.
32　David Penington, 'Nation's Needs Are What Count in Education Reform', *Australian Financial Review*, 8 September 1989.
33　Brian Wilson in AVCC Media Release, 26 July 1988; John Ward, 'Strangulation by Regulation', *The Australian*, 10 August 1988; 'Know Your Product', *Farrago*, no. 68, 1989.
34　'Notes on meeting between Vice-Chancellors and the Minister', 1 September 1988; John Dawkins to John Scott, 2 September 1988; Scott to Dawkins, 2 September 1988; AVCC 5–35–5.
35　Don Aitkin, 'Trends in Funding Arrangements', *Higher Education Quarterly* 42, no. 2 (1988), pp. 144–51; Geoff Maslen, 'A Difficult Birth, a Tougher Future', *The Age*, 21 July 1988; Simon Marginson, *Monash: Remaking the University* (Sydney: Allen & Unwin, 2000), p. 66.
36　Brian Wilson to John Dawkins, 21 September 1988; Dawkins to Robert Smith, chair of NBEET, and to Bob Hawke, 30 September 1988, AVCC 5–35–5; David Penington to Dawkins, 7 October 1988, UMR 11–60–6, Part 9; Glenn Milne, 'Government Plans New Education Review', *Sydney Morning Herald*, 30 September 1988.
37　'Plan for Campus Mergers Criticised', *The Age*, 18 July 1988; 'Education: Merge or Miss Out', *Courier-Mail*, 28 July 1988; 'Some Progress for Dawkins on Tertiary Amalgamations', *Australian Financial Review*, 1 March 1989; 'Education "Empire Building"', *Courier-Mail*, 5 April 1989.
38　National Board of Employment, Education and Training, *Report of the Task Force on Amalgamations in Higher Education* (Canberra: AGPS, 1989), p. 8.
39　States managed this process differently. Governments in South Australia, Victoria and Western Australia left arrangements to the institutions within guidelines, while New South Wales took a more interventionist approach. At first Queensland planned to elevate all its CAEs to university status, but Dawkins rejected this on the ground that proposals must bring educational benefits as well as cost savings; Macintyre, Brett and Croucher, *No End of a Lesson*, pp. 84–88.
40　Terry Hogan, *Coming of Age* (Carlton, Vic.: Melbourne University Publishing, 2016), pp. 61–64.
41　Commonwealth Tertiary Education Commission, *Advanced Education Statistics* 1985, 1986.
42　AVCC 1–30–15 1986; White, *WAIT to Curtin*.
43　Debra Adelaide, Paul Ashton and Annette Salt (eds), *Stories from the Tower: UTS 1988–2013* (Sydney: Xoum, 2013), pp. 22, 93, 189–91.
44　Noeline Kyle, Catherine Manathunga and Joanne Scott, *A Class of its Own: A History of Queensland University of Technology* (Sydney: Hale & Iremonger, 1999), ch. 8.
45　Alison Mackinnon, *A New Kid on the Block: The University of South Australia in the Unified National System* (Carlton, Vic.: Melbourne University Publishing, 2016), pp. 18–49.

46 Brian Carroll, *A Decade of Achievement: Phillip Institute of Technology* (Melbourne: RMIT Press, 1995).
47 Mark Hutchinson, *A University of the People: A History of the University of Western Sydney* (Sydney: Allen & Unwin, 2013).
48 Chris McConville, *Rising in the West: From Western Institute to Victoria University of Technology, 1987–1992* (Melbourne: Western Institute, 1991); Peter Love assisted by Sara Jervis, *Practical Measures: 100 Years at Swinburne* (Melbourne: Swinburne University of Technology, 2007), pp. 108–11.
49 The earlier Canberra University College was not forerunner to the Canberra CAE. It had already merged with ANU when it was established.
50 P Tannock, *The Founding and Establishment of the University of Notre Dame Australia, 1986–2014* (Fremantle, WA: University of Notre Dame Australia, 2014).
51 AVCC, *Foundations for the 'Clever Country': Report for the 1992–94 Triennium* (Canberra: AVCC, 1991), p. 44.
52 O'Brien, *The National Tertiary Education Union*, pp. 1–44.
53 'AVCC Guidelines on the Criteria for a Recognised University', 24 February 1989; AVCC L–01–008; Christopher Dawson, 'Colleges Strike Back', *The Australian*, 22 May 1989; AVCC Media Release, 12 November 1989, AVCC G–4–031.
54 AVCC, 'The Nature of a University', June 1989.
55 Department of Employment, Education and Training, *National Report on Australia's Higher Education Sector* (Canberra: AGPS, 1993), p. 147, table 7.14; David Mahony, 'Counter Images of Australia's Move to an Entrepreneurial Higher Education System: An Analysis', *Higher Education* 28, no. 3 (1994), pp. 301–23.
56 AVCC 3/83 File Number C5501224479–02.
57 Don Smart, 'Education', in Brian W Head and Allan Patience (eds), *From Fraser to Hawke: Australian Public Policy in the 1980s* (Melbourne: Longman Cheshire, 1989), pp. 317–18; Don Smart and Janice Dudley, 'Education Policy', in Christine Jennett and Randal G Stewart (eds), *Hawke and Australian Public Policy: Consensus and Restructuring* (Melbourne: Macmillan, 1990), pp. 213–14.
58 WL Hansen and MS Rhodes, *Student Debt Crisis: Are Students Incurring Excessive Debt* (Madison, WI: Wisconsin Center for Education Research, School of Education, University of Wisconsin-Madison, 1985); FM Edwards, 'Piecemeal Solutions Won't Reduce the Default Rate on Guaranteed Loans', *The Chronicle of Higher Education* 17, no. 44 (1988); R Wilson, 'Student-Aid Analysts Blast Loan Program, Urge Big Overhaul; Observers Doubt that Congress Will Approve Sweeping Changes', *The Chronicle of Higher Education* 27, no. 1 (1988).
59 It included a senior bureaucrat, Meredith Edwards, along with two ANU economists: Bob Gregory, with expertise in labour markets, and Bruce Chapman, who acted as consultant.
60 Glenn Milner, 'Minister Warns on Leaks', *Sydney Morning Herald*, 8 March 1988; Meredith Edwards, *Social Policy, Public Policy: From Problem to Practice* (Sydney: Allen & Unwin, 2001), pp. 116, 127–32; Bruce Chapman, 'Economics and Policy-Making: The Case of the Higher Education Contribution Scheme', *Canberra Bulletin of Public Administration*, no. 90 (1998), pp. 120–24.

61 AVCC, 1988; Sally Heath, 'Graduate Tax is "Wild Speculation"', *Herald*, 19 April 1988. The AVCC's commissioned research was later published as Gerald Burke, 'How Large are the Cuts in Operating Grants Per Student?' *Australian Universities Review* 31, no. 2 (1988), pp 42–43.
62 Higher Education Round Table, Media Release, 18 May 1988, Noonan papers; Roy Morgan Research Poll, 19 May 1988, Noonan papers; Saulwick & Associates Poll, *The Age*, 19 May 1988.
63 Cabinet Submission 5922, 'Establishing a Higher Education Contribution Scheme', 4 August 1988, NAA: A14039, 5922; AVCC Press Release, 5 May 1988; ACDP Press Release, 5 May 1988, TRPB responses to Wran Committee on Higher Education, NAA: A1642, 88/15701; Glenn Milne, 'Dawkins in Attack on Academics over Tax', *Sydney Morning Herald*, 11 May 1988; Brian Wilson to John Dawkins, 24 May 1988, Noonan papers.
64 Dawkins, *Higher Education: A Policy Statement*; Anderson, 'Access to University Education in Australia 1852–1990'.
65 CTEC, *Selected University Statistics*, various years.
66 National Board of Employment, Education and Training, *A Fair Chance for All: Higher Education that's within Everyone's Reach* (Canberra: The Department, 1990).
67 L Martin, 'Framing the Framework: The Origins of A Fair Chance For All', in A Harvey, C Burnheim and M Brett (eds), *Student Equity in Australian Higher Education* (Singapore: Springer, 2016), p. 22.
68 Dawkins, *Higher Education: A Policy Statement*, p. 21.
69 Peter Baldwin to Frank Hambly, 21 January 1991, AVCC F-10–003.
70 Peter Baldwin to Frank Hambly, 21 January 1991, AVCC F-10–003.
71 AVCC 5/89, 13 November 1989.
72 Department of Prime Minister and Cabinet, Access and Equity (A&E) Strategy Evaluation – Request for Submissions, 1991, AVCC F-10–003.201.
73 Martin, 'Framing the Framework', p. 24.
74 National Board of Employment, Education and Training, *A Fair Chance for All*.
75 Martin, 'Framing the Framework', p. 25. The targets were: 'All institutions to develop special entry arrangements for socio-economically disadvantaged groups by 1992'; 'An increase of 50 per cent in Aboriginal enrolments in higher education by 1995'; 'An improvement in the graduation rates of Aboriginal students to a level comparable to the total student population by 1995'; 'To increase the proportion of women in non-traditional courses from their current levels to at least 40 per cent by 1995';'To improve the proportion of women in engineering courses from 7 per cent to 15 per cent by 1995'; 'To increase the numbers of women in post-graduate study, particularly in research, relative to the proportion of female undergraduates in each field by 1995'; 'All institutions with significant proportions of Non-English Speaking Background groups in their catchment area to provide tertiary awareness programs and adequate support programs by 1992'; and 'To double present commencing enrolments of people with disabilities by 1995'.
76 AVCC 5/89, 13 November 1989, F-10–003, p. 1.
77 Frank Hambly to Peter Baldwin, 26 November 1989, AVCC F-10–003; AVCC 4/90, 18 September 1990.

78 For instance, *3 Times Less Likely: A Report on the Access of Country Students to Tertiary Institutions* (Melbourne: Victorian Country Education Project, 1988).
79 *A Fair Go: The Federal Government's Strategy for Rural Education and Training* (Canberra: Department of Employment, Education and Training, 1989).
80 Glenda Korporaal, *AARNet: 20 Years of the Internet in Australia: 1989–2009* (North Ryde, NSW: AARNet, 2009), p. 16.
81 *Sydney Alumni Magazine* (University of Sydney), Winter 2006, p. 12.
82 Doug McCann and Peter Thorne, *The Last of the First. CSIRAC: Australia's First Computer* (Melbourne: Department of Computer Science and Software Engineering, University of Melbourne, 2000).
83 ARPA was renamed DARPA in 1971.
84 AVCC 3/88, 12 July 1988.
85 Korporaal, *AARNet*.
86 Korporaal, *AARNet*, p. 39.
87 AVCC submission to the ARC, September 1989; Korporaal, *AARNet*, p. 36.
88 Korporaal, *AARNet*, p. 41.
89 AVCC 4–5–22.
90 Korporaal, *AARNet*, p. 46.
91 G Croucher and P Woelert, 'Institutional Isomorphism and the Creation of the Unified National System of Higher Education in Australia: An Empirical Analysis', *Higher Education* 71, no. 4 (2016), pp. 439–53; P Woelert and G Croucher, 'The Multiple Dynamics of Isomorphic Change: Australian Law Schools 1987–1996', *Minerva* 56, no. 4 (2018), pp. 479–503.
92 Peter Karmel, 'Funding Universities', in Tony Coady (ed.), *Why Universities Matter: A Conversation about Values, Means and Directions* (St Leonards, NSW: Allen & Unwin, 2000), p. 183.
93 AVCC, *Australian Universities: Partners in Australia's Future: Policy Statement for the 1995–97 Triennium* (Canberra: AVCC, 1994), p. 5.

CHAPTER 8 – INTERNATIONAL UNIVERSITIES

1 OECD, *Benchmarking Higher Education System Performance: Conceptual Framework and Data, Enhancing Higher Education System Performance* (Paris: OECD, 2017); Times Higher Education Rankings; National Science Foundation Comparative Research Performance.
2 Glyn Davis, *The Australian Idea of a University* (Carlton, Vic.: Melbourne University Publishing, 2017).
3 Seamus O'Hanlon, *City Life: The New Urban Australia* (Sydney: NewSouth, 2018), ch. 6.
4 Malcolm I Thomis, *A Place of Light and Learning: The University of Queensland's First Seventy-Five Years* (St Lucia, Qld: University of Queensland Press, 1985), p. 75.
5 Australian Government Department of Education, *Selected Student Statistics*, various years.
6 Sophia Laderman, 'State Higher Education Finance: Financial Year 2016' (Denver: State Higher Education Executive Officers Association), p. 16.

7   Australian Government Department of Education, *Selected Student Statistics*, various years.
8   UIS.Stat, UNESCO Institute for Statistics, 2018.
9   Ian Chubb, 'Foreword', in AVCC, *The Internationalisation of Australian Universities* (Canberra: AVCC, 2001), p. 5.
10 'Business of Education Export Looms as Potential Goldmine', *Canberra Times*, 21 February 1989, p. 11.
11 Stuart Macintyre, André Brett and Gwilym Croucher, *No End of a Lesson: Australia's Unified National System of Higher Education* (Carlton, Vic.: University of Melbourne Publishing, 2017); Lyndon Megarrity, 'Regional Goodwill, Sensibly Priced: Commonwealth Policies Towards Colombo Plan Scholars and Private Overseas Students, 1945–72', *Australian Historical Studies* 38, no. 129 (2008), pp. 88–105; David Lowe, 'Australia's Colombo Plans, Old and New: International Students as Foreign Relations', *International Journal of Policy* 21, no. 4 (2015), pp. 448–62.
12 Dorothy Violet Davis and Bruce Mackintosh (eds), *Making a Difference: Australian International Education* (Sydney: University of New South Wales Press, 2011); Alec Lazenby, Denis Blight and IDP Education Australia, *Thirty Years in International Education and Development: The IDP Story* (Canberra: IDP Education Australia, 1999).
13 *The Internationalisation of Australian Universities*.
14 Davis and Mackintosh (eds), *Making a Difference*, p. 73.
15 AVCC, *Code Of Ethical Practice in the Provision of Education to International Students by Australian Universities* (Canberra: AVCC, 1998). The AVCC released the *Code of Ethical Practice in the Provision of Education to Overseas Students by Australian Higher Education Institutions* in January 1990, and revised it in December 1994. It also released a *Code of Ethical Practice in the Provision of Offshore Education and Educational Services by Australian Higher Education Institutions* in April 1995. In March 1998, the two codes were combined into one document.
16 Minutes, AVCC, B-02-003.
17 AVCC, *Australian Universities, International Universities* (Deakin, ACT: AVCC, 1999); *The Internationalisation of Australian Universities*.
18 Australian Committee of Directors and Principals and AVCC, *Code of Ethical Practice in the Provision of Full-Fee Courses to Overseas Students by Australian Higher Education Institutions* (Braddon, ACT: The Committees, 1989).
19 'Code Calls for Quality', *The Australian*, 12 August 1998.
20 'Education Honeymoon Adds Up to Uni Accord', *The Australian*, 22 December 1997.
21 'Export Boom Forecast Despite Bali Fears', *The Australian*, 13 November 2002.
22 'Britain's Foreign Bonanza', *The Australian*, 2 April 2008.
23 HM Government, *International Education: Global Growth and Prosperity*, July 2013.
24 Australian Government Department of Education, *Selected Student Statistics*, various years; J Arvanitakis, 'Massification and the Large Lecture Theatre: From Panic to Excitement', *Higher Education* 67, no. 6 (2014), pp. 735–45.

25 Glenda Korporaal, *AARNet: 20 Years of the Internet in Australia: 1989–2009* (North Ryde, NSW: AARNet, 2009).
26 AVCC, UN-01-001.
27 Open Universities Australia, 'Media Release: Australia's First Online Higher Education Platform Marks 25 Years of Making Education Accessible to All', 12 September 2018, <www.open.edu.au/about-us/media-centre/news-and-media-releases/2018/09/12/00/20/australias-first-online-higher-education-platform-marks-25-years-of-making-education-accessible-to-all>.
28 Open Universities Australia, 'Media Release', 12 September 2018.
29 Australian Government Department of Education, *Selected Student Statistics*, various years.
30 Annie Talvé, 'Libraries as Places of Invention', *Library Management* 32, no. 8/9 (2011), pp. 493–504; Jurgen Schulte, Belinda Tiffen, Jackie Edwards, Scott Abbott and Edward Luca, 'Shaping the Future of Academic Libraries: Authentic Learning for the Next Generation', *College & Research Libraries* 79, no. 5 (2018), pp. 685–96; M Tripathi and S Kumar, 'Use of Web 2.0 Tools in Academic Libraries: A Reconnaissance of the International Landscape', *The International Information & Library Review* 42, no. 3 (2010), pp. 195–207; Alan Bundy, 'Better, More Accessible, Libraries for All in Australia: Progress and Potential', *Australasian Public Libraries and Information Services* 25, no. 3 (2011), p. 138.
31 WC Jacobsen and R Forste, 'The Wired Generation: Academic and Social Outcomes of Electronic Media Use among University Students', *Cyberpsychology, Behavior, and Social Networking* 14, no. 5 (2011), pp. 275–80; PA Tess, 'The Role of Social Media in Higher Education Classes (Real and Virtual) – A Literature Review', *Computers in Human Behavior* 29, no. 5 (2013), pp. 60–68.
32 DF Onah, J Sinclair and R Boyatt, 'Dropout Rates of Massive Open Online Courses: Behavioural Patterns', in *Proceedings of the 6th International Conference on Education and New Learning Technologies (EDULEARN14), At Barcelona, Spain, July 2014*, doi: 10.13140/RG.2.1.2402.0009; D Clow, 'MOOCs and the Funnel of Participation', in *Proceedings of the Third International Conference on Learning Analytics and Knowledge 2013*, pp. 185–89; B Stewart, 'Massiveness + Openness = New Literacies of Participation', *Journal of Online Learning and Teaching* 9, no. 2 (2013), pp. 228–38.
33 Carleton Coffrin, Linda Corrin, Paula de Barba and Gregor Kennedy, 'Visualizing Patterns of Student Engagement and Performance in MOOCs', in *Proceedings of the Fourth International Conference on Learning Analytics and Knowledge, 24 March 2014*, pp. 83–92.
34 Kim Jackson, 'The Higher Education Contribution Scheme, E-Brief, Parliament of Australia', 12 August 2003, <www.aph.gov.au/About_Parliament/Parliamentary_Departments/Parliamentary_Library/Publications_Archive/archive/hecs>, accessed 3 September 2019.
35 'Let's Make a Budget Deal – AVCC', *The Australian*, 31 July 1996.
36 Minutes, AVCC, 16 September 1996.
37 'Uni Management under Microscope', *The Australian*, 23 August 1996.
38 *Learning for Life: Review of Higher Education Financing and Policy* (West Review) (Canberra: AGPS, 1998).

39 'Uni Fees Scheme "a Bit Rich"', *The Australian*, 14 October 1999; John Niland, 'Kemp's Plan a Bit Too Academic', *The Australian*, 15 October 1999.
40 'Real-Rate Loans Still on Cards – Howard', *The Australian*, 16 October 1999; Minutes, AVCC, 9 November 1999.
41 Bruce Chapman and Chris Ryan, *Higher Education Financing and Student Access* (Deakin, ACT: AVCC, 2003).
42 'Bleak Future for AVCC', *The Australian*, 24 August 2005.
43 QUT left this group in 2018.
44 James Cook University joined in 2007, and Charles Darwin University joined in 2009. Macquire University left in 2008 and Newcastle University left this group in 2014. Western Sydney University joined in 2017.
45 Charles Sturt University joined in 2019.
46 'Peak Body Poised for Change', *The Australian*, 8 February 2006.
47 Minutes, AVCC, 16 March 2006.
48 Minutes, AVCC, 4 September 2006.
49 PhillipsKPA report to AVCC, August 2006.
50 'New Council for Chancellors', *The Australian*, 4 April 2007.
51 'Funding Shakeout Now Inevitable', *The Australian*, 20 December 2006.
52 Minister for Education, 'Media Release: Higher Education Revolution', 13 May 2008.
53 Denise Bradley, Peter Noonan, Helen Nugent and Bill Scales, *Review of Australian Higher Education: Final Report* (Canberra: Commonwealth of Australia, 2008).
54 'Bradley Receives a Cautious Thumbs Up', *The Australian*, 18 June 2008.
55 Vin Massaro, 'Cui Bono? The Relevance and Impact of Quality Assurance', *Journal of Higher Education Policy and Management* 32, no. 1 (2010), pp. 17–26.
56 AVCC, *Code of Practice for Maintaining and Monitoring Academic Quality and Standards in Higher Degrees* (Canberra: AVCC, 1990); AVCC, *Academic Standards in Higher Education: Report of the Academic Standards Panel, Physics* (Canberra: AVCC, 1990); AVCC, *Academic Standards in Higher Education: Report of the Academic Standards Panel, History* (Canberra: AVCC, 1991); AVCC, *Academic Standards in Higher Education: Report of the Academic Standards Panel, Economics* (Canberra: AVCC, 1992); AVCC, *Academic Standards in Higher Education: Report of the Academic Standards Panel, Psychology* (Canberra: AVCC, 1992); AVCC, *Grades of Pass for Undergraduate Degree Subjects* (Canberra: AVCC, 1993); AVCC, *Academic Standards in Higher Education: Report of the Academic Standards Panel, Computer Science* (Canberra: AVCC, 1993); AVCC, *Academic Standards in Higher Education: Report of the Academic Standards Panel, Biochemistry* (Canberra: AVCC, 1993); AVCC, *Grades of Pass for Undergraduate Degree Subjects* (Canberra: AVCC, 1995); Ian Dobson, Raj Sharma and Anthony Haydon, *Commencing Undergraduates in Australian Universities: Enrolment and Performance Trends, 1993–1995* (Canberra: AVCC, 1997).
57 Minutes, AVCC, 19 November 1996.
58 *Persons Referred to in the Senate: Certain Faculty Members of Greenwich University* (Canberra: Commonwealth of Australia, June 1999).
59 Bradley, et al., *Review of Australian Higher Education*.

60 'VCs Voice Unease over Regulatory Blueprint', *The Australian*, 10 March 2010; Universities Australia, 18 May 2010; 'Canberra Appeasing Unis on Regulator', *The Australian*, 19 May 2010.
61 Vin Massaro, 'TEQSA and the Holy Grail of Outcomes-Based Quality Assessment', in Simon Marginson (ed.), *Tertiary Education Policy in Australia* (Melbourne: Centre for the Study of Higher Education, 2013).
62 Terms of Reference, Standing Group on TEQSA, Universities Australia, July 2011.
63 *Transforming Australia's Higher Education System* (Canberra: Australian Government, 2009).
64 *Transforming Australia's Higher Education System*.
65 Universities Australia Workshop Program, 22 August 2011.
66 Department of Education, *Selected Higher Education Statistics*, various years (Canberra: 2018).
67 *Education and Work, May 2018* (Canberra: Australian Bureau of Statistics, 2018).
68 'Evans off to India to Calm "Hysteria"', *The Australian*, 16 August 2009.
69 'Evans off to India to Calm "Hysteria"'.
70 Department of Education, *Selected Higher Education Statistics: 2017 Student Data* (Canberra: 2018).
71 *National Science Foundation Indicators 2018, 5–22; S&E Articles in All Fields, by Country or Economy: 2006 and 2016* (National Science Foundation, 2018).
72 Frank Larkins, *Australian Higher Education Research Policies and Performance, 1987–2010* (Carlton, Vic.: Melbourne University Publishing, 2011); Office of the Chief Scientist, *Health of Australian Science Report* (Canberra: Commonwealth of Australia, 23 May 2012).
73 Australian Government Department of Education, *Selected Higher Education Statistics*, various years.
74 Australian Government Department of Education, *Portfolio Budget Statements* (various years, 2008–09 to 2012–2013).
75 Universities Australia Issue Brief, No. 2/14, 2 May 2014; National Commission of Audit, Towards Responsible Government, 14 February 2014.
76 'Slugging Students More', *The Australian*, 2 May 2014; 'We'll Take That as a Comment', *The Australian*, 6 May 2014; 'Don't Rush Fee Deregulation: UA', *The Australian*, 5 May 2014.
77 Department of Education, 'Building a World-Class Higher Education System', in *Budget 2014–15* (Canberra: 2014).
78 Universities Australia, Media Release No. 15/14, Tuesday 13 May 2014, 'Budget Drives Sweeping Changes to Higher Education'.
79 The government removed the most contentious proposals for change to the loan scheme but even this was not enough, and a final attempt was made in December 2014, without success.
80 Croucher G, W Wen, H Coates and L Goedegebuure, 'Framing Research into University Governance and Leadership: Formative Insights from a Case Study of Australian Higher Education', *Educational Management Administration & Leadership* (accepted 9 November 2019).
81 Minister for Employment and Education Services, 'Media Release: A Fair Chance for All', 16 May 1990.

BIBLIOGRAPHY

This history has drawn on the Universities Australia collection, identified with file numbers where these are available.

This history has also drawn extensively on newspapers through the National Library, and academic journals dedicated to higher education, including:
The Australian Dictionary of Biography
The Australian University, 1963–1976
Australian Universities Review, 1985—
Vestes, 1958–1984

This history has drawn actively on statistical collections, including:
Australian Government Department of Education, *Selected Student Statistics*
Australian Government Department of Education, *uCube*
Calendars of Australian Universities
CTEC *Selected University Statistics*
Official Year Book of the Commonwealth of Australia

AVCC PUBLICATIONS
Auchmuty, JJ. *Australian Vice-Chancellors' Committee: Chairman's Report on the Years 1967–1970*. Surry Hills, NSW: The Wentworth Press, 1971.
Australian Committee of Directors and Principals and AVCC. *Code of Ethical Practice in the Provision of Full-Fee Courses to Overseas Students by Australian Higher Education Institutions*. Braddon, ACT: The Committees, 1989.

BIBLIOGRAPHY

Australian Research Grants Committee, Australian Science and Technology Council, AVCC. *Australian Research Grants Scheme: Research Funding Survey*. Australian Research Grants Committee, Australian Science and Technology Council. Adelaide: AVCC, 1984.
AVCC. *A Crisis in the Finances and Development of the Australian Universities*. AVCC, 1952.
AVCC. *Aboriginal Education*. Canberra: AVCC, 24 July 1981.
AVCC. *Academic Standards in Higher Education: Report of the Academic Standards Panel, Biochemistry*. Canberra: AVCC, 1993.
AVCC. *Academic Standards in Higher Education: Report of the Academic Standards Panel, Computer Science*. Canberra: AVCC, 1993.
AVCC. *Academic Standards in Higher Education: Report of the Academic Standards Panel, Economics*. Canberra: AVCC, 1992.
AVCC. *Academic Standards in Higher Education: Report of the Academic Standards Panel, History*. Canberra: AVCC, 1991.
AVCC. *Academic Standards in Higher Education: Report of the Academic Standards Panel, Physics*. Canberra: AVCC, 1990.
AVCC. *Academic Standards in Higher Education: Report of the Academic Standards Panel, Psychology*. Canberra: AVCC, 1992.
AVCC. *Academic Tenure*. Canberra: AVCC, November 1981.
AVCC. *Appointment of Staff: Fractional Appointments*. Canberra: AVCC, November 1981.
AVCC. *Australian Universities, International Universities*. Deakin, ACT: AVCC, 1999.
AVCC. *Australian Universities: Partners in Australia's Future: Policy Statement for the 1995–97 Triennium*. Canberra: AVCC, 1994.
AVCC. *Code of Ethical Practice in the Provision of Education to Overseas Students by Australian Higher Education Institutions*. Canberra: AVCC, 1990.
AVCC. *Code of Ethical Practice in the Provision of Offshore Education and Educational Services by Australian Higher Education Institutions*. Canberra: AVCC, 1995.
AVCC. *Code of Ethical Practice in the Provision of Education to International Students by Australian Universities*. Canberra: AVCC, 1998.
AVCC. *Code of Practice for Maintaining and Monitoring Academic Quality and Standards in Higher Degrees*. Canberra: AVCC, 1990.
AVCC. *Conference on University Education, 1960*. Revised edn. Carlton, Vic.: AVCC, 1961.
AVCC. *Examination for PhD Degree*. Braddon, ACT: AVCC, March 1980.
AVCC. *Foundations for the 'Clever Country': Report for the 1992–94 Triennium*. Canberra: AVCC, 1991.
AVCC. *Grades of Pass for Undergraduate Degree Subjects*. Canberra: AVCC, 1993.
AVCC. *Grades of Pass for Undergraduate Degree Subjects*. Canberra: AVCC, 1995.
AVCC. *The Internationalisation of Australian Universities*. Canberra: AVCC, 2001.
AVCC. *Junior Teaching Staff: Conditions of Employment*. Canberra: AVCC, 9 February 1979.
AVCC. *Junior Teaching Staff: Conditions of Employment*. Canberra: AVCC, November 1981.
AVCC. *Limited Term Appointments: Academic Staff*. Canberra: AVCC, November 1981.

AVCC. *Long Service Leave: Academic and General Staff.* Canberra: AVCC, June 1981.
AVCC. *Maternity Leave.* Canberra: AVCC, October 1979.
AVCC. *Probationary Period of Employment.* Canberra: AVCC, November 1981.
AVCC. *Promotion of Academic Staff.* Canberra: AVCC, November 1981.
AVCC. *Submission by the AVCC to the Committee on Australian Universities, 4 July 1957.* Carlton: Melbourne University Press, 1957.
AVCC. *Survey of Academic Links Between Australian and Overseas Institutions.* Occasional Papers, no 3. Canberra: AVCC, 1980.
AVCC. *Universities' Post-Graduate Scholarships.* Canberra: AVCC, June 1981.
AVCC. *University Unions: Subsidies.* Canberra: AVCC, April 1981.
Cochrane, D. *Report to Australian Vice-Chancellors' Committee on Year-Round Teaching.* Canberra: AVCC, 1970.
Dobson, Ian, Raj Sharma and Anthony Haydon. *Commencing Undergraduates in Australian Universities: Enrolment and Performance Trends, 1993–1995.* Canberra: AVCC, 1997.
Gibson, Boyce. 'The Australian Universities and Public Opinion.' In *A Symposium on 'The Place of the Australian University in the Community' and 'Post-Graduate Studies in the Australian Universities'.* Canberra: AVCC, 1955.
Inter-University Research Committee. *University Research 1982.* Canberra: AVCC, 1982.
Macmillan, David S. *Australian Universities: A Descriptive Sketch.* Sydney: Sydney University Press, 1968.
Mitchell, AG and SW Cohen. *The Australian University Student: Admission, Selection and Progress.* Canberra: AVCC, 1968.
Myers, DM. *University Staffing in a Static Situation: An Inquiry for the Australian Vice-Chancellors' Committee.* AVCC Occasional Papers, no. 1. Canberra: La Trobe University for AVCC, 1979.
Partridge, PH. 'Accountability and Evaluation.' In *Australian Universities to the Year 2000: Conference of University Governing Bodies,* AVCC Occasional Papers, no. 2. Canberra: ANU, 1979.
Sanders, C. *Universities and Educational Institutions in South East Asia: Report on Standards.* AVCC, 1958.

GOVERNMENT REVIEWS

3 Times Less Likely: A Report on the Access of Country Students to Tertiary Institutions. Melbourne: Victorian Country Education Project, 1988.
A Fair Go: The Federal Government's Strategy for Rural Education and Training. Canberra: Department of Employment, Education and Training, 1989.
Commonwealth Advisory Committee on Advanced Education, First Report: Colleges of Advanced Education, 1967–1969. Canberra: Commonwealth of Australia, 1966.
Education, Training and Employment: Report of the Committee of Inquiry into Education and Training, vol. 1. Canberra: AGPS, 1979.
Learning for Life: Review of Higher Education Financing and Policy (West Review). Canberra: AGPS, 1998.
Ministerial Statement: Review of Commonwealth Functions. Canberra: AGPS, 1981.
Persons Referred to in the Senate: Certain Faculty Members of Greenwich University. Canberra: Commonwealth of Australia, June 1999.

BIBLIOGRAPHY

Post-Secondary Education in South Australia. Adelaide: Government Printer, 1979.
Post-Secondary Education in Western Australia: Report of the Committee on Post-Secondary Education, appointed by the Minister for Education in Western Australia under the Chairmanship of Professor P.H. Partridge. Perth: Government Printer, 1976.
Report of the Australian Universities Commission on Australian Universities, 1958–1963. Canberra: AJ Arthur, 1960.
Report of the Committee of Inquiry into Post-Secondary Education. Melbourne: Government Printer, 1978.
Report of the Ministerial Working Party on Tertiary Education, Tasmania. Hobart: University of Tasmania Printer, 1978.
Report of the Murray Committee on Australian Universities, September 1957. Canberra: AJ Arthur, Commonwealth Government Printer, 1957.
Review of Efficiency and Effectiveness in Higher Education: Report of the Committee of Enquiry. Canberra: Commonwealth Tertiary Education Commission, 1986.
Royal Commission on the University of Melbourne: Minutes of Evidence on Administration, Teaching Work, and Government of the University of Melbourne. Melbourne: Robt S Brain, Government Printer, 1903.
Tertiary Education in Australia: Report of the Committee on the Future of Tertiary Education in Australia to the Australian Universities Commission, Volume 1, August 1964 (Canberra: Australian Government Printer, 1964).
Transforming Australia's Higher Education System. Canberra: Australian Government, 2009.
Bradley, Denise, Peter Noonan, Helen Nugent and Bill Scales. *Review of Australian Higher Education: Final Report.* Canberra: Commonwealth of Australia, 2008.
Commonwealth of Australia. *Report of the Inquiry into Academic Salaries.* Canberra: Commonwealth Government Printer, 1964.
Dawkins, JS. *The Challenge for Higher Education in Australia.* Canberra: AGPS, 1987.
Dawkins, JS. *Higher Education: A Policy Discussion Paper.* Canberra: AGPS, 1987.
Dawkins, JS. *Higher Education: A Policy Statement.* Canberra: AGPS, 1988.
Department of Employment, Education and Training. *National Report on Australia's Higher Education Sector.* Canberra: AGPS, 1993.
Higher Education Statistics Agency. *Provider Mergers and Changes.* Canberra: 2019.
HM Government. *International Education: Global Growth and Prosperity.* London: HM Government, July 2013.
National Board of Employment, Education and Training. *A Fair Chance for All: Higher Education that's within Everyone's Reach.* Canberra: The Department, 1990.
National Board of Employment, Education and Training. *Report of the Task Force on Amalgamations in Higher Education.* Canberra: AGPS, 1989.
Office of the Chief Scientist. *Health of Australian Science Report.* Canberra: Commonwealth of Australia, 23 May 2012.

SECONDARY LITERATURE

'The Centenary of the University of Sydney.' *Building and Engineering*, 24 October 1950, pp. 20–22.
'Editorial – A New University in New South Wales'. *The Australian University* 1, no. 3 (1963): pp. 235–37.

'FCUSAA Committee of Inquiry into the Orr Case'. *Vestes* 4, no. 1 (1961): pp. 70–88.
Inauguration of the University of Queensland: Queensland's Jubilee Day, 10th December, 1909. Brisbane: Anthony James Cumming, Government Printer, 1909.
'King v. The University of Sydney; ex parte Drummond'. *Australian Law Journal* 17, (16 July 1943): pp. 103–106.
Murdoch Voices: The First 40 Years at Murdoch University. Perth: Murdoch University, 2015.
'Political Tests for University Appointments: The Russel Ward Case.' *Vestes* 4, no. 1 (1961), pp. 51–68.
Record of the Jubilee Celebrations of the University of Sydney, September 30th, 1902. Sydney: William Brooks and Co., 1902.
'Rolph, William Kirby (1919–1954)', *Obituaries Australia*, National Centre of Biography, Australian National University, <oa.anu.edu.au/obituary/rolph-william-kirby-875/text876>, accessed 27 May 2019.
Up the Right Channels. St Lucia: University of Queensland, 1970.
Ack, Tess Lee. 'Student Politics.' In *Breaking Out: Memories of Melbourne in the 1970s*, edited by Susan Blackburn. Willoughby, NSW: Hale & Iremonger, 2015.
Adelaide, Debra, Paul Ashton and Annette Salt, eds. *Stories from the Tower: UTS 1988–2013*. Sydney: Xoum, 2013.
Aitkin, Don. 'Trends in Funding Arrangements.' *Higher Education Quarterly* 42, no. 2 (1988): pp. 144–51.
Alexander, Fred. *Campus at Crawley: A Narrative and Critical Appreciation of the First Fifty Years of the University of Western Australia*. Melbourne: FW Cheshire, 1963.
Anderson, DS. 'Access to Higher Education: The Link between Admissions and Social Class.' *Critical Studies in Education* 25, no. 1 (1983): pp. 91–111.
Anderson, DS. 'Access to University Education in Australia 1852–1990: Changes in the Undergraduate Social Mix.' *Australian Universities Review* 33, nos. 1 & 2 (1990): pp. 37–50.
Anderson, DS, and AE Vervoorn. *Access to Privilege: Patterns of Participation in Australian Post-Secondary Education*. Canberra: Australian National University Press, 1983.
Anderson, DS. 'The Prospect of Student Power in Australia.' *The Australian University* 6, no. 3 (1968): pp. 207–21.
Anderson, DS, R Boven, PJ Fensham and JP Powell. *Students in Australian Higher Education: A Study of Their Social Composition since the Abolition of Fees*. Canberra: AGPS, 1980.
Anderson, Fay. *An Historian's Life: Max Crawford and the Politics of Academic Freedom*. Carlton, Vic.: Melbourne University Publishing, 2005.
Anderson, Warwick. 'Knowing Natives: Instituting Social Anthropology in Australia after the Great War.' In Kate Darian-Smith and James Waghorne, eds, *The First World War, the Universities and the Professions in Australia*. Carlton, Vic.: Melbourne University Publishing, 2019.
Anonymous. 'Letter to the editor.' *Vestes* 12, no. 2 (1969): p. 150.
Arvanitakis, J. 'Massification and the Large Lecture Theatre: From Panic to Excitement' *Higher Education* 67, no. 6 (2014): pp. 735–45.
Ashby, Eric. *Community of Universities: An Informal Portrait of The Association of*

BIBLIOGRAPHY

Universities of the British Commonwealth, 1913–1963. Cambridge: Cambridge University Press, 1963.
Ashby, Eric. 'The Diversity of Universities in the Commonwealth.' *The Australian University* 2, no. 1 (1964): pp. 1–16.
Auchmuty, JJ. 'The Idea of the University in its Australian Setting – A Historical Survey.' *The Australian University* 1, no. 2 (1963): pp. 146–70.
Auchmuty, JJ. 'Jubilee Account of the Australian Vice-Chancellors' Committee.' *The Australian University* 8, no. 3 (1970): pp. 238–76.
Australian Academy of Technological Sciences and Engineering, 'Pest and Disease Control.' In *Technology in Australia 1788–1988*, Australian Academy of Technological Sciences and Engineering, <www.austehc.unimelb.edu.au/tia/043.html#158>, accessed 9 December 2019.
Baldwin, Jenny. 'World War I and the Development of Language Study at Australian Universities.' In *The First World War, the Universities and the Professions in Australia, 1914–1939*, edited by Kate Darian-Smith and James Waghorne. Carlton, Vic: Melbourne University Publishing, 2019.
Barcan, Alan. 'The Australian Student, 1961.' *Meanjin Quarterly* 20, no. 2 (1961): pp. 194–208.
Barcan, Alan. *Radical Students: The Old Left at Sydney University*. Carlton: Melbourne University Press, 2002.
Barnard, Clift. *Profile of a Student: College and University Students*. Kensington, NSW: Tertiary Education Research Centre, 1976.
Barnard, Clift and Denis Kelly. *Socio-Economic Background and Enrolment Characteristics of Commencing Students in 1974*. Kensington, NSW: Tertiary Education Research Centre, 1976.
Baxter, JP. 'A Short History of the University of New South Wales to 1964.' *The Australian University* 3, no. 1 (1965): pp. 74–114.
Baxter, JP. 'The Role of the Vice-Chancellor in the University of New South Wales.' *The Australian University* 6, no. 1 (1968): pp. 4–13.
Beasley, AW. *The Mantle of Surgery: The First Seventy-Five Years of the Royal Australasian College of Surgeons*. Melbourne: Royal Australasian College of Surgeons, 2002.
Bell, Peter. *Our Place in the Sun: A Brief History of James Cook University, 1960–2010*. Townsville: James Cook University, 2010.
Beloff, Michael. *The Plateglass Universities*. London: Secker & Warburg, 1968.
Bennett, JM. 'Cullen, Sir William Portus (1855–1935).' *Australian Dictionary of Biography*, National Centre of Biography, Australian National University, <adb.anu.edu.au/biography/cullen-sir-william-portus-5838/text9919>, published first in hardcopy 1981, accessed online 23 April 2019.
Berdahl, Robert O. *British Universities and the State*. Berkeley: University of California Press, 1959.
Bessant, Bob. 'Robert Gordon Menzies and Education in Australia.' *Critical Studies in Education* 19, no. 1 (1977): pp. 75–101.
Bessant, Bob. '"A Climate of Fear": From Collegiality to Corporatisation.' In *The Subversion of Australian Universities*, edited by John Biggs and Richard Davis. Wollongong: Fund for Intellectual Dissent, 2002.

Bhathal, Ragbir and Graeme White. *Under the Southern Cross: A Brief History of Astronomy in Australia*. Kenthurst: Kangaroo Press, 1991.

Binnie, AE. *From Atomic Energy to Nuclear Science: A History of the AAEC*. Sydney: Macquarie University, 2003.

Blainey, Geoffrey. *A Centenary History of the University of Melbourne*. Carlton: Melbourne University Press, 1957.

Board, P. *A Report Following Upon Observations of American Education*. Sydney: William Applegate Gullick, 1909.

Bolt, Bruce A. 'The FSM Affair at Berkeley.' *Vestes* 8, no. 3 (1965): pp. 155–63.

Booth, Edgar. *New England University College: Decentralisation of University Education*. Armidale: Armidale Express Print, 1943.

Borchardt, DH. 'Some Administrative and Professional Issues in Australian University Libraries.' *The Australian University* 7, no. 3 (1969).

Borrie, WD and Ruth M Dedman. *University Enrolments in Australia 1955–1970: A Projection*. Maryborough, Vic.: Hedges & Bell, 1957.

Bowen, Jennifer. '"A Capable Army of Experts": The Broadcasting Profession between the Wars.' In *The First World War, the Universities and the Professions*, edited by Kate Darian-Smith and James Waghorne. Carlton, Vic.: Melbourne University Publishing, 2019.

Braga, Stuart. *Anzac Doctor: The Life of Sir Neville Howse, Australia's First VC*. Alexandria, NSW: Hale & Iremonger, 2000.

Bramston, Troy. *Robert Menzies: The Art of Politics*. Melbourne: Scribe, 2019.

Breen, William J, ed. *Building La Trobe University: Reflections on the First 25 Years 1964–1989*. Melbourne: La Trobe University Press, 1989.

Brennan, HG. 'Fee Abolition: An Appraisal.' *The Australian University* 9, no. 2 (1971): pp. 81–149.

Brett, Judith. *Robert Menzies' Forgotten People*. Chippendale, NSW: Macmillan Australia, 1992.

Brogan, AH. *Committed to Saving Lives: A History of the Commonwealth Serum Laboratories*. South Yarra, Vic.: Hyland House, 1990.

Brown, Nicholas. *A History of Canberra*. Port Melbourne, Vic.: Cambridge University Press, 2014.

Brown, Nicholas. 'Student, Expert, Peacekeeper: Three Versions of International Engagement.' *Australian Journal of Politics and History* 57, no. 1 (2011): pp. 34–52.

Brubacher, John. *Higher Education in Transition: History of American Colleges and Universities*. New York: Routledge, 2017.

Bryan, Harrison. 'Australian University Library – A Measure of Success.' *The Australian University* 2, no. 1 (1964): pp. 17–41.

Bryan, Harrison. 'The Fisher "Sit-Ins" of April 1967.' *Vestes* 11, no. 2 (1968): pp. 153–59.

Bryan, Harrison. 'Rationalisation of Australian Library Holdings.' *The Australian University* 9, no. 3 (1971): pp. 222–36.

Bundy, Alan. 'Better, More Accessible, Libraries for All in Australia: Progress and Potential.' *Australasian Public Libraries and Information Services* 25, no. 3 (2011): pp. 138–44.

Burke, Gerald. 'How Large are the Cuts in Operating Grants Per Student?' *Australian Universities Review* 31, no. 2 (1988): pp 42–43.

BIBLIOGRAPHY

Burke, Gerald. 'The Politics of Bonded Service: The Case of Graduate Secondary Teachers in Victoria, Australia.' *Higher Education* 5 (1976): pp. 35–47.
Butlin, M, R Dixon and P Lloyd. 'Statistical Appendix: Selected Data Series, 1800–2010.' In *The Cambridge Economic History of Australia*, edited by S Ville & G Withers. Cambridge: Cambridge University Press, 2014. doi:10.1017/CHO9781107445222.033.
Butlin, SJ and CB Shedvin. *War Economy, 1942–1945. Australia in the War of 1939–1945*. Series 4, Civil, vol. 4. Canberra: Australian War Memorial, 1977.
Butterfield, Merrelyn. 'Towards Equality through Inequality in Educational Opportunities at the Tertiary Level.' *The Australian University* 8, no. 2 (1970): pp. 169–92.
Butterfield, Merrelyn and L Kane. 'A New Look at the Part-Time Student: Academic Performance.' *The Australian University* 7, no. 3 (1969): 226–49.
Cable, KJ. 'The University of Sydney and its Affiliated Colleges, 1850–1880.' *The Australian University* 2, no. 3 (1964): pp. 183–214.
Caiden, Gerald E. *Career Service: An Introduction to the History of Personnel Administration in the Commonwealth Public Service of Australia 1901–1961*. Carlton, Vic.: Melbourne University Press, 1965.
Caiden, Naomi. 'Student Failure in Australian Universities: A Bibliographical Review.' *Vestes* 7, no. 1 (1963): pp. 48–56.
Campbell, Richard. 'Flexibility in a Steady State University.' *Vestes* 20, no. 3 (1977): pp. 9–16.
Carroll, Brian. *A Decade of Achievement: Phillip Institute of Technology*. Melbourne: RMIT Press, 1995.
Castle, Josie. *University of Wollongong: An Illustrated History*. Wollongong: University of Wollongong, 1991.
Chapman, Bruce. 'Economics and Policy-Making: The Case of the Higher Education Contribution Scheme.' *Canberra Bulletin of Public Administration*, no. 90 (1998).
Chapman, Bruce and Chris Ryan. *Higher Education Financing and Student Access*. Deakin, ACT: AVCC, 2003.
Christy, Ralph D and Lionel Williamson, eds. *A Century of Service: Land-grant Colleges and Universities, 1980–1990*. New Brunswick, NJ: Transaction Publishers, 1992.
Clarke, Alex M and L Michael Birt. 'Some Current Issues in the Administration of Australian Universities.' *Higher Education* 8 (1979): pp. 491–512.
Clarke, Alex M and L Michael Birt. 'Australian Universities in the Post-Williams Period: The Impact of Public Policy on the Small Universities.' *Higher Education* 10 (1981): pp. 181–97.
Clarke, Alex M and Lynn M Edwards. 'The Williams Committee of Inquiry into Education and Training in Australia: Recommendations for Universities.' *Higher Education* 9, no. 5 (1980): pp. 495–528.
Clements, MA. 'Frank Tate and the Politics of Agricultural Education in Victoria, 1895–1905.' *Critical Studies in Education* 19, no. 1 (1977): pp. 190–226.
Clow, D. 'MOOCs and the Funnel of Participation'. In *Proceedings of the Third International Conference on Learning Analytics and Knowledge* 2013: pp. 185–89.
Coaldrake, Peter and Lawrence Stedman. *Raising the Stakes: Gambling with the Future of Universities*. St Lucia, University of Queensland Press, 2013.

Coffrin, Carleton, Linda Corrin, Paula de Barba and Gregor Kennedy. 'Visualizing Patterns of Student Engagement and Performance in MOOCs.' In *Proceedings of the Fourth International Conference on Learning Analytics and Knowledge, 24 March 2014*: pp. 83–92.

Coleman, William, Selwyn Cornish and Alf Hagger. *Giblin's Platoon: The Triumphs and Trials of the Economist in Australian Public Life*. Canberra: ANU E Press, 2006.

Collins, J Maxwell. 'Review Article: The Williams Report.' *Higher Education* 9, no. 5 (1980): pp. 633–37.

Collis, KF, P Hughes and P Byers. 'Institutional Rationalization in Tasmania in the Late 1970s Early 1980s: College and University.' In *Institutional Amalgamations in Higher Education: Process and Outcomes in Five Countries*, edited by Grant Harman and V Lynn Meek. Armidale: Department of Administrative and Higher Education Studies, University of New England, 1988.

Connell, WF. *The Australian Council of Educational Research*. Hawthorn, Vic.: Australian Council of Educational Research, 1980.

Connell, WF, Geoffrey Sherington, BH Fletcher, Clifford Turney and Ursula Bygott. *Australia's First: A History of the University of Sydney, Vol. 2, 1940–1990*. Sydney: Hale & Iremonger, 1995.

Connell, William. *The Foundations of Secondary Education*. Melbourne: ACER, 1962.

Cope, RL. 'The Rise of the Library of Congress: Lessons for Australia?' *The Australian University* 2, no. 2 (1964): pp. 152–61.

Cowan, HJ. 'University Autonomy.' *Vestes* 12, no. 2 (1969): pp. 121–26.

Cowen, Zelman. 'Some Thoughts on the Australian Universities.' *The Australian University* 9, no. 3 (1971): pp. 159–74.

Crawford, JG. 'The Accountable of Universities.' In *Opportunity in Education*. Carlton, Vic.: The Australian College of Education, 1968.

Crawford, JG. *The Australian National University: Its Concept and Role*. Melbourne: University of Melbourne, 1968.

Crawford, JG. *The University and Government: The Robert Garran Memorial Oration, 24 November 1969*. Canberra: Royal Institute of Public Administration, 1969.

Crawford, RM. 'Humanities and Social Sciences in Australian Universities: Effects of the Bulge and the Trend.' *The Australian University* 6, no. 2 (1968): pp. 122–35.

Croucher, G and P Woelert. 'Institutional Isomorphism and the Creation of the Unified National System of Higher Education in Australia: An Empirical Analysis.' *Higher Education* 71, no. 4 (2016): pp. 439–53.

Croucher, G., W. Wen, H. Coates and L. Goedegebuure. 'Framing Research into University Governance and Leadership: Formative Insights from a Case Study of Australian Higher Education'. *Educational Management Administration & Leadership* (accepted 9 Nov 2019).

Currie, George and John Graham. *The Origins of CSIRO: Science and the Commonwealth Government, 1901–1926*. Melbourne: Commonwealth Scientific and Industrial Research Organisation, 1966.

Curthoys, Ann. 'Television before Television.' *Continuum: Journal of Media & Cultural Studies* 4, no. 2 (1991): pp. 152–70.

Curthoys, Ann. *Freedom Ride: A Freedom Rider Remembers*. Sydney: Allen & Unwin, 2002.

BIBLIOGRAPHY

Damousi, Joy. 'Universities and Conscription: The "Yes" Campaigns and the University of Melbourne.' In *The Conscription Conflict and the Great War*, edited by Robin Archer, Joy Damousi, Murray Goot and Sean Scalmer. Clayton, Vic.: Monash University Publishing, 2016.

Darian-Smith, Kate and James Waghorne. 'Australian-Asian Sociability, Student Activism, and the University Challenge to White Australia in the 1950s.' *Australian Journal of Politics and History* 62, no. 2 (2016): pp. 203–18.

Darian-Smith, Kate and James Waghorne. 'Introduction.' In *The First World War, the Universities and the Professions in Australia, 1914–1939*, edited by Kate Darian-Smith and James Waghorne. Carlton, Vic.: Melbourne University Publishing, 2019.

Darian-Smith, Kate and James Waghorne, eds. *The First World War, the Universities and the Professions in Australia 1914–1939*. Carlton, Vic.: Melbourne University Publishing, 2019.

Darroch, JN, RA Layton and WH Maze. *Report by the Steering Committee to the Australian Vice-Chancellors' Committee on Greater Utilisation of University Facilities*. Canberra: Australian Vice-Chancellors' Committee, 1968.

Davies, Susan. *The Martin Committee and the Binary Policy of Higher Education in Australia*. Melbourne: Ashwood House, 1989.

Davis, Dorothy Violet and Bruce Mackintosh, eds. *Making a Difference: Australian International Education*. Sydney: University of New South Wales Press, 2011.

Davis, Glyn. *The Australian Idea of a University*. Carlton, Vic.: Melbourne University Publishing, 2017.

Davis, Richard. *Open to Talent: The Centenary History of the University of Tasmania, 1890–1990*. Hobart: University of Tasmania, 1990.

Davis, Richard. 'The Battle for Collegiality in Tasmania: The 1955 Royal Commission and the Orr Aftermath.' In *The Subversion of Australian Universities*, edited by John Biggs and Richard Davis. Wollongong: Fund for Intellectual Dissent, 2002.

Davison, Graeme and Kate Murphy. *University Unlimited: The Monash Story*. Sydney: Allen & Unwin, 2012.

Dean, Katrina. 'The Physicist's Homestead: Alexander Mcaulay, Hydroelectricity and Mathematical Physics in Tasmania.' *Tasmanian Historical Studies* 8 (2003).

Deery, Phillip. 'Scientific Freedom and Post-War Politics: Australia, 1945–55.' *Historical Records of Australian Science* 13, no. 1 (2000): pp. 1–18.

Deery, Phillip. 'Remembering ASIO.' *Overland*, no. 203 (2011), <https://overland.org.au/previous-issues/issue-203/feature-phillip-deery/>, accessed 9 December 2019.

Dhondt, Pieter. 'Introduction.' In *University Jubilees and University History Writing: A Challenging Relationship. Scientific and Learned Cultures and Their Institutions*, edited by Pieter Dhondt. Leiden: Brill, 2015.

Doherty, RL. 'The Faculty Resolves to Recommend ... The University of Queensland Faculty of Medicine, 1936–1985.' In *A Medical School for Queensland*, edited by RL Doherty. Brisbane: Boolarong Publications, 1986.

Drummond, DH. *A University Is Born: The Story of the Founding of the University College of New England*. Sydney: Angus & Robertson, 1959.

Duncan, WGK and Roger Ashley Leonard. *The University of Adelaide, 1874–1974*. Adelaide: Rigby, 1973.

Dyke, Timothy and Warwick P Anderson. 'A History of Health and Medical Research in Australia.' *Medical Journal of Australia* 201, no. 1 Suppl (2014): pp. 33–36.
Easson, Michael. 'Ross, Lloyd Robert Maxwell (1901–1987).' *Australian Dictionary of Biography*. National Centre of Biography, Australian National University, <adb.anu.edu.au/biography/ross-lloyd-robert-maxwell-15927/text27128>, published first in hardcopy 2012, accessed online 4 August 2018.
Eddy, WHC. *Orr*. Brisbane: Jacaranda Press, 1961.
Edgeloe, VA. *The Medical School of the University of Adelaide: A Brief History from an Administrative Viewpoint*. Adelaide: University of Adelaide, 1991.
Edwards, FM. 'Piecemeal Solutions Won't Reduce the Default Rate on Guaranteed Loans.' *The Chronicle of Higher Education* 17, no. 44 (1988): p. A44.
Edwards, Meredith. *Social Policy, Public Policy: From Problem to Practice*. Sydney: Allen & Unwin, 2001.
Edwards, P. *Australia and the Vietnam War*. Sydney: NewSouth Publishing, 2014.
Egerton, John and Hannah Forsyth. 'Veterinary Science, World War I and the Professions.' In *World War I, the Universities and the Professions in Australia*, edited by Kate Darian-Smith and James Waghorne. Carlton, Vic.: Melbourne University Publishing, 2019.
Eggleston, RM. *Report of the Inquiry into Academic Salaries*. Canberra: AJ Arthur, 1964.
Ellis, DR. 'Participation or Tokenism.' *Vestes* 14, no. 1 (1971): pp. 25–28.
Encel, S. 'Science, Education and the Economy.' *The Australian University* 3, 1 (1965): pp. 54–73.
Fitzpatrick, Brian. 'An Injustice Has Been Done.' *Meanjin* 20, no. 1 (1961): pp. 107–11.
Fitzpatrick, Brian. 'The Arts, and the Upsurge of the PTM Class.' *Meanjin* 20, no. 1 (1960): pp. 73–79.
Forsyth, Hannah. *A History of the Modern Australian University*. Sydney: NewSouth, 2014.
Forsyth, Hannah. 'Expanding Higher Education: Institutional Responses in Australia from the Post-War Era to the 1970s.' *Paedagogica Historica* 51, no. 3 (2015): pp. 365–80.
Forsyth, Hannah. 'Post-War Political Economics and the Growth of Australian University Research, c.1945–1965.' *History of Education Review* 46, no. 1 (2017): pp. 15–32.
Forsyth, Hannah. 'The Russel Ward Case: Academic Freedom in Australia During the Cold War.' *History Australia* 11, no. 3 (2014): pp. 31–52.
Foster, Leonie. *High Hopes: The Men and Motives of the Australian Round Table*. Melbourne: Melbourne University Press, in association with the Australian Institute of International Affairs, 1986.
Foster, SG and Margaret M Varghese. *The Making of the Australian National University: 1946–1996*. Canberra: ANU E Press, 2009.
Gallagher, AP. 'One in All In: FAUSA and the Origins of the Academic Salaries Tribunal.' *Vestes* 25, no. 2 (1982): pp. 35–41.
Gamage, DT. 'La Trobe and Lincoln Merger: The Process and Outcome.' *Journal of Educational Administration* 30, no. 4 (1992): pp. 73–89.
Geiger, Roger L. *American Higher Education since World War II: A History*. Princeton, NJ: Princeton University Press, 2019.

BIBLIOGRAPHY

Geiger, Roger L. *The History of American Higher Education: Learning and Culture from the Founding to World War II.* Princeton, NJ: Princeton University Press, 2015.

Goodchild, Lester and Harold Wechsler, eds. *The History of Higher Education*, 2nd ed. Needham Heights, MA: Simon & Schuster, 1997.

Goot, Murray and Sean Scalmer. 'Party Leaders, the Media, and Political Persuasion: The Campaigns of Evatt and Menzies on the Referendum to Protect Australia from Communism.' *Australian Historical Studies* 44, no. 1 (2013): pp. 71–88, doi:10.1080/1031461X.2012.760635.

Gregory, Jenny and Jean Chetkovich, eds. *Seeking Wisdom: A Centenary History of the University of Western Australia.* Crawley, WA: UWA Publishing, 2013.

Hambly, FS. 'Australian Vice-Chancellors' Committee.' *Journal of Tertiary Education Administration* 1, no. 1 (1979): pp. 64–71.

Hammond, SB. 'The Students and the University.' *Critical Studies in Education* 4, no. 1 (1960): pp. 95–124.

Hansen, WL and MS Rhodes. *Student Debt Crisis: Are Students Incurring Excessive Debt?* Madison, WI: Wisconsin Center for Education Research, School of Education, University of Wisconsin-Madison, 1985.

Harloe, Lori. 'Anton Breinl and the Australian Institute of Tropical Medicine.' In *Health and Healing in Tropical Australia and New Guinea*, edited by Roy MacLeod and Donald Denoon. Townsville, Qld: James Cook University, 1991.

Harman, Grant. 'Academic Staff and Academic Drift in Australian Colleges of Advanced Education.' *Higher Education* 6 (1977): pp. 313–35.

Harman, Grant. 'Introduction.' In *Academia Becalmed: Australian Tertiary Education in the Aftermath of Expansion*, edited by GS Harman, AH Miller, DJ Bennett and BI Anderson. Canberra: Australian National University Press, 2000.

Harman, Grant. 'The "Razor Gang" Decisions, the Guidelines to the Commissions and Commonwealth Education Policy.' *Vestes* 24, no. 1 (1981): pp. 28–40.

Harman, Grant and V Lynn Meek, eds. *Australian Higher Education Reconstructed?: Analysis of the Proposals and Assumptions of the Dawkins Green Paper.* Armidale: Department of Administrative and Higher Education Studies, University of New England, 1988.

Harman, Grant and C Selby Smith, eds. *Australian Higher Education: Problems of a Developing System.* Sydney: Angus & Robertson, 1972.

Harman, Grant and C Selby Smith, eds. *Readings in the Economics and Politics of Australian Education.* Rushcutters Bay, NSW: Pergamon Press, 1976.

Harman, Grant and Don Smart, eds. *Federal Intervention in Australian Education.* Melbourne: Georgian House, 1982.

Harper, Marjorie. *Douglas Copland: Scholar, Economist, Diplomat.* Carlton, Vic.: The Miegunyah Press, 2013.

Harris, Robin S. 'On Higher Education in Australia and Canada.' *The Australian University* 7, no. 3 (1969): pp. 190–203.

Hasluck, Paul. *The Government and the People, 1939–41. Australia in the War of 1939–1945.* Canberra: Australian War Memorial, 1952.

Haynes, Raymond. *Explorers of the Southern Sky: A History of Australian Astronomy.* Cambridge University Press, 1996.

Herbst, P. 'Honours Courses in Australian Universities.' *The Australian University* 2, no. 1 (1964), pp. 42–51.

Hilliard, David. *Flinders University: The First 25 Years, 1966–1991*. Adelaide: Flinders University of South Australia, 1991.
Hobbins, Peter. '"Outside the Institute there Is a Desert": The Tenuous Trajectories of Medical Research in Interwar Australia.' *Medical History* 54, no. 1 (2010): pp. 1–28.
Hocking, Jenny. *Gough Whitlam, His Time, vol. 2*. Carlton, Vic.: The Miegunyah Press, 2012.
Hogan, Terry. *Coming of Age: Griffith University in the Unified National System*. Carlton: Melbourne University Publishing, 2016.
Holme, ER. '"Universities and the State": Paper by ER Holme, to the Third Imperial Congress on Higher Education, Cambridge, July 1926'.
Holt, Stephen. *A Veritable Dynamo: Lloyd Ross and Australian Labor 1901–1987*. St Lucia: University of Queensland Press, 1996.
Home, RW, ed. *Australian Science in the Making*. Cambridge: Cambridge University Press, 1988.
Home, RW. 'A World-Wide Scientific Network and Patronage System: Australian and Other "Colonial" Fellows of the Royal Society of London.' In *International Science and National Scientific Identity: Australia between Britain and America*, edited by RW Home and Sally Gregory Kohlstedt. Dordrecht: Kluwer Academic Publishers, 1991.
Home, RW. 'Origins of the Australian Physics Community.' *Historical Studies* 20, no. 80 (1983): pp. 383–400.
Hore, Terry. 'Implications for Academic Staff of the "Steady State".' *Vestes* 20, no. 3 (1977): pp. 21–23.
Horne, Julia. 'Looking from the Inside Out: Rethinking University History' *Journal of Educational Administration and History* 46, no. 2 (2014): pp. 174–89.
Horne, Julia and Geoffrey Sherington. *Sydney: The Making of a Public University*. Carlton, Vic.: Melbourne University Publishing, 2012.
Howard, John. *The Menzies Era: The Years that Shaped Modern Australia*. Sydney: HarperCollins, 2014.
Hutchinson, Mark. *A University of the People: A History of the University of Western Sydney*. Sydney: Allen & Unwin, 2013.
Hyde, Jim. 'The Development of Australian Tertiary Education to 1939.' *Critical Studies in Education* 24, no. 1 (1982): pp. 125–27.
Jackson, Kim. 'The Higher Education Contribution Scheme', E-Brief, Parliament of Australia, 12 August 2003, <www.aph.gov.au/About_Parliament/Parliamentary_Departments/Parliamentary_Library/Publications_Archive/archive/hecs>, accessed 3 September 2019.
Jacobsen, WC and R Forste. 'The Wired Generation: Academic and Social Outcomes of Electronic Media Use among University Students.' *Cyberpsychology, Behavior, and Social Networking* 14, no. 5 (2011): pp. 275–80.
Jordan, Matthew, *A Spirit of True Learning: The Jubilee History of the University of New England*. Sydney: UNSW Press, 2004.
Karmel, Peter. 'Funding Universities.' In *Why Universities Matter: A Conversation about Values, Means and Directions*, edited by Tony Coady. Sydney: Allen & Unwin, 2000.
Karmel, Peter. *Reflections on a Revolution*. AVCC Papers, no. 1. Canberra: AVCC, 1989.

BIBLIOGRAPHY

Karmel, Peter. 'Tertiary Education in a Steady State.' In *Academia Becalmed: Australian Tertiary Education in the Aftermath of Expansion*, edited by GS Harman, AH Miller, DJ Bennett and BI Anderson. Canberra: Australian National University Press, 1980.
Kerr, Clark. 'Higher Education: Paradise Lost?' *Higher Education* 7 (1978): pp. 261–78.
Kerr, Clark. *The Uses of the University*. Cambridge, MA: Harvard University Press, 1963.
Koder, LM and R McLintock. 'The Sydney College of Advanced Education Amalgamation.' In *Institutional Amalgamations in Higher Education: Process and Outcomes in Five Countries*, edited by Grant Harman and V Lynn Meek. Armidale, NSW: Department of Administrative and Higher Education Studies, University of New England, 1988.
Korporaal, Glenda. *AARNet: 20 Years of the Internet in Australia: 1989–2009*. North Ryde, NSW: AARNet, 2009.
Kyle, Noeline, Catherine Manathunga and Joanne Scott. *A Class of its Own: A History of Queensland University of Technology*. Sydney: Hale & Iremonger, 1999.
Laby, TH. 'A University for the Commonwealth.' *The Australian Quarterly* 1, no. 1 (1929): pp. 32–42.
Laderman, Sophia. 'State Higher Education Finance: Financial Year 2016.' Denver, Col.: State Higher Education Executive Officers Association.
Lamb, Paul. 'The Merger that Never Was.' In *Institutional Amalgamations in Higher Education: Process and Outcomes in Five Countries*, edited by Grant Harman and V Lynn Meek. Armidale, NSW: Department of Administrative and Higher Education Studies, University of New England, 1988.
Larkins, Frank. *Australian Higher Education Research Policies and Performance, 1987–2010*. Carlton, Vic.: Melbourne University Publishing, 2011.
Lazenby, Alec, Denis Blight and IDP Education Australia. *Thirty Years in International Education and Development: The IDP Story*. Canberra: IDP Education Australia, 1999.
Lees, S and J Senyard. *The 1950s: ... How Australia Became a Modern Society and Everyone got a House and a Car*. Melbourne: Hyland House, 1987.
Lewis, Milton J. 'The Idea of a National University: The Origins and Establishment of the Australian National University.' *Journal of the Australian and New Zealand History of Education Society* 8, no. 2 (1979): pp. 40–55.
Lewis, Milton J. *The People's Health: Public Health in Australia, 1788–1950*. Westport, Conn.: Praeger, 2003.
Little, Graham. 'Students' Conceptions of the University.' *The Australian University* 7, no. 1 (1969): pp. 22–36.
Lodewycks, KA. 'The Departmental Book Collection in Relation to Library Provision in Institutes of Tertiary Education.' *The Australian University* 13, no. 1 (1975).
Love, Peter, assisted by Sara Jervis. *Practical Measures: 100 Years at Swinburne*. Melbourne: Swinburne University of Technology, 2007.
Lowe, David. *Australia Between Empires: The Life of Percy Spender*. London: Routledge, 2010.
Lowe, David. 'Australia's Colombo Plans, Old and New: International Students as Foreign Relations.' *International Journal of Policy* 21, no. 4 (2015): pp. 448–62.

Lowe, David. 'The Colombo Plan.' In *Australia and the End of Empire*, edited by David Lowe. Geelong: Deakin University Press, 1996.
Lowe, David and Daniel Oakman, eds. *Australia and the Colombo Plan*. Canberra: Department of Foreign Affairs and Trade, Documents on Australian Foreign Policy, 2004.
Lucas, Christopher J. *American Higher Education: A History*. New York: St. Martin's Press, 1994.
McCann, Doug and Peter Thorne. *The Last of the First. CSIRAC: Australia's First Computer*. Melbourne, Vic.: Department of Computer Science and Software Engineering, University of Melbourne, 2000.
McConville, Chris. *Rising in the West: From Western Institute to Victoria University of Technology, 1987–1992*. Melbourne: Western Institute, 1991.
Macintyre, Stuart. *Australia's Boldest Experiment: War and Reconstruction in the 1940s*. Sydney: NewSouth, 2015.
Macintyre, Stuart. 'Looking up the Right Channels', *Farrago*, 48, no. 22 (1970): pp. 12–13.
Macintyre, Stuart. *The Poor Relation: A History of Social Sciences in Australia*. Carlton, Vic.: Melbourne University Publishing, 2010.
Macintyre, Stuart. 'Useful Knowledge: The Contribution of Universities to Government between the Wars'. In *The First World War, the Universities and the Professions in Australia 1914–1939*, edited by Kate Darian-Smith and James Waghorne. Carlton, Vic.: Melbourne University Publishing, 2019.
Macintyre, Stuart, André Brett and Gwilym Croucher. *No End of a Lesson: Australia's Unified National System of Higher Education*. Carlton, Vic.: University of Melbourne Publishing, 2017.
Macintyre, Stuart and RJW Selleck. *A Short History of the University of Melbourne*. Carlton, Vic.: Melbourne University Press, 2003.
Mackinnon, Alison. *A New Kid on the Block: The University of South Australia in the Unified National System*. Carlton, Vic.: Melbourne University Publishing, 2016.
McKinnon, KR. 'United We Stand ... the Process of Amalgamation at Wollongong University.' In *Institutional Amalgamations in Higher Education: Process and Outcomes in Five Countries*, edited by Grant Harman and V Lynn Meek. Armidale: Department of Administrative and Higher Education Studies, University of New England, 1988.
McLean, D. 'American and Australian Cold Wars in Asia.' *Australasian Journal of American Studies* 9, no. 2 (1990): pp. 33–46.
MacLeod, Roy M. 'Science, Progressivism, and "Practical Idealism": Reflections on Efficient Imperialism and Federal Science in Australia, 1895–1915.' *Scientia Canadensis: Canadian Journal of the History of Science, Technology and Medicine* 17, nos 1–3 (1993): pp. 7–25.
MacLeod, Roy M, ed. *The Commonwealth of Science: ANZAAS and the Scientific Enterprise in Australasia, 1888–1988*. Melbourne: Oxford University Press, 1988.
Macmillan, David S. 'The University of Sydney – The Pattern and the Public Reaction, 1850–1870', *The Australian University* 1, 1 (1963): pp. 27–59.
McPhee, Peter. *'Pansy': A Life of Roy Douglas Wright*. Carlton, Vic.: Melbourne University Press, 1999.

BIBLIOGRAPHY

Mahony, David. 'Counter Images of Australia's Move to an Entrepreneurial Higher Education System: An Analysis.' *Higher Education* 28, no. 3 (1994): pp. 301–23.

Maling, Jillian. 'The Impact of an Amalgamation on the Career Prospects of Women Staff in a Newly Amalgamated College of Advanced Education.' In *Institutional Amalgamations in Higher Education: Process and Outcomes in Five Countries*, edited by Grant Harman and V Lynn Meek. Armidale, NSW: Department of Administrative and Higher Education Studies, University of New England, 1988.

Mansfield, Bruce and Mark Hutchinson. *Liberality of Opportunity: A History of Macquarie University 1964–89*. Sydney: Macquarie University in association with Hale & Iremonger, c1992.

Marginson, Simon. *Educating Australia: Government, Economy and Citizen since 1960*. Cambridge: Cambridge University Press, 1997.

Marginson, Simon. *Education and Public Policy in Australia*. Cambridge: Cambridge University Press, 1993.

Marginson, Simon. *Markets in Education*. Sydney: Allen & Unwin, 1997.

Marginson, Simon. *Monash: Remaking the University*. Sydney: Allen & Unwin, 2000.

Marginson, Simon. *The Dream Is Over: The Crisis of Clark Kerr's California Idea of Higher Education*. Oakland: University of California Press, 2016.

Marginson, Simon and Mark Considine. *The Enterprise University: Power, Governance and Reinvention in Australia*. Cambridge: Cambridge University Press, 2000.

Martin, Allan. *Robert Menzies, A Life*, vol. 2. Carlton, Vic.: Melbourne University Press, 1999.

Martin, L. 'Framing the Framework: The Origins of a Fair Chance for All.' In *Student Equity in Australian Higher Education*, edited by A Harvey, C Burnheim and M Brett. Singapore: Springer, 2016.

Massaro, Vin. 'Cui Bono? The Relevance and Impact of Quality Assurance' *Journal of Higher Education Policy and Management* 32, no. 1 (2010): pp. 17–26.

Massaro, Vin. 'TEQSA and the Holy Grail of Outcomes-Based Quality Assessment.' In *Tertiary Education Policy in Australia*, edited by Simon Marginson. Melbourne: Centre for the Study of Higher Education, 2013.

Matheson, JAL. 'Australian Multiversities?' *The Australian University* 3, no. 3 (1965): pp. 204–24.

Matheson, JAL. 'Authority and Responsibility: Who Should Run the Universities?' *Vestes* 14, no. 2 (1971): pp. 110–13.

Matthew, HGC. *The Liberal Imperialists: The Ideas and Politics of a Post-Gladstonian Elite*. London: Oxford University Press, 1973.

Medley, JDG. *The Present and Future of Australian Universities*. Melbourne: Melbourne University Press, 1945.

Medlin, EH. 'A Case for an Association of Australian Universities.' *Vestes* 19, no. 1 (1976): pp. 5–13.

Meek, Lynn and Leo Goedegebuure. *Higher Education: A Report*. Armidale: Department of Administrative and Higher Education Studies, University of New England, 1989.

Meek, V Lynn and Grant Harman, eds. *The Binary Experiment for Higher Education: An Australian Perspective*. Armidale: Department of Administrative, Higher and Adult Education Studies, University of New England, 1993.

Megarrity, Lyndon. 'Regional Goodwill, Sensibly Priced: Commonwealth Policies Towards Colombo Plan Scholars and Private Overseas Students, 1945–72.' *Australian Historical Studies* 38, no. 129 (2008): pp. 88–105.
Melbourne, ACV. *Report on a Visit to the Universities of China and Japan*. Brisbane: University of Queensland, 1936.
Mellor, DP. *The Role of Science and Industry. Australia in the War of 1939–1945*. Series 4, Civil. Vol. 5. Canberra: Australian War Memorial, 1958.
Menzies, Robert. 'Message from the Prime Minister.' *The Australian University* 1, no. 1 (1963): p. 5.
Moore, AL. 'The History, Machinery and Scope of Direct Grants by the Commonwealth Government to Australian Universities, 1935–1964.' *The Australian University* 3, no. 3 (1965): pp. 225–34.
Moorhouse, CE and Barbara Falk. 'The University Teaching Project of the University of Melbourne.' *The Australian University* 1, no. 3 (1963): pp. 294–307.
Moran, Carmen. *Student Opinions on the Influence of Tuition Fee Abolition Upon Their Choice of Course*. Kensington, NSW: Tertiary Education Research Centre, UNSW, 1975.
Moran, Carmen and Denis Kelly. *The Effect of the Abolition of Fees on Commencing Students in 1974*. Kensington, NSW: Tertiary Education Research Centre, UNSW, 1976.
Morgan, Alexander. *Scottish University Studies*. London: Humphrey Milford, 1933.
Moyal, Ann. *A Bright and Savage Land: The Science of a New Continent Australia – Where All Things Were 'Queer and Opposite'*. Ringwood, Vic.: Penguin Books, 1986.
Murphy, John. *A Harvest of Fear: A History of Australia's Vietnam War*. Sydney: Allen & Unwin, 1993.
Murphy, John. *Imagining the Fifties*. Sydney: UNSW Press, 2000.
Murphy, Kate. '"In the Backblocks of Capitalism": Australian Student Activism in the Global 1960s.' *Australian Historical Studies* 46, no. 2 (2015): pp. 252–68.
Murphy, Kate. 'Student Activism at the University of New England in Australia's "Long 1960s".' *Journal of Australian Studies* 43, no. 2 (2019): pp. 174–87.
Murray-Smith, Stephen. 'A History of Technical Education in Australia: With Special Reference to the Period before 1914.' PhD thesis, University of Melbourne, 1966.
Newton, Andrew. 'The History of the Royal Australasian College of Surgeons from Foundation to 1935.' BA (Hons) Thesis, Monash University, 1979.
Oakman, Daniel. *Facing Asia: A History of the Colombo Plan*. Canberra: ANU E Press, 2010.
O'Brien, John Michael. *The National Tertiary Education Union: A Most Unlikely Union*. Sydney: UNSW Press, 2015.
O'Connor, B, A Chivas, D Mather, J Studdert and A Binnie. *AINSE – An Institute for Research and Training Excellence in Nuclear Science: The First 50 Years*. NSW: AINSE, 2008.
OECD, *Benchmarking Higher Education System Performance: Conceptual Framework and Data, Enhancing Higher Education System Performance*. Paris: OECD, 2017.
O'Farrell, Patrick. *UNSW: A Portrait, the University of New South Wales, 1949–1999*. Sydney: UNSW Press, 1999.
O'Hanlon, Seamus. *City Life: The New Urban Australia*. Sydney: NewSouth, 2018.

BIBLIOGRAPHY

Onah, DF, J Sinclair and R Boyatt. 'Dropout Rates of Massive Open Online Courses: Behavioural Patterns.' In *Proceedings of the 6th International Conference on Education and New Learning Technologies (EDULEARN14), At Barcelona, Spain*, July 2014, DOI: 10.13140/RG.2.1.2402.0009.

O'Neil, WM. 'Government Support for University Research in Australia, Canada, the United Kingdom and the United States of America.' *Vestes* 13, no. 1 (1970): pp. 11–19.

Oppenheimer, Melanie. 'The Professionalisation of Nursing through the 1920s and 1930s: The Impact of War and Volunteerism.' In *The First World War, the Universities and the Professions in Australia*, edited by Kate Darian-Smith and James Waghorne. Carlton, Vic.: Melbourne University Publishing, 2019.

Otten, C Michael. *University Authority and the Student: The Berkeley Experience*. Berkeley: University of California Press, 1970.

Partridge, PH. 'The University System.' *Critical Studies in Education* 4, no. 1 (1960): pp. 49–71.

Passmore, JA, SW Cohen, Ernest Roe and LN Short. *Teaching Methods in Australian Universities: Report Based on a Survey Conducted by a Committee on Research into Teaching Methods*. Canberra: AVCC, 1963.

Pelikan, Jaroslav. *The Idea of the University: A Re-examination*. New Haven: Yale University Press, 1992.

Phillips, AEB. 'Colleges of Advanced Education: In Search of Identity.' *The Australian University* 8, no. 2 (1970): pp. 126–51.

Philp, Hugh. 'The Piper and the Tune – from Murray to the Fourth A.U.C. Report.' *The Australian University* 8, no. 1 (1970): pp. 3–33.

Piccini, Jon. 'Transnational Protest, Australia and the 1960s.' In *Palgrave Studies in the History of Social Movements*, edited by Stefan Berger and Holger Nehring. London: Palgrave Macmillan, 2016.

Pietsch, Tamson. *Empire of Scholars: Universities, Networks and the British Academic World, 1850–1939*. Manchester: Manchester University Press, 2013.

Pietsch, Tamson. 'Out of Empire: The Universities' Bureau and the Congresses of the Universities of the British Empire, 1913–36.' In *Universities for a New World: Making a Global Network in International Higher Education, 1913–2013*, edited by Deryck M Schreuder. Thousand Oaks, Cal.: SAGE Publications, 2013.

Pietsch, Tamson. '"They Do Not Go as Strangers": Academic Connections between Australia and Britain, 1880–1939.' *Australian Studies* 5 (2013): pp. 1–13.

Polesel, John and Richard Teese. *The 'Colleges': Growth and Diversity in the Non-University Tertiary Studies Sector (1965–1974)*. University of Melbourne: Educational Outcomes Research Unit, 1998.

Powell, JP. 'The Idea of a Liberal Education.' *The Australian University* 3, no. 1 (1965): pp. 1–18.

Powell, JP. 'Tutorial Teaching and the University Ideal.' *The Australian University* 4, no. 1 (1966): pp. 19–36.

Poynter, John and Carolyn Rasmussen. *A Place Apart: The University of Melbourne: Decades of Challenge*. Carlton South, Vic.: Melbourne University Press, 1996.

Prescott, SL. '*The Australian University* an Introduction.' *The Australian University* 1, no. 1 (1963): pp. 1–4.

Priestley, Raymond E. *The Diary of a Vice-Chancellor: University of Melbourne 1935–1938*, edited by Ronald T Ridley. Carlton South, Vic.: Melbourne University Press, 2002.

Priestley, RE. *The Problems of the English-Speaking University World*. Adelaide: The Hassell Press, 1937.

Professorial Board, University of Sydney, 'Academic Administrative Structure.' *The Australian University* 1, no. 2 (1963): pp. 123–34.

Pybus, Cassandra Jane. *Gross Moral Turpitude: The Orr Case Reconsidered*. Port Melbourne: William Heinemann, 1993.

Quirke, Noel. *Preparing for the Future: A History of Griffith University 1971–1996*. Nathan, Qld: Boolarong Press for Griffith University, 1996.

Rae, Ian D. 'False Start for the PhD in Australia' *Historical Records of Australian Science* 14, no. 2 (2002): pp. 129–41.

Ramsay, Gregor. 'Future Directions for Tertiary Education: The Next Decade.' In *Setting the Agenda for Australian Tertiary Education: Planning Mechanisms, Policy Issues and Government Guidelines for the 1985–87 Triennium: Papers from a National Conference held at the University of Melbourne, 13–14 August 1984*, edited by JE Anwyl and GS Harman. Parkville, Vic.: Centre for the Study of Higher Education, University of Melbourne, 1984.

Rasmussen, Carolyn. '"Constructive Work": The Engineering Profession in Australia and World War I.' In *The First World War, the Universities and the Professors in Australia, 1914–1939*, edited by Kate Darian-Smith and James Waghorne. Carlton, Vic.: Melbourne University Publishing, 2019.

Rasmussen, Carolyn. *Increasing Momentum: Engineering at the University of Melbourne, 1861–2004*. Carlton, Vic.: Melbourne University Press, 2004.

Rasmussen, Carolyn. *Shifting the Boundaries: The University of Melbourne, 1975–2015*. Carlton, Vic.: Melbourne University Publishing, 2018.

Raymond, Phillip. 'The Decline of Melbourne's Affiliated Colleges: The Effect of the Report of the Royal Commission on the University of Melbourne, 1904' *Melbourne Studies in Education* 39, no. 2 (1998): pp. 91–113.

Rechter, Bernard and John Scott. 'The Proposed Merger between La Trobe University and Lincoln Institute of Health Sciences.' In *Institutional Amalgamations in Higher Education: Process and Outcomes in Five Countries*, edited by Grant Harman and V Lynn Meek. Armidale: Department of Administrative and Higher Education Studies, University of New England, 1988.

Rees, Anne. 'A War of Card Indexes: From Political Economy to Economic Science.' In *The First World War, the Universities and the Professions in Australia 1914–1939*, edited by Kate Darian-Smith and James Waghorne. Carlton, Vic.: Melbourne University Publishing, 2019.

Rivett, ACD. 'Pan-Pacific Science Congress, Australia, 1923.' *Nature* 112 (1923): pp. 378–79.

Rivett, ACD. 'Paper on the Relations between the Commonwealth Council for Scientific and Industrial Research and the Universities.' In *Australian and New Zealand Universities' Conference, Adelaide 1937: Report of Proceedings*. Adelaide: The Hassell Press, 1937.

Robinson, Eric E. *The New Polytechnics*. Harmondsworth: Penguin, 1968.

BIBLIOGRAPHY

Rootes, CA. 'The Development of Radical Student Movements and Their Sequelae.' *Australian Journal of Politics and History* 34, no. 2 (1988): pp. 173–85.

Rothblatt, Sheldon. *The Modern University and its Discontents: The Fate of Newman's Legacies in Britain and America*. Cambridge: Cambridge University Press, 1997.

Rowe, AP. *If the Gown Fits*. Carlton, Vic.: Melbourne University Press, 1960.

Rüegg, Walter, ed. *A History of the University in Europe: Vol. 3, Universities in the Nineteenth and Early Twentieth Centuries (1800–1945)*. Cambridge: Cambridge University Press, 1992.

Rüegg, Walter, ed. *A History of the University in Europe: Vol. 4, Universities since 1945*. Cambridge: Cambridge University Press, 2011.

Rüegg, Walter. 'Themes.' In *A History of the University in Europe: Vol. 3: Universities in the Nineteenth and Early Twentieth Centuries (1800–1945)*, edited by Walter Rüegg. Cambridge: Cambridge University Press, 2004.

Russell, KF. *The Melbourne Medical School, 1862–1962*. Carlton, Vic.: Melbourne University Press, 1977.

Salmond, John A. 'The Academic Structure.' In *Building La Trobe University: Reflections on the First 25 Years 1964–1989*, edited by William J Breen. Melbourne: La Trobe University Press, 1989.

Samuel, Bernard. *Imperialism and Social Reform: English Social-Imperial Thought, 1895–1914*. London: George Allen & Unwin, 1960.

Schedvin, Carl Boris. *Australia and the Great Depression*. Sydney: Sydney University Press, 1970.

Schedvin, Carl Boris. *Shaping Science and Industry: A History of Australia's Council for Scientific and Industrial Research, 1926–49*. Sydney: Allen & Unwin, 1987.

Schonell, Fred. 'Student Adaptation and its bearing on Student Achievement.' *The Australian University* 1, no. 1 (1963): pp. 60–88.

Schonell, Fred. *The University in Contemporary Society: Tenth Commonwealth Universities Congress, Sydney, 17–23 August 1968*. Sydney: Association of Commonwealth Universities, 1968.

Schreuder, Deryck M., ed. *Universities for a New World*. Thousand Oaks, Cal.: SAGE Publications, 2013.

Schulte, Jurgen, Belinda Tiffen, Jackie Edwards, Scott Abbott and Edward Luca. 'Shaping the Future of Academic Libraries: Authentic Learning for the Next Generation.' *College & Research Libraries* 79, no. 5 (2018): pp. 685–96.

Scott, Ernest. *A History of the University of Melbourne*. Melbourne: Melbourne University Press, 1936.

Searle, Geoffrey. *The Quest for National Efficiency: A Study in British Politics and Political Thought, 1899–1914*. Oxford: Blackwell, 1971.

Selby-Smith, R. 'The Amalgamation and Closure of Tertiary Institutions.' In *Academia Becalmed: Australian Tertiary Education in the Aftermath of Expansion*, edited by GS Harman, AH Miller, DJ Bennett and BI Anderson. Canberra: Australian National University Press, 1980.

Selleck, RJW. *Finding Home: The Masson Family*. North Melbourne: Australian Scholarly Publishing, 2013.

Selleck, RJW. *The Shop: The University of Melbourne, 1850–1939*. Carlton, Vic., Melbourne University Press, 2003.

Shattock, Michael. *The UGC and the Management of British Universities*. Buckingham: Open University Press, 1994.

Short, LN. 'Universities and Colleges of Advanced Education: Defining the Difference.' *The Australian University* 11, no. 1 (1973): pp. 3–25.

Simpson, Renate. *The Development of the PhD Degree in Britain, 1917–1959 and Since: An Evolutionary and Statistical History in Higher Education*. Lewiston: The Edwin Mellen Press, 2009.

Smart, Don. 'Education.' In *From Fraser to Hawke: Australian Public Policy in the 1980s*, edited by Brian W Head and Allan Patience. Melbourne: Longman Cheshire, 1989.

Smart, Don and Janice Dudley. 'Education Policy.' In *Hawke and Australian Public Policy: Consensus and Restructuring*, edited by Christine Jennett and Randal G Stewart. Melbourne: Macmillan, 1990.

Smith, Julian Ormond. 'The History of the Royal Australasian College of Surgeons, 1920–1935.' *Australian & New Zealand Journal of Surgery* 41, no. 1 (1971): pp. 1–19.

Souter, Gavin. *Acts of Parliament: A Narrative History of the Senate and House of Representatives, Commonwealth of Australia*. Carlton, Vic.: Melbourne University Press, 1988.

Spaull, AD. *John Dedman: A Most Unexpected Labor Man*. South Melbourne: Hyland House, 1998.

Stackpole, Stephen H. *Commonwealth Program 1911–1961*. New York: Carnegie Corporation of New York, 1963.

Stavropoulos, Pam. *Short Circuit: The Melbourne University Assembly, 1974–1989*. Parkville, Vic.: The Assembly, 1989.

Stewart, B. 'Massiveness + Openness = New Literacies of Participation.' *Journal of Online Learning and Teaching* 9, no. 2 (2013): pp. 228–38.

Strangio, Paul, Paul T Hart and James Walter. *The Pivot of Power: Australian Prime Ministers and Political Leadership, 1949–2016*. Carlton, Vic.: Melbourne University Publishing, 2017.

Syme, Patrick Kenny, ed. *The Founders of the Royal Australasian College of Surgeons*. Melbourne: Royal Australasian College of Surgeons, 1984.

Taft, R, Patricia Strong and PJ Fensham. 'National Background and Choice of Tertiary Education in Victoria.' *International Migration* 9, nos 1–2 (1971): pp. 36–54.

Talvé, Annie. 'Libraries as Places of Invention.' *Library Management* 32, no. 8/9 (2011): pp. 493–504.

Tannock, P. *The Founding and Establishment of the University of Notre Dame Australia, 1986–2014*. Fremantle, WA: University of Notre Dame Australia, 2014.

Tannock, PD. 'A Study of the Role of the Government of the Commonwealth of Australia in Education since Federation, 1901–1968.' PhD Thesis, The Johns Hopkins University, 1969.

Tannock, PD. *The Government of Education in Australia: The Origins of Federal Policy*. Nedlands, WA: UWA Press, 1975.

Tannock, PD and IK Birch. 'Defining the Limits of Commonwealth Education Power: The Drummond Case, the Federal Government and the Universities.' *Critical Studies in Education* 15, no. 1 (1973): pp. 163–74.

BIBLIOGRAPHY

Tess, PA. 'The Role of Social Media in Higher Education Classes (Real and Virtual) – A Literature Review.' *Computers in Human Behavior* 29, no. 5 (2013): pp. 60–68.
Thomis, Malcolm I. *A Place of Light and Learning: The University of Queensland's First Seventy-Five Years.* St Lucia, Qld: University of Queensland Press, 1985.
Thomis, Malcolm I. 'Melbourne, Alexander Clifford Vernon (1888–1943).' *Australian Dictionary of Biography* (National Centre of Biography, Australian National University), <adb.anu.edu.au/biography/melbourne-alexander-clifford-vernon-7552/text13177>, published first in hardcopy 1986, accessed online 23 May 2019.
Tripathi, M and S Kumar. 'Use of Web 2.0 Tools in Academic Libraries: A Reconnaissance of the International Landscape.' *The International Information & Library Review* 42, no. 3 (2010): pp. 195–207.
Trow, Martin. 'Problems in the Transition from Elite to Mass Higher Education.' In OECD, *Policies for Higher Education: Conference on Future Structures of Post-Secondary Education, Paris, 26–29 June 1973, General Report.* Paris: OECD, 1974.
Trow, Martin. 'The Implications of Low Growth Rates for Higher Education.' *Higher Education* 5 (1976): pp. 377–96.
Tucker, Thomas. *The Place of Classics in Education: An Inaugural Address Delivered in the Wilson Hall of the University of Melbourne, 22nd March, 1886.* Melbourne: S Mullen, 1886.
Turney, C, U Bygott and P Chippendale. *Australia's First: A History of the University of Sydney, Vol. 1, 1850–1939.* Sydney: Hale & Iremonger, 1991.
Twomey, Christina and Jodie Boyd. 'Class, Social Equity and Higher Education in Postwar Australia.' *Australian Historical Studies* 47, no. 1 (2016): pp. 8–24.
Vernon, Keith. 'Calling the Tune: British Universities and the State, 1880–1914.' *History of Education* 30, no. 3 (2001): pp. 251–71.
Waghorne, James. 'Civil Liberties and the Referendum.' *Australian Historical Studies* 44, no. 1 (2013): pp. 105–16.
Waghorne, James. 'Growth and Specialisation: The Medical Profession in Interwar Australia.' In *The First World War, the Universities and the Professions in Australia 1914–1939*, edited by Kate Darian-Smith and James Waghorne. Carlton, Vic.: Melbourne University Publishing, 2019.
Waghorne, James and Stuart Macintyre. *Liberty: A History of Civil Liberties in Australia.* Sydney: UNSW Press, 2011.
Walsh, Richard. 'Australian Protest: Odious International Comparisons.' *Vestes* 11, no. 2 (1968): pp 126–30.
Waters, Christopher. 'Cold War Liberals: Richard Casey and the Department of the External Affairs, 1951–60.' In *Ministers, Mandarins and Diplomats: Australian Foreign Policy Making, 1941–1969*, edited by Joan Beaumont. Carlton, Vic.: Melbourne University Press, 2003.
Welch, Jim. 'Shaping the Box: The Cultural Construction of American Television, 1948–1952.' *Continuum: Journal of Media & Cultural Studies* 13, no. 1 (1999): pp. 97–117.
White, Michael. *WAIT to Curtin: A History of the Western Australian Institute of Technology.* Perth: Paradigm Books, 1996.
Williams, Brian. 'A Scholar Goes to War: K.S. Cunningham 1914–18.' *Critical Studies in Education* 35, no. 1 (1994): pp. 149–67.

Williams, Brian. *A Tertiary Education Commission?* AVCC, 27 February 1975.
Wilson, R. 'Student-Aid Analysts Blast Loan Program, Urge Big Overhaul; Observers Doubt that Congress will Approve Sweeping Changes.' *The Chronicle of Higher Education* 27, no. 1 (1988): p. A1–2.
Winkler, A. *The Cold War: A History in Documents*. Oxford: Oxford University Press, 2011.
Woelert, P and G Croucher. 'The Multiple Dynamics of Isomorphic Change: Australian Law Schools 1987–1996.' *Minerva* 56, no. 4 (2018): pp. 479–503.
Wright, DI. *Looking Back: A History of the University of Newcastle*. Callaghan: University of Newcastle, 1992.
Young, Nigel. *An Infantile Disorder? The Crisis and Decline of the New Left*. London: Routledge, 1977.

INDEX

1851 Exhibition Trust 11
1902 Jubilee 15
1973 'oil shock' 133
1988 White Paper on higher education 161–62

AARNet *see* Australian Academic Research Network
AAUCS *see* Australian–Asian Universities' Cooperation Scheme
ABC *see* Australian Broadcasting Commission
Aboriginal and Torres Strait Islanders *see also* Indigenous rights
   fair chance for all discussion paper 173
   increased higher education participation 182
   participation and advancement in universities 200–1
   staff policies 152
   student encouragement 152
academic professional associations 115–19
   on salaries and work conditions 117–18
Academic Salaries Tribunal 119
access widening to education 141–45
ACDP *see* Australian Committee of Directors and Principals
ACER *see* Australian Council for Educational Research
ACTU, the 161
ACU *see* Australian Catholic University
Advertiser (Adelaide) 48
Advisory Council of Science and Industry 17, 34

Age (Melbourne) 60
AINSE *see* Australian Institute of Nuclear Science and Engineering
Aitken, Don 163
Alcock, Henry 32
Anderson, Don
   criticisms of CAEs 128
Antarctica 46
ANU Council 75
ARC *see* Australian Research Council
ARGC *see* Australian Research Grants Committee
ARPANET 175
Ashby, Eric 55
ASIO *see* Australian Security Intelligence Organisation
Association of the Universities of the British Commonwealth
   Quinquennial Congress, 1953 97–98
Association of the Universities of the British Commonwealth (AUBC) 97
   1955 Conference 100–1
   national policy 101–2
ASTEC *see* Australian Science, Technology and Engineering Council
Astronomy 138
AUBC *see* Association of the Universities of the British Commonwealth
AUC *see* Australian Universities Commission
AUQA *see* Australian Universities Quality Agency
Australasian Association for the Advancement of Science 24
Australian Academic Research Network (AARNet)

establishment of 175–77
Australian and New Zealand Universities
  Conference 46, 48
Australian Atomic Energy Agency 118
AAEC *see* Australian Atomic Energy
  Commission
Australian Atomic Energy Commission
  (AAEC) 137
Australian Broadcasting Commission
  'Design in Australia' 96
  'University of the Air' 96
Australian Broadcasting Commission
  (ABC) 96, 187
Australian Catholic University (ACU)
  167
Australian Committee of Directors and
  Principals (ACDP) 156
Australian Constitution 27
Australian Council for Educational
  Research (ACER) 63, 119–20
Australian Federation 2, 5
Australian Forestry School 36
Australian Institute of Nuclear Science
  and Engineering (AINSE) 137
Australian Labor Party
  on abolition of university fees 131
Australian National Airways 97
Australian National University (ANU)
  101
  criticisms of proposed 70
  establishment of 51, 75
  foundation ceremony 76
  national research scholarships 72
Australian Nuclear Science and
  Technology Association 176
Australian Nursing Federation 31
Australian Railways Union 61
Australian Research Council (ARC) 159,
  162
Australian Research Grants Committee
  (ARGC) 126
  1984 survey and funding shortfalls
    152
Australian Science, Technology and
  Engineering Council (ASTEC) 139
  1984 survey, funding shortfalls 152
Australian Security Intelligence
  Organisation (ASIO) 80
  University of Melbourne
    investigations 90
Australian Technology Network 192
Australian universities
  1920 conference of 5–7
  academic networks, British Empire
    11–14
  Access and Equity Strategy 173
  accountability of 150
  and advocacy 43
  and the Australian Vice-Chancellors'
    Committee (AVCC) 43–44
  barriers to state cooperation 10
  changing politics of, early twentieth
    century 14–18
  and the Cold War 89–91
  Colonial and Allied Universities
    conference 12
  Commonwealth funding impasse 99
  Commonwealth funding,
    administration of 68
  and Commonwealth Government
    relations 33–37, 44–45
  grants for facilities 67
  cooperation between 26–33
  creation of 1
  crisis in financing 91–96
  and Curtin Labor Government
    55–56
  definition of the AVCC's role, 1968
    129–31
  on developing a national computer
    network 176
  difficulties in commitments, 1920s
    48–50
  early curricula 7
  early funding of 7
  effects of Second World War 51–65
    collaboration with military 54
    courses for military needs 54
    enrolment quotas 58, 64
    fall in enrolments 59–60
    treatment of students who failed 59
    women and enrolment 60
  establishment of job titles 42
  expansion in number 109

INDEX

on fair opportunities for access to 201–2
and the Great Depression 37–40
staff salary reductions 39–40
increased enrolments, 1989 to 2017 179
independence of 1
Indigenous participation and advancement in 200–1
informal conference of 1906 20–21
internal administration 40–43
internal composition 8–9
international recognition 179
and international students 87–89
internationalisation of 182–86
investment in research 198
numbers of papers and students 198–99
and mergers 151–52, 163
Murray Committee recommendations 105–6
network with British universities 6
organisation of 8
and pensions 32
and postwar reconstruction 65–77
research funding 71–74
postwar scholarships 86
professional associations 29–30
public roles of 4
and public sector qualifications and expertise 35
redesign of study spaces 187
roles played by 1
sabbatical leave 11
sabbatical travel 97
scholarships and fee programs 10
secular nature of 7
social equality through education 143
social standing 10–11
Standing Advisory Committee of Australian Universities 22, 26
standing committee, creation of 3
state government research programs 46–47
student and staff representation 3
support for the Colombo Plan 97
and tenure 33

Whitlam funding proposals 132
women in 200
Australian Universities Commission (AUC) 106, 145, 146
authority over higher education 112–15
building new universities 111–12
computer funding 175
determination of student fees 141–42
establishment of 108
on student numbers 107
Australian Universities Conference, 1969 128
Australian Universities Quality Agency (AUQA) 195
Australian Vice-Chancellors' Committee (AVCC) 3, 43, 45, 65, 85, 92, 145 *see also* Universities Australia
'Survey of University Needs' 99–100
1980 university research survey 139
1984 survey and funding shortfalls 152
1989 nature of university statement 169
1994 policy statement 178
1999 action plan for women employed in universities 200
absorption of the ACDP 169–70
academic salaries and conditions 117–18
agricultural research, inter-university 138–39
The Australian University 120, 125
campaign against funding cuts 189
changes in 75
collaboration with Universities Commission 67
conference on university education 121–22
Conferences of Australian Universities, 115
criticisms of 191, 192, 193
definition of its role, 1968 129–31
delegation to Curtin University of Technology 157
delegation to Dawkins, John 158
determination of student fees 141

developing a national computer network 176
differences with the FCUSAA 118
diminished university advocacy role 147
efficiency surveys 152
establishing of computer architecture 155
FAUSA criticisms of 136
on future role of universities 159
higher education and the AUC 112–15
and international students 87
internet establishment of 174
on joining the Unified National System 163
National Health and Medical Research Council 47
omission from AUC decision planning 106
reports on higher education academic standards 195
research on student contribution to education 171
role of 116
and scholarships 97
and Second World War 52
secretariat expansion 161
on students missing out on placement 156
submission to Murray Committee 103–4
Tenth Commonwealth Universities Congress 127
UniOn 187
Australian–Asian Universities' Cooperation Scheme (AAUCS) 138
AUSTUDY 167
AVCC see Australian Vice-Chancellors' Committee
AVCC–ACDP working paper 156
Aynsley, Brenda 177

Bailey, Kenneth 53–59, 58
Bainbridge, Joseph 23
Barff, Henry 28, 41
Barker, FP 61

Barraclough, Henry 43
Barrett, James 31
Basser, Adolph 175
Baxter, Phillip 113, 137
Beasley, Frank 53
BHP Research Laboratories 176
'binary' system 123–29
  changes in 154
  overlapping CAE and universities functions 168
  removal of 163
Birt, Michael 158
Black, Hermann 96
Blood-Type Dryer 55
Board, Peter 16
Boeing Computer Services 176
Bond University 167
Boyd, Robin 96
Bradley Review 196
Bradley, Denise 4, 194
Brain, Hugh 102
Brennan, Geoffrey 131
Brigden, James 32
British Broadcasting Corporation 33–34
British Commonwealth 86
British Commonwealth of Nations 86
British Empire
  academic networks in 11–14
  Australia's place in 14
British Medical Association 30
British universities' pension fund 32
British University Grants Committee 94, 98, 104
Brown, Allen 95
Bruce, Stanley 36
Buckley, Dr Ken 115
Burton, Joe 90, 100
Butlin, Sydney 53, 62

CAE see College of Advanced Education
Cambridge University 10
Cameron, Robert 38
Canberra University College 37, 90, 101
  affiliation with University of Melbourne 37
Carnegie Corporation (NY) 44, 97, 138
Caro, David 158

INDEX

Casey, Richard 45, 79, 88
Catholic universities 157
Central Queensland University 165
CFAS *see* Commonwealth Financial Assistance Scheme
Chapman, Bruce 171–72
Charles Darwin University 166
Charles Sturt University 165
Chifley, Ben 65, 76
Chisholm Institute of Technology 164
Clunies Ross, Sir Ian 92, 102
Cochrane, Donald 130
Cold War, the 79, 80, 86, 89–91, 137
    Public Service (Cth) security checks 90
College of Advanced Education (CAE) 109, 124–26, 143
    dependence on government support 145–46
    expansion of 148, 156
    mergers 151, 163
    Whitlam funding proposals 132
Colombo Plan 80, 86
    and international students 87
Colonial and Allied Universities conference 12
Commission on Advanced Education 145
Committee on Uniform Taxation (Cth) 61
Commonwealth Advisory Committee on Advanced Education 125
Commonwealth Capital Grants 125
Commonwealth Financial Assistance Scheme (CFAS) 62, 66
Commonwealth Government of Australia 2, 181
    1962 increase in scholarships 123
    1981 razor gang 151
    1988 White Paper on higher education 161–62
    block grants to universities 84
    cuts to higher education, 1996 190
    fair chance for all policy statement 201
    First World War undertakings 14
    full costs of study, meeting of 79
    funding cuts to universities 38–39
    government-supported bachelor enrolments 197
    on graduates entering the Public Service 35
    grants for new university facilities 67
    and the Great Depression 37
    Higher Education Loan Program (HELP) 199
    increase in assistance to universities 95
    increased range of activities 33
    interest in research 137–39
    lowering of HECs thresholds 189
    means-tested allowances 142
    mergers, universities and colleges 163
    and Mills Committee of Inquiry 81–83
    postwar scholarships and living allowances 66
    relations with Public Service Board 36
    research support of universities 17, 47, 72–74, 136–39
    and Second World War 52
    statutory organisation funding roles for universities 2
    student financial assistance scheme 70
    support for international and postgraduate education 182
    support for university research 45
    university administration funding 67
    university fee reintroduction 151
    university funding impasse 99
    University of Canberra proposal 49
    use of university staff expertise 44–45
Commonwealth Industrial Court 118
Commonwealth Office of Education 82, 86
Commonwealth Pan-Pacific Sciences Congress 36
Commonwealth Reconstruction Training Scheme (CRTS) 66, 68
    funding of university facilities 74
    opportunities and threats 67
    surge of post-Second World War enrolments 79

Commonwealth Scholarships 84
  national survey, 88
Commonwealth Scientific and Industrial Research Organisation (CSIRO) 80, 92
  internet infrastructure 174–75
  work with universities 137
Commonwealth Serum Laboratories 27
Commonwealth Tertiary Education Commission (CTEC) 146, 159
  1986 review 160
  abolition of 178
  establishment of 146
  freezing of triennial system funding 147
  quotas on student places 148
  role of 146–47
Commonwealth–State funding relationship 118
Commonwealth–State relationship principle 83
Commonwealth Department of Education 141
Communist Party 89, 117
  1949 royal commission into the Communist Party 89
Conferences of Australian Universities 115
Considine, Mark 139
Cook, Dr James 102
Coombs 'Nugget', HC 65, 66
  proposed Canberra university 69
Coplan Plan *see* Premiers' Plan 1931
Copland, Douglas 32, 38, 44, 53, 75, 76
  as member of Mills Committee of Inquiry 81–82
  Vice-Chancellor at Australian National University 72
correspondence courses 180–81
Council of Australian Postgraduate Associations 189
Council of Scientific and Industrial Research (CSIR) 34, 45–46
  grants negotiations, 1941 55
  proposed research university 68–69
Coursera 188
CQUniversity 165
cross-disciplinary curriculum approaches 128

CRTS *see* Commonwealth Reconstruction Training Scheme
CSIR *see* Council of Scientific and Industrial Research
CSIRAC and CSIR computers 175
CSIRO *see* Commonwealth Scientific and Industrial Research Organisation
CSIRONET 176
CTEC *see* Commonwealth Tertiary Education Commission
Culgoora Radio Heliograph 138
Cullen, Sir William 5–6
curriculum in secondary schools 10
Currie, George 48, 75, 87, 91
Curtin Labor Government
  support for university research 55–56
Curtin University of Technology 156–57
Curtin, John 60
  and student financial assistance 61

Darling, James 61–62
David, Sir Edgeworth 16, 23–24
Dawkins, John 4, 154, 191
  'purple circle' (advisory group) 158
  The Challenge for Higher Education in Australia 158
  expansion of size of university system 157–58
  Green Paper on higher education 159–61
  HECS fees 170
  reforms by 154–55
Deakin University 128
  establishment of 141
Dedman, John 56–57, 65, 66, 76
Department of Defence (US) 175
Department of External Affairs 88
Department of Labour and National Service (Cth) 55
Department of Post-War Reconstruction 65
Department of War Organisation 62
Derham, David 119
Distant Education Centres 174
Domino Theory 80
Drummond, John 64

INDEX

Edith Cowan University 166
Education
    national coordination of 18–22
education means tests 66
edX 188
Eggleston, Richard 118
Engineering courses
    different organisation of 28
enrolment quotas 197

Farrer, William 17
FAUSA *see* Federal Association of University Staff Associations
FCUSAA *see* Federal Council of University Staff of Australia
Federal Association of University Staff Associations (FAUSA) 119
    criticisms of the AVCC 136
    symposium, governing universities 135
    symposium, university autonomy 135
    Vestes 120
Federal Council of University Staff of Australia (FCUSAA) 98
    differences with the AVCC 118
    increasing prominence of 115–16
Federal Examining University initiative 32
Federation University 166
financial assistance for enrolments 60–61
First World War 2, 6, 13
    student enlistment in 14
Fitzgerald, Sir Alexander 102
flexible work conditions 148
Flinders University 128
    establishment of 140
    faculty reorganisation 177
Florey, Sir Howard 69
Ford Foundation 138
Ford, John 75, 98
Foster, John 52, 63, 75
'four conditions of entry' 144
Fraser Liberal Government 149
    appointment of Williams Committee 149
Free University, Sydney 136
Fulbright Scholarships 97

Gale, Fay 200
Gardner, Margaret 200
Garran, Sir Robert 49–50
Geelong Grammar School 62
Geelong Teachers' College 141
George V 15–16
Giblin, Lyndhurst 38
Gillard, Julia 194
    2009 education inquiry recommendations 194–95
Gippsland Institute of Advanced Education 164
global financial crisis 181
Go8 *see* Group of Eight
Goodes, FJ 82
Gordon Institute of Technology 141
Grants Committee (Cth) 61
Graylands CAE 151
Great Depression, the 37–40
    boost in university enrolments 40
    Commonwealth funding cuts to universities 38–39
Green Paper on higher education, 1987 159–61
Greenwich University 195
Gregory, JW 16
Griffith University 128, 140
    faculty reorganisation 177
Group of Eight (Go8) 191–92
    2005 public statement 192
'gumtree' universities 139

Hambly, Frank 161, 189
Hamilton, Stuart 193
Harding, Sandra 200
Harris, Robin 108
Hartwell, Max 116–17
Hasluck, Paul 91–92
Hawke Government
    Access and Equity Strategy 173
    fair chance for all discussion paper 173
    National Economic Summary 172
    White and Green papers 172–73
Hawke, Bob 170 *see also* Hawke Government
HELP *see* Higher Education Loan Program

HES *see* Higher Education Contribution Scheme
HESF *see* Higher Education Standards Framework
Hewitt, Sir Lenox 119
High Court 64
　decision against bank nationalisation 81
　Orr case 116
Higher Education Administration Charge 170
Higher Education Contribution Scheme (HECS) 155, 162, 170–72, 178, 181, 190
　changes to 191
　implementation of 172
　lowering of thresholds 189
Higher Education Loan Program (HELP) 199
Higher Education Standards Framework (HESF) 196
Higher Education Support Act 194
higher education, accessibility to 10
Hill, Alex 21
Holme, Ernest 13, 31
Howse, Neville 34
Hughes, William (Billy) 17
Hytten, Torleiv 43, 92

imperial connections between universities 11–14
Indigenous rights *see also* Aboriginal and Torres Strait Islanders
　'Freedom Rides' 133
Innovative Research Universities Australia 192
Institute of Science and Industry (ISI) 17–18
Institute of Technical and Adult Teacher Education 164
Institute of Technology (NSW) 68
　New South Wales Government proposals 74
Institute of Tropical Health 27
Institute of Tropical Medicine 17
international students 86–89
　entrance requirement 88
　increases in number 198

national survey 88
preparation for Australian education 88–89
internet and online courses 187
internet, establishment of 174–77
Isles, Keith 113

Jackson, Catriona 200
James Cook University 110
Jennings, Ivor 87
John Curtin School of Medical Research 69
　foundation ceremony 76
Jones, Ken 141, 145
Julius, George 34

Karmel, Peter 123–24, 140, 142, 145
　on mergers 151
　petitioning of 146
　on role of CTEC 147
　on university accountability 150
Kemp, David 190
　fee increase recommendations 190
Keppel, Frederick P 44
Kerr, Clark 134
King, Robert 64
Korean War, the 90
　national service 90–91
Kuring-gai CAE 164

Laby, Thomas 34, 68
Land Grant Universities (US) 15, 16
Lang, Jack 37
La Trobe University 128, 167
　establishment of 140
Lawson, Harry 21
Learning Management Systems 186
Leeper, Alexander 24
Liberal Party, the 81
Loans Council 33
Lowe, Sir Charles 89
Lucas Heights 137
Lyons, Joseph 38

MacCallum, Mungo 15, 42
MacFarland, John 21, 42
Macmahon Ball, W 96

INDEX

Macmillan, David 128–29
  on CAEs 129
Macquarie University 128
Macrossan Lectures, 1946 69
Madgwick, Robert 100, 114
Makinson, Richard 90
Marginson, Simon 3, 139
Martin report, 1965 126
Martin, Leslie 4, 106, 111–12, 113–14
  inquiry into tertiary education, 1961 123–24
Massive Open Online Courses (MOOCs) 188
Masson, Orme 19
Matheson, Louis 135–36
Matriculation Conference 21
Mawson, Sir Douglas 23–24, 46
McKinnon, Ken 158
medical research 137–38
Medley, John 52, 57–58, 69–71, 76
  1949 resignations 74–75
Medlin, Harry 136
Melbourne Bruce, Stanley 91
Melbourne Studies in Education (publication) 120
Melbourne Town Hall 20
Melbourne Union Theatre 106
Melbourne University Magazine 18
Melbourne, ACV 47
Menzies, Robert 4
  as Attorney-General 45
  as editor of Melbourne University Magazine 18
  as prime minister 78
  1961 Marin inquiry 123
  acceptance of Murray report 104, 105–6
  agreement to AVCC–FCUSAA proposal 118
  anti-communist platform 89–90
  on CAEs 127
  defence of parliamentary democracy 80
  endorsement of *The Australian University* 123
  increased student support 84–85

Martin Report, 1965 126
  and Mills Committee of Inquiry 81–82
  reduced university support 84
  on states' rights 81, 83
  university deputation 95
  on university internal affairs 100
mergers, CAEs and universities 151–52, 163
merging of AUC and CTEC 145–47
Mills Committee of Inquiry 76–77, 81–82, 91, 103
Mills, Richard 18, 32, 53, 59, 61, 63, 76, 85
Mitchell, Sir William 58
Monash University 110–11, 112, 130
  campus disruptions 134
Monash, Sir John 35
MOOCs *see* Massive Open Online Courses
Moratorium marches 133
Morris, Sir Charles 98, 102
Morris, Sir Phillip 102
Mount Stromlo Observatory 45, 138
Mullarvey, John 193
Murdoch University 128, 157
  establishment of 140
Murdoch, Walter 96
Murray Committee 103, 104, 109, 117
  criticisms of the AVCC 104–5
  on failure rates 120–21
  national university structure 115
  on second Victorian university 110
  on student numbers 106–7
Murray, Keith 4
Murray, Sir Keith 102

National Aboriginal and Torres Strait Islander Higher Education Consortium 201
National Aeronautics and Space Administration (NASA) 176
National Board of Employment, Education and Training (NBEET) 159, 162
National Economic Summit 172
National Health and Medical Research Council (NHMRC) 47

university funding 138
National Institute of International Education (US) 22
National Library of Australia 176
National Security Act 52
National Territory Education Union (NTEU) 168
   campaign against funding cuts 189
National Union of Australian Students (NUAUS) 52, 62
   1944 conference 66
   on abolition of university fees 131
National Union of Students 189
NBEET *see* National Board of Employment, Education and Training
Nelson, Brendan 191
   changes to HECS 191
   Greenwich University intervention 195
   Higher Education at the Crossroads 191
'new Australians' and Commonwealth scholarships 86
New England University
   affiliation with Sydney University 37
   independence from Sydney University 110
New Left 133
New South Wales Government 68
   Institute of Technology proposals 74
   support to University of Sydney 71
New South Wales University of Technology 80, 111
   establishment of 51
NHMRC *see* National Health and Medical Research Council
Niemeyer, Sir Otto 37
NTEU *see* National Territory Education Union
NUAUS *see* National Union of Australian Students

Oliphant, Marcus 137
online courses 187
Open Learning Agency of Australia 187
Open Universities Australia (OUA) 187
Open University (UK) 96
Orr, Sparkes
   dismissal of 116
OUA *see* Open Universities Australia
Oxford University 10, 12

Paris 1968 protests 134
Parkes Radio Telescope 138
Parnell, Thomas 63
Partridge, Percy 119, 129
Passmore, John 122
Paton, George 96, 102, 106
   on student numbers 113
Pearl Harbour 56
Penington, David 163
PhD examination regulations 152
PhDs, establishment of 71–72
philanthropic gifts 109
'plateglass' universities 140
post-Second World War reconstruction 65–77
post-Second World War research funding 71–74
postwar 'babyboom' 108
postwar assisted-immigration scheme 86
postwar expansion, education 110–12
Premiers' Conference, 1953 95
Premiers' Plan, 1931 37–38
Prescott, Sir Stanley 120
Priestley, Raymond 42
private universities 157
professional associations 29–30
Public Service Act 35
Public Service Board (Cth) 35
   entry examinations 35
   on qualifications and expertise 35
   relations with Commonwealth Government 36
'purple circle' (advisory group) 158

Queensland and Commonwealth Advisory Committee on Eastern Trade 47
Queensland Conservatorium of Music 165
Queensland Institute of Technology 112
Queensland Institute of Technology (QIT) 164, 165

Regional Universities Network 192

INDEX

Reid, Alex J 103
Research and Experiment into Educational Matters 130 *see also* Partridge, Percy
Rhodes scholarships 11
Richards, Jack C 103
Rivett, David 34, 46
RMIT *see* Royal Melbourne institute of Technology
Roberts, Stephen 92
Robertson, Sir Bob 126
Robinson, Belinda 200
Rockefeller Foundation 31, 44
Rolph, Ruth 98
Roseworthy Agricultural College 17
Ross, AD 20
Ross, Dr Lloyd 61
Rowe, Albert 42–43, 87, 96, 100, 121
Roxby Downs 139
Royal Australasian College of Surgeons 29–30
Royal College of Physicians 30
Royal Melbourne institute of Technology (RMIT) 154, 164
Royal Melbourne Technical College 110, 112
Rum Jungle uranium mine 137

sabbatical travel 97
Saint Regis University (US) 195
Sanders, Col 88–89
Schonell, Fred 121, 122, 127
    on students receiving scholarships 123
Scientific Liaison Bureau 55–56
Second World War
    effects on Australian universities 51–65
    and quotas 64
    fall of France 53
    mobilisation 53
Shann, Edward 29, 38
Sharpley, Cecil 89
Short, Laurence 127–28
SILLIAC (computer) 175
Smith's Weekly 64
South Australian Institute of Technology (SAIT) 164
Standing Advisory Committee of Australian Universities 22, 26, 43
    central offices of 22
    first meeting of 27–29
    introduction of PhDs 28
Stanford University 134
Stantke, Victor 59
Star, Dr KH 131
State Electricity Commission of Victoria 35
state government postwar education initiatives 79
state government, education responsibilities 81–88
States Grants (Universities) Act 1951 83, 91
'steady state' 147–53
Story, John 42
student and staff movement 133–36
    disruptive protests 134
    opposition to student deferred payments 171
student failure rates 120–22
student financial assistance 61
student hostels 85
student movement criticisms of universities 136
student visas 180
Supplementary Grants 142
Supreme Court (NSW) 64
Supreme Court (Tasmania)
    Orr case 116
Southern Cross University 166
Sutton, Gerard 192
Swanson, Thomas 145
Swinburne University of Technology 166
Sydney Morning Herald 25
Sydney Teachers College 119
Sydney University Press 129
Syme, George 30

TAFE 162
TEAS *see* Tertiary Assistance Scheme
Telecom 175, 177
Tenth Commonwealth Universities Congress 127

tenure 148
TEQSA *see* Tertiary Education Quality Standards Agency
Terry, Deborah, 200
Tertiary Assistance Scheme (TEAS) 141
Tertiary Education Commission 145
    powers of 146
Tertiary Education Quality Standards Agency (TEQSA) 196
The Australian National University Act of Incorporation 1946 69
The Australian University Student
    on student selection 122
The Challenge for Higher Education in Australia (pamphlet) 158
The Network University of New England 166
Thorp, Roland 115
Timbs, Maurice 118
Tivey, Sir John 102
Trueman, Sir Arthur 98
Tucker, Thomas 20
Turner, John 71–72

Udacity 188
UNS *see* Unified National System
Unified National System (UNS) 154, 162, 163, 168, 179
    changes effected in higher education 177–78
    control of supply of places 197
Union of Australian College Academics 169
United States, the 15 *see also* Land Grant Universities
Universities Australia (UA) 3, 193–94, 199
    Indigenous Strategy 201
Universities Commission 61, 76
    collaboration with Australian Vice-Chancellors' Committee 67
    and the Commonwealth Financial Assistance Scheme 62
    student hostels scheme 85
    tasks and powers 62
Universities Educational Committee of the Australian Imperial Force 13

Universities in France and Germany 16
Universities' Bureau of the British Empire 12, 44, 75
    1917 and 1918 congresses 13
    1920 congress 21–22
    Doctor of Philosophy (PhD) program 13
    limited powers of 12–13
university allocations per student 83
university and college mergers, 1988 to 1992 164–68
University Assembly 136
University College of Townsville 112
university fees 84 *see also* Higher Education Contribution Scheme
University Grants Committee (Britain) 27, 49, 94, 98, 102
University House 102
University of Adelaide
    establishment of 7
    on final place selections 63
    royal commission into 16
University of Ballarat 166
University of Calcutta 47
University of California 32, 134
University of Canberra 166
University of Leeds 98
University of London 32
University of Madras 47
University of Malaya 87
University of Melbourne 2
    affiliation with Canberra University College 37
    ASIO investigations 90
    CSIRAC and CSIR computers 175
    establishment of 7
    establishment of Commerce faculty 30
    fee increases 84
    introduction of PhDs 28–29, 71
    jubilee celebrations 12
    Riverina enrolments 19–20
    royal commissions into 16, 17, 19, 41
    training programs 118
    University Assembly 136
University of Melbourne Council 24
University of New South Wales (UNSW) 111, 117

INDEX

training programs 118
University of New Zealand 32
University of Notre Dame Australia 167
University of Papua and New Guinea 128
University of Queensland
  correspondence courses 180
  establishment of 7, 17
  prickly pear eradication 18
  student input in course materials 136
  training programs 118
University of South Australia 165
University of Southern Queensland 112, 165
University of Sunshine Coast 166
University of Sussex 128
University of Sydney
  1920 Conference of the Australian Universities 5–7, 24
  1950 centenary 78, 80
  Act of Incorporation 8
  affiliation with University of Sydney 37
  establishment of 7
  establishment of Australian Chair of Anthropology 30–31
  Federal Examining University initiative 32
  Free University 136
  and international students 88
  jubilee celebrations 12, 20
  national meeting on entry requirements 20
  SILLIAC (computer) 175
  support from New South Wales Government 71
  training programs 118
University of Tasmania
  dismissal of Orr, Sparkes 116
  establishment of 7
  interviewing of candidates 64
University of Technology, Sydney (UTS) 164
University of Toronto 22
University of Western Australia
  establishment of 7, 17
  on final place selection 63

and international students 88
resource management problems 49
training programs 118
university quotas
  during Second World War 64
university, meaning of 168–70
UNSW *see* University of New South Wales
UNSW Tertiary Education Research Centre 131, 143
UNSW Tertiary Education Research Centre 143

Vanstone, Amanda 190
Victoria University of Technology 166
Victorian College of Pharmacy 164
Victorian Government
  education support by 18
Vietnam War, the 133

Wadham, Sir Samuel 102
WAIT *see* Western Australian Institute of Technology
Walker, Kenneth 53
Walker, Ronald 66
Wallace, Robert 48, 63
Walter and Eliza Hall Institute of Medical Research 138
Ward, John 162
Ward, Russell 116–17
Watts, Don 157
West Australian 9 *see also* Winthrop Hackett, Sir John
West, Roderick 190
  review of higher education 190
Western Australian Institute of Technology (WAIT) 124–25, 156, 164
White Australia Policy 133
White, Sir Brudenell 35
Whitfeld, Hubert 42
  death of 48
Whitlam Government
  1975 Budget cuts 147
  freeze of triennial system funding 147
  higher education funding 141
  means-tested student allowances 142–43

277

social equality through education 143
Whitlam, Gough 155–56 *see also*
　Whitlam Government
　　on abolition of university fees 132, 145, 172
　　on funding for universities and CAEs 132
　　Tertiary Education Commission 145
Willet, F John 140
Williams Committee 149–50
　recommendations of 151
Williams, Bruce 145, 146, 191
Wilson, Brian 158, 162
Windeyer, Major-General Victor 102

Winthrop Hackett, Sir John 9, 11–12, 17 *see also West Australian*
　bequest to University of Western Australia 9
Withers, Glen 193
Workers' Educational Association 61
Wran Committee 171
Wran, Neville 171 *see also* Wran Committee
Wright 'Pansy', RD 69

Yearbook, British universities 13
Yerbury, Dianne 200